East From Brazosport

By William B. Seward

EAST FROM BRAZOSPORT
is published by The Dow Chemical Company
Midland, Michigan 48640
Printed in U.S.A. by the McKay Press.
© 1974, The Dow Chemical Company
All rights reserved.
Design: Packard Graphics, Inc.
Illustrations: Robert Heindel

Library of Congress Catalog
Card Number: 74-19938
ISBN: 0-915150-01-8

Table of Contents

Foreword

East From Brazosport is about big business, multinational business. It's also about The Dow Chemical Company. But most of all, it's about people—white, brown, black; men and women; young, middle-aged, and one remarkable 76-year-old; executives and managers, scientists and salesmen, skilled and unskilled workers; some employed by Dow and many not. The people are in Texas, aboard a Dutch ship on the Atlantic, and in Brazil, Argentina, Holland, Switzerland, Italy, and Germany.

The thread tying these people together begins in Brazosport—which you won't find on many maps. Not yet, anyway. Today, Brazosport is a group of communities gradually growing together on the Gulf Coast of Texas about 60 miles south of Houston. These communities surround a Dow complex, itself divided into Plants A and B of Dow's Texas Division, and the company's Oyster Creek Division. At one time Plant A was identified as being at Freeport, and Plant B at Velasco. But those two communities have merged into one, called Freeport. Close neighbors are Clute, Gulf Park, Jones Creek, Lake Barbara, Lake Jackson, Oyster Creek, Richwood, and Surfside.

This land, at the mouth of the Brazos River, is a flat coastal prairie threaded by waterways, crisscrossed by roads, and with bunchy salt grass as the predominant vegetation. The landward horizon is a great maze of towers and structures built for the manufacture of chemicals in large volume and, incidentally, providing a spectacular nighttime panorama of lights. There are dikes to thwart hurricane-driven tides. And there are inlets with docks and tie-up bollards for ocean-going tankers and cargo carriers, intracoastal barges, the shrimp boats long a part of the Brazosport scene, and the steadily increasing number of pleasure craft manned by both local residents and weekenders from Houston. The Gulf of Mexico provides—besides a means of transportation—one source of a salt and of cooling water for Dow production processes; beaches for sunbathing, swimming, and surfing; and shrimp to be taken, frozen, and shipped to market.

Statistics—either tons or dollars—won't be a major part of this book. But it needs saying that ships and barges carry away from Brazosport each year thousands of tons of Dow products, derived mainly from the salt and petroleum resources native to Texas. And all these flow toward the east because that's the way you get out of Brazosport by water, even if you're headed for Canada up the Mississippi River and through the Great Lakes, or for the Far East via the Panama Canal.

There's also a return flow. Millions of dollars come into Brazosport in a year—in paychecks to Dow employees and pensions to Dow retirees, as dividends to stockholders, for purchases from local suppliers and contractors, and as tax payments to various units of government. Both movements reflect the fact that applications of petrochemicals continue to increase, and an increasing number of the world's people are becoming users of these products.

Earle Barnes, president of Dow Chemical U.S.A., sparked the idea for this book with a comment on that flow of chemical products. He suggested that a step-by-step tracking of a single product—from raw material and first processing to end use in an everyday consumer application—could tell more about a multinational company than charts, graphs, statistics, and analytic studies. And he emphasized that what would make it a good story would be the people involved.

The idea was intriguing. Pick a basic Dow product. Find out all the activities the product spawns, and who gets involved in those activities. Then follow a typical shipment from its Dow-plant origin until—in whatever form—it reaches the ultimate consumer. And all along the way to talk with the people involved, not to gather historical data or predictions of the future, but to meet each person as an individual so as to learn a little about how he or she affects—and is affected by—a multinational business.

For the people in this book—the researcher in Brazosport, the deck officer on the *Bilderdyk*, the engineer in Guaruja, the sales manager in Cremona, the man-and-wife consumers in Berlin, and all the others—the common bond is thus a Dow product. More accurately, it's a group of related products in the family of urethane chemicals.

The choice of the urethanes dictated Brazosport, rather than Dow's corporate headquarters at Midland, Michigan, as my starting point. Brazosport—the company's largest production location, and the largest originator of American chemical industry exports—is the home base for Dow research and production activities in urethane chemicals.

For the author there's been a lot of fun in this venture, particularly in not knowing where the product would lead me—except that one leg of the trail would cross the Atlantic Ocean and the other would go south of the Equator. Here and there the chemistry and hardware of the business come to the fore, but the tight focus stays on what makes the business of chemicals and plastics and urethanes both multinational and very healthy—providing expanding opportunities for employees, profitable returns for investors, thriving markets for suppliers, and useful process materials and end products for customers.

The one apology I want to offer is to the many people, both in and out of Dow, who contributed information but who are not mentioned in the text. They helped educate me on a great variety of subjects, from managing a chemical business to piloting a ship and manufacturing picture frames.

It is characteristic of the chemical industry that even people working day-to-day close to the manufacture of a product may not know exactly where it ends up. It's quite possible, for instance, to walk into a store and see a suit of clothes, a pail of paint, or a chair, and—while knowing a number of chemicals were used in the article—not know whether the chemicals involved came from a plant just down the street or from halfway around the world. So part of my adventure was not knowing where in Europe my urethane trail would lead once it reached Rotterdam. And similarly in South America, where the product would go after leaving the polyol production plant at Guaruja.

It's my intent to get out of the way and let the people I met tell most of the story. But for the reader who knows as little about urethane chemicals as I did when this journey started, it may be helpful to identify them. Urethane chemicals are materials used to manufacture urethane plastic foams. In some formulations, urethane foam is so soft as to be ideal for pillows. In other formulations, the somewhat different foam that results is so utilitarian that it is a superior insulation material. And in still other formulations, urethane chemicals produce a material that can be molded to look exactly like wood—even matching the grain of an old tree—and either heavier or lighter as desired, and better than wood in some respects since it will neither expand nor contract with changes in temperature.

In a book about people, however, it would be out of place to dwell interminably on the product. So don't be misled by these comments.

Because *East From Brazosport* is about people—the people in and around and touched by a multinational business. The multinational trail of a product in movement simply provides the string that ties the people together.

1 | Sami From Iraq

"I got to watch for two minutes—one minute for Willys and one minute for GM."

He was born in Mosul, Iraq, and studied industrial chemistry at the university in Baghdad. After receiving his degree Sami Koudsi decided to specialize in rubber technology. Because Iraq had little industry he went to Lebanon where, at 22, he quickly landed a job. But before long Lebanon's rubber markets dried up—thanks to strong foreign competition and the turmoil of political upheavals in other Middle Eastern countries.

In the Bahrein Islands of the Persian Gulf, the oil business was booming. Sami, combining a job with cultural studies, worked there for a year. Then in Kuwait, where the oil business was even better. But the Persian Gulf climate is very hot; and besides, Sami wanted to get back into the rubber business which he'd studied at the university.

Because Iraq is a former British mandate, Sami had learned English in school. As he considered leaving the Middle East, Sami thought first of Britain, then the United States, Canada, and Australia. In each case there was a problem, such as waiting years for an opening in the U.S. immigration quota. His thoughts turned to South America.

"I thought first of Argentina because it is well known and more developed than Brazil. I went to the Argentine Embassy in Beirut to apply for a visa, and when I was leaving another boy told me, 'Go to the Brazilian Embassy, and you can get one right away.' I went there and the man asked, 'What's your work?' I said industrial chemistry, and in two minutes he gave me a visa for Brazil."

Two days later, carrying several books on Portuguese, the Brazilian language, he sailed for Italy where, at Genoa, he boarded the *Marco Polo*, bound for Santos in Brazil. When he reached South America, the 25-year-old Sami had $144. Today, business associates estimate his worth at $20 million.

In 1973 he was elected "Industrial Man of the Year" by Centro das Industrias de Estado de Sao Paulo, the leading industrial organization in the State of Sao Paulo. As we talked in his factory office in a suburb of Sao Paulo, Latin America's largest city, the story of Sami Koudsi was unfolded almost dollar by dollar, product by product.

The Brazilian magazine *Banas* started an article on Sami like this:

"Sami Koudsi does not have any of the mysteries and secrets that fiction lends to old Baghdad. He's an open and simple man who says what he wants with the will of one who knows what he wants."

Aside from the obvious variety of races—Indians, blacks, Orientals, whites, and all sorts of in-betweens (I was told that wherever the Portuguese have settled they have mixed with the local population)—there is little doubt the industrial part of Brazil was the most multinational I visited in two months of traveling. Here I talked with people born in Argentina, Chile, the People's Republic of China, Colombia, Hungary, Macao, Switzerland, the United States, and now Iraq. Except for Sami, they all worked for Dow. And they all—including Sami—had a part in one of the company's best businesses, the production and sale of urethane chemicals.

For Sami, it was only 30 days from the time he bought those Portuguese language books until he reached Brazil. En route, he studied Portuguese 14 to 18 hours a day. When he was four days from Brazil, he put his tongue to the test by asking another passenger to quiz him on any part of a 180-page book he'd found especially helpful.

By the time he reached Santos he was confident of his ability to answer questions, carry on a conversation in the language of his new country. He now spoke Arabic, English, Portuguese, some Aramaic, and some Kurdish.

Once landed, Sami headed for Sao Paulo, on a plateau 40 miles up the hills from Santos.

"With only $144 in my pocket, I needed to find a job right away. The first day after I arrived, I got a list of the 240 rubber companies in Sao Paulo. That night, in the *pension*, the house where I had a room, I took a map and started locating the 240 companies.

"On the second day, when I was calling on the 14th company, the man asked what salary I wanted. I said that for two months I would accept the minimum worker's salary, which was $40 a month, and during that time he could see how I did my job.

"After two months the company gave me not the salary of the worker or the salary of the technician, but $80 a month, and I was managing a plant with 350 workers. I was speaking Portuguese, and I was the number two man in the technical part of the business."

But Sami soon decided technicians were not paid good salaries in Sao Paulo and, unless he could find a better opportunity, he would leave Brazil. He found his opportunity 200 miles away, in Rio de Janeiro, where he tripled his salary by signing a six-month contract to work on the development of mattresses made of natural foam rubber.

At the end of the sixth month, when he'd been in Brazil less than a year, Sami decided he was ready to go into business for himself. He had a thousand dollars, and he had continued studying three to four hours a day, especially on innovations in rubber products. He calculated that what was sold for three cruzeiros could be manufactured for one cruzeiro, and that with his own company he could make ten times what he would earn working for someone else.

"I met a broker who took me to a small company that made parts for washing machines and brakes. The company was in very bad shape and losing money. The owners said, 'If you know the business, we'll give you 30 per cent of the profits and a small salary.' "

But they also offered Sami another deal: When the profits equalled the book value of the company, $10,000, they would take the profits and get out—and Sami could have the company. That was what appealed to him.

"To my surprise, after ten months with the company, the profits were 80 per cent of the value of the company."

Sami thought he was on the verge of owning the company. But he did not have a written contract.

"The owners said to me, 'Sami, it seems you don't yet understand Portuguese very well. We never made that kind of agreement.' "

And now I understood why Sami had emphasized he knew Portuguese even before leaving the ship at Santos. And why he detailed that he was speaking Portuguese in managing 350 workers on the first job in Sao Paulo.

Still, the situation was not all dark. The owners did give Sami the 30 per cent of the profits mentioned in the beginning. And in the next 12 months the company earned another 200 per cent of book value.

With his share of the earnings, Sami and a partner started their own company in 1955. This was the first Piramides company, a predecessor to Piramides Brasilia S.A., of which he is president.

At the start he continued on his old job, managing the new company during the Brazilian two-hour lunch period. But he soon

Sami Koudsi

9

decided the new venture needed his attention full time.

"During all this time I was always keeping up to date on the innovations in the rubber business in Europe and the United States. I subscribed to all the rubber magazines."

One thing he read about was rubber hoses for cars. In Brazil, such hoses were being made with textile reinforcement in an effort to withstand the high operating temperatures of engines. But, Sami learned by reading, manufacturers in the United States used no textiles in their hoses—having found the textile reinforcement of little or no practical value in hoses on modern passenger cars.

Sami decided to try the American approach, despite warnings of "you'll go broke" if he made hoses without the reinforcing material. Eliminating the reinforcement cut the cost, of course, and soon "I had 80 per cent of the market for rubber hoses, simply by following what had been successful in other countries. The big companies—Firestone, Goodyear, and Goodrich—didn't want to go into such things as small hoses in Brazil, so this is one of the things that made Piramides go very big. And we also made hoses that were reinforced with steel or textiles for the big trucks."

All this happened about 1956, when cars were being manufactured in Brazil for the first time, by Willys Jeep.

"When I saw that Brazil was starting a new era, I said this is the time and this is the place to grow. I began to contact the Americans working for Willys. One thing Willys found was that in Brazil, because we have lots of red mud, they needed rubber mats in the cars. But in Brazil rubber mats had never been made by the vacuum process.

"I decided to go to the United States, to

Toledo and Akron, and find out how they made the rubber mats. But the rubber companies didn't want to show me how they made the mats. I said I needed only one minute, but they said it was very complicated and one minute wouldn't help. I knew General Motors also needed the mats in Brazil, so I tried to get their help. Finally, in Akron, I got to watch for two minutes—one minute for Willys and one minute for GM.

"I saw that the secret was in the molds. So I got a book that listed all the tool companies in Akron, and I called each one to see who made the molds for rubber mats. After about 35 calls, one man finally said, 'Yes, I made all the molds for those mats. But that mat isn't being made any more, and just five

days ago we sent all the tools to Brazil.' "

Back in Brazil, Sami obtained the tools from Willys, and just two days later he delivered the first mat—with an offer to make any quantity wanted at seven cruzeiros each. GM, Ford, and Simca all became his customers and Sami became known as "the king of the molded rubber mats" in Brazil.

"Today 15 big companies are making molded rubber products by the same process we used then. But when I saw one company, then five, six companies start doing it, I got out of this business."

It was while he was still making mats that Sami was walking along 42nd Street in New York City one day. His eye caught a display of one-thong rubber sandals selling,

in a plastic bag, at three pairs for a dollar.

"In the United States you can't get lunch for a dollar, so I knew they must be imported from Japan. I said these would be good for Brazil, this is the type of thing that I can sell."

Back home he started experiments on how to make the sandals in mass production. With his brother-in-law, Antonio Haddad, and other partners he had started another company, Brasilia, for making shoes. He knew the sandals would be a good product for Brazilians, not just for the beaches but for everyday wear.

"There was no problem in putting them on the market. The people were anxious to get them. We soon had orders for our pro-duction 90 days ahead. They didn't cost much, and we made big profits, 300 per cent at times.

"Twenty-five million people began using these sandals, and more than 300 companies were founded to make them. Fifty per cent of the sandals are made not for the beaches but for regular wear."

As you might guess, Sami was moving on to other things before the 300 other companies joined in the sandal business. By this time, he had bought out his former partner in Piramides. Then, in 1963, he merged the Piramides and Brasilia compa-nies into Piramides Brasilia S.A.

Another U.S. idea he picked up through Brazilian friends was white sidewalls for tires. This was a rubber whitewall adhered to the tire with centrifugal pressure—again something that he thought would go even better in Brazil than in the United States.

"In Brazil, people like to make their cars very beautiful. There isn't anyone who doesn't wash his car on Saturday or Sunday. A lot of money was spent to make the tools needed to get the white sidewalls on the market. And I had already spent the money when one of my salesman said, 'Listen, Sami, this isn't going to sell. This time we are going to fail.' "

But Sami asked the salesman to give it a try for 10 or 15 days.

"I knew there were more than 1,500 taxi stops in Sao Paulo. So I told the salesman to go to these taxi stops and pick out the very nice taxis, the black cars, and give them the white sidewalls free. And at the taxi stop, just leave a card with our company's phone number.

"After one week of giving these away, we had a constant flow of cars that wanted the white sidewalls. The big parts shops began to buy our production, and for seven years we sold all we could make."

Sami's next idea led him into the ure-thane foam business. This one also started with Willys, which wanted to reduce the noise coming into its cars from the transmis-sions. Sami told Willys, "I can supply you with a floor mat that has one layer of ure-thane foam and one of jute. There will be an insulating space between the two layers, and this will hold out the noise and heat."

The heat from the engine is more of a problem in a tropical country than in the United States and GM also became interested.

At first Sami was a customer for ure-thane foam, buying from two Brazilian companies, Vulcan and Trorion. These two companies had introduced urethane foam in Brazil with technological and capital help from two large chemical manufacturers, Bayer of Germany and Union Carbide of the United States.

Sami became "so enthusiastic about the future for urethane foam in Brazil that I was suspicious there wouldn't be enough foam to meet our needs. I decided the only way to do was to go to the States and learn to make foam."

In the United States he received red-carpet treatment from manufacturers of the two major raw materials for urethane foam, polyols and toluene diisocyanate (TDI).

"Dow was very small in the urethane business at the time. They made polyols, they also were selling in Brazil the silicon stabiliz-er made by Dow Corning. But with the help of Dow, DuPont, and Union Carbide, I had the opportunity to learn the business in American laboratories.

"I came back to Brazil and began to make experiments for moving everything from rubber to urethane foam. In 1966, the foam business was so good that we shut down all our rubber business and put all our strength in urethane foam. The business was increasing everywhere—for mattresses, pillows, and automotive cushioning.

"We did not buy our first polyol from Dow, but when we tried the Dow CP-3000 product we discovered it was the best polyol at that time, and we increased the volume we bought from Dow.

"In the United States, only 10 to 15 per cent of the mattress business was in urethane, very small in relation to box springs. But one day I received a call from a French company; they were having a very big celebration for their manufacture of the one-millionth urethane mattress.

"In Brazil, some people said urethane mattresses would never be big sellers because the foam would feel too warm. But I went to France for that celebration and found one very good idea, designing the mattresses so that there was some air between the cloth and the foam.

"It wasn't long before the mattress business doubled for our company, and for the other companies in Brazil. Piramides has now manufactured more than two million mattresses. Dow saw what was happening and decided this business was going to be very big."

So Dow and Piramides Brasilia agreed to a joint venture, the Propenasa company, for the construction and operation of a polyol production plant at Guaruja, Brazil. At this site Dow already had a dock and tanks for unloading and storing bulk chemicals shipped from the United States, and was planning for a plant to produce styrene-butadiene latex.

From Brazosport come the major raw materials, propylene oxide and ethylene oxide, for the Propenasa plant, owned 80 per cent by Dow and 20 per cent by Piramides Brasilia.

"This plant is very good for the urethane foam business in Brazil because the foam companies now have assurance of the availability of the polyol. The top people at Dow are very interested in the plant. The people who work for Dow like the company. They show enthusiasm. And they are proud of their company. Even when someone leaves the company, they speak well of Dow. Because they always are looking to the future, the top people keep in close contact with Brazil and this helps the company to grow."

Business growth is something Sami and his partner Antonio know well. Piramides Brasilia has its headquarters and its largest factory, with 1,300 employees, in Santo Amaro, a suburb of Sao Paulo. But it also employs 500 people at its subsidiary plants in six other Brazilian locations—Rio Grande do Sul, Curitiba, Rio de Janeiro, Votuporanga, Recife, and Salvador.

Twenty-five per cent of the company's stock is now owned publicly, and more than 1,000 Brazilians are stockholders. When entering the Propenasa venture, Dow acquired a 30 per cent interest in Piramides Brasilia. This was reduced to 23 per cent when Piramides put six million shares on the open market.

Because of its fast growth, Piramides has caught up with the pioneers and is probably Brazil's largest company in urethane foam. Vulcan and Trorion, both technically strong and aggressive in market expansion, also continue to grow rapidly. Other companies also are growing. All are customers of the Propenasa polyol plant and thus users of the products manufactured by Dow in Texas.

Piramides, meanwhile, has expanded into other plastics—polyvinyl chloride, low-density polyethylene, polystyrene, ABS (acrylonitrile-butadiene-styrene). In a sepa-

rate company, Sami and Antonio have invested in the steel industry. They also build apartment houses, including one near the Santo Amaro factory where employees can buy apartments with a ten per cent down payment. They recently bought a ranch with 4,000 cattle and have organized a trading company called Interpetrol. The combined sales of Piramides and the steel company will reach $80 million in 1974.

"My opinion is that this economy will grow very fast during the next ten years. Brazil will be the giant of South America, like the U.S. in North America. The greatness of any country depends on the natural resources and the people, sometimes the two together with the leaders. Brazilians are a very patient people, and they are hard working.

"Out of 100 million people, only 35 million are today really consumer buyers of manufactured products, but every year three to five more million are becoming consumers.

"During my first year in Brazil I received calls from more than 100 salesmen a month, but only five per cent had cars. Today, we have more than 500 salesmen a month, and 99 per cent have cars.

"I have 150 salesmen in my company, and the 150 all have cars. Today our plant has parking for 180 to 220 cars while only seven years ago there were only 20 cars here.

"There are 750,000 cars sold in one year in Brazil, and each car represents three or four persons. Look at all the new apartments. The cheapest is $10,000, and some cost $50-100,000.

"There are two philosophies in the world today. One is for revolution to redistribute the wealth. That's what the socialists and communists believe.

"The other way is by evolution—to create jobs and the wealth and then redistribute the wealth as the economy can support it. Brazil has chosen the second alternative. If there's no savings from the rich and middle classes to make jobs, you cannot grow.

"The Brazilian government is putting great emphasis on seeing that these savings are reinvested to stimulate economic growth. A just redistribution of the wealth created by this growth policy will be made by heavier taxation when the Brazilian economy is large enough to support it. This will minimize the great differences between the classes that exist today."

So that "from the beginning he will live with the workers and see what it takes to get ahead," Sami's 18-year-old son Eduardo, oldest of four children, has worked in the Santo Amaro plant for five years. He works from 8 a.m. to 6 p.m. and attends school at night, taking business administration from 7 to 11 p.m.

It was during his third year in Brazil that Sami married a Brazilian, her father of Lebanese descent and her mother a German. When he had been in Brazil ten years, he phoned his father and mother to invite them for a visit. It was a time of political problems and instability in the Middle East and they, along with Sami's three brothers and sister, all decided to move to Brazil.

Today there's scant trace of the Koudsi family in the Arab world where Sami grew up, except for a project that he cares about a great deal. It's the home in Beirut that he built and supports to care for 60 people who have no other homes—one way of remembering whence he got the education and the means for reaching Brazil.

2 | Not Like a Cruise

"On a cruise ship, you can have a little fun...Some people call it being a 'gigolo,' but we like 'entertainer.'"

On dry land you may hear a lot about the romance of life at sea. But not on a cargo carrier or a tanker. It's not like a pleasure cruise.

That is why most of the officers of the Dutch cargo carrier *Bilderdyk* were incredulous at my choice of the ship for travel from the United States to the Dow terminal at Rotterdam. I made the 14-day trip in the early summer—along with 179 drums of VORANOL RS-350 polyol, a few thousand bags and drums of other Dow products, and tons of magnesium metal. All the cargo was loaded in barges that had been lifted directly onto the *Bilderdyk* after being towed to rendezvous points off the coasts of Texas and Louisiana.

It's not that work aboard a cargo carrier is hard. And for someone like me, on his first voyage, the whole trip can be a lark. But for those who have made dozens of trips—and the *Bilderdyk* had men who knew most of the ports of Africa and Central and South America, as well as the busier harbors of the North Atlantic—there's a constant struggle against boredom, and a countdown of days till vacation.

And this is easy to understand. Even on my first crossing of the North Atlantic by ship, the nine days from Savannah to Sheerness, England, would have become dull were

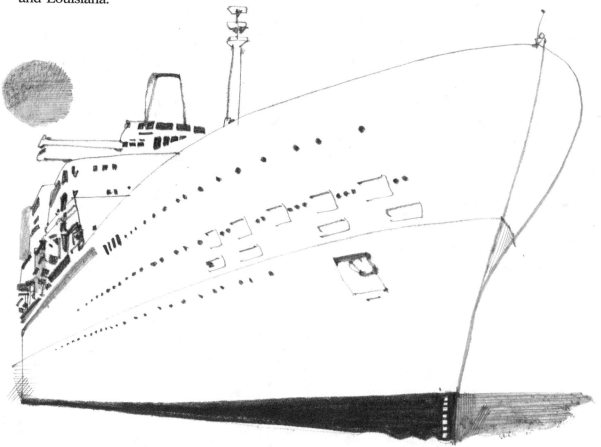

it not for the interesting people aboard. Perhaps it's because the ship is owned and manned by the Holland-America Line, long renowned in running pleasure cruises, that the officers and crew were so hospitable. Certainly I debarked with great admiration for their capability and the hope that our paths would cross again, even if my first trip on a freighter probably was also the last. So it was that, one day weeks later in Sao Paulo, I remembered that this very day the *Bilderdyk* was due to dock in Texas.

I wondered whether Ben de Haas, second officer of the *Bilderdyk*, had succeeded in winning an assignment on a cruise ship following his one-month vacation, or if he was back on the bridge of the big cargo carrier. It had been three years ago, 28 years after he was born in a Japanese prison camp, that Ben had met all the requirements for a master's certificate—a license to captain any ship of any tonnage in the Dutch merchant navy. But the Holland-America Line today operates only a fraction of the ships it had when passenger transport was a going business. Today Ben's prospects are not bright for soon becoming a captain, or even a "chief mate." (And the younger officers will tell you that it really is the chief mate who runs a ship; the captain is there to take the responsibility.) After nine voyages on the *Bilderdyk*, and ten previous weeks getting acquainted with this then-new type of ship while it was in dry dock at Rotterdam, Ben was hoping he could go back to the caviar and champagne of the cruises.

Duty on a cruise ship is different than on a freighter. And it's also a great contrast to Ben's first ocean voyage, when he was deported from Indonesia. Because they were Dutch citizens, Ben's mother, his two brothers, and his two sisters had been put in prison camps when the Japanese occupied

Indonesia early in 1942. His father was shipped to Burma to work for the Japanese in building the military railroad that included the bridge over the River Kwai. After the war the Indonesians, revolting against return of Dutch rule, sent the family to another prison camp—worse than the one they'd been in during the war.

"But as a matter of fact, when my mother laughs in recalling incidents in the Japanese camp, I can't believe that it really was so bad." The Indonesian government offered his mother a choice: Give up her Dutch citizenship and remain, or be deported to Holland. His father was born in Holland, but his mother's ancestry is a mixture of Dutch, Indonesian, and French. Ben himself is dark, a slim 5 feet 7, with an Oriental glint in his eyes.

In the Indonesian prison camp in 1946, Ben's mother had no idea where her husband was, and she chose deportation to Holland. Ben was only four years old, so he has only faint recollections of the trip. But he does remember going to the large port city of Surabaja on an Australian airplane. "The door was missing from the plane, and I remember there was a soldier naked from the waist up who had a tommy gun and wouldn't let us talk. My mother had made all our clothes from bedsheets, and everything else we owned was wrapped in a handkerchief."

They traveled to Amsterdam on the Dutch ship *New Holland*, with some 2,500 to 3,000 other deportees. At a small island near the Suez Canal they went ashore to receive shirts, pants, and rain shoes from the American Red Cross. Either en route to Holland, or shortly after they arrived—Ben doesn't remember just where—they were joined by his father. Not for many months, though, because his father returned to Indo-china and divorced his mother.

"In Amsterdam, we were put in a house that is very, very nice, by European standards at least, and my mother still lives there. It was a rather awkward location, quite a distance from the city, and we didn't even have a bike. But today it's in an area where the millionaires live. The neighbors all have a number of cars, but my mother still takes the bus."

All of which helps explain why Ben is a deck officer of a ship. As a schoolboy he wanted to be an artist or an actor. His vocational testing and his school activities—in acting, writing for the school magazine, and painting—all pointed in the same direction, as did his marks in painting and sculpture.

"My mother and oldest brother, for reasons very easy to understand, didn't want money thrown away on something as doubtful as being an artist." His mother lived on a government allowance, and Ben went to college on government funds—to the Nautical College in Amsterdam, close to his home. "I was chasing girls then, and my mother said I'd better go where there was a stick behind the door. 'They'll teach you some manners there.'"

Ben was among 150 students who came out of that school, Holland's oldest nautical college, to go to sea as an apprentice in 1960. The captain on Ben's first voyage was Arie Van Dijk, the same master captaining the *Bilderdyk* on my trip. Ben and the captain, who was substituting for the regular master, hadn't seen each other in 13 years.

What Ben remembers most about his first voyage was a fire at night halfway to Vera Cruz, Mexico, and Captain Van Dijk going below deck carrying a fire extinguisher and wearing a breathing apparatus. There was a thick swell of smoke, and the fire seemed worse than it actually proved to be when brought under control after an hour.

"I thought this was the usual routine and described it that way when I wrote home. My mother showed the letter to my brother who also had been in the merchant navy, and he said, 'There Ben goes, exaggerating as usual.'"

Most of Ben's time in the 1960s was at sea, calling at ports in India, Pakistan, Burma, Saudi Arabia, Israel, the United States, all over the European coast except Scandinavia, and in many of the small countries of Africa. At the same time—meeting the experience requirements, taking tests, and returning to school for brief periods—he was progressing toward his master's certificate.

By this summer it all had become very routine, unloading and loading barges onto the *Bilderdyk*, going back and forth across the ocean. "I'd like a little variety in this job. On a cruise ship, you can have a little fun—you can have anything, being an entertainer all night. Some people call it being a 'gigolo,' but we like 'entertainer,'" he laughed.

"My wife would like me back on a cruise ship too, because then she would want to go along. I love to take my wife on cruises from New York to the Caribbean. On the first day, during the bad weather before we reach the horse latitudes, everybody is getting acquainted. Then it's to the swimming pool and ashore at the ports. And by the time we are coming home the passengers are spending so much time with each other they don't even care about the bad weather."

Ben's wife is Louisa—he calls her "Loeky"—a girl from The Hague whom he met when they were both 14 and watching a rowing match between nautical colleges. It was eight years later, in 1964, that they were married, and both still were young.

His wife doesn't go on many trips, cruise or freighter, because she tends to get seasick, and Ben says he'd never take her on a ship lacking stabilizers. (A stabilizer, Ben noted, "is an airplane wing that we shove out the side of the ship. We can reduce the rolling about 40 per cent, but there's nothing we can do about pitching, the ship's too long." He also explained that the "horse latitudes" were given that name in the days of sail-driven ships when horses were dumped in this region of the ocean after they died from the heat in the holds of ships becalmed by lack of wind.)

And what does his wife think about the cruises when she is not aboard?

"She says that it's when I stop chasing

women that she'll get worried. She says it's good for my ego.

"Seamen's wives have to be very independent. I'm not saying they are, but you'd better get one who is. My wife is very independent. She's fun, she's not jealous, I detest jealous people.

"She came right from her mother. I'd prefer a girl who had her wild years before she married. She left me once, and that was a mess. Oh, that was a mess. Now she knows how important she is to me."

When they married, Loeky had just completed her schooling to become a hair dresser, and for 10 to 12 years after her marriage she had worked. But now she had quit, and she'd accompanied Ben on the *Bilderdyk's* previous trip. And Ben was looking forward to his vacation after reaching Rotterdam.

"She's never home. She's always moving around and doing something. I don't know what. She'd really like to have a little shop, a boutique, with perfume and exclusive things. That's quite an investment, and I don't have that kind of money. But if that's what she's got in her head, I wouldn't be surprised if that's what she did."

For vacations, they seldom do much planning. "If we want to go somewhere, we just go, but I'm never sure when I'll have time off." And it wasn't until five days before we reached Rotterdam that a radio message confirmed a leave for Ben when the ship reached home port.

"Last year I had only one month of holidays because of the shortness of people (deck officers). I intend to have more this year. I can't stand it any more. When I go on vacation it means I'm sick and tired of the water. A job that would appeal to me is the Peace Corps in Africa. Of course, you don't get any money, but I like the idea of doing

Ben de Haas

something different."

Except that an office job—"sitting behind a desk eight to five"—isn't Ben's idea of doing something different. He's turned down three desk jobs, even though they offered better pay.

So I wondered what's next for Ben de Haas? His hopes were high he'd land aboard Holland-America's newest cruise ship, scheduled for 14-day voyages out of Singapore. Among the countries to be visited is Indonesia, and Ben would like that. Though he's seen much of the world, he's never been back to Java since that day in 1946 when he left barefoot and clothed in bedsheets.

3 | "B" for Broaddus

"We have things to keep doing, so we don't have time to sit down and concentrate on the rat race. Most of our life has been raising kids."

Bill Broaddus is lean, red-haired, freckled, 6 feet 4¾ inches—a foot and a half taller than his mother—and a 20-year employee of Dow in Texas. He is an operator in the plant that produces polyols for the manufacture of rigid-urethane products—foam for the insulation of refrigerators, for example, and synthetic wood for sculptured furniture.

At the time we talked at the plant, and at Bill's home in Clute, this plant manufactured all the polyols sold by Dow anywhere in the world for use in making rigid urethanes and also some of those for flexible urethanes. The drums of RS-350 aboard the *Bilderdyk* were produced in this plant.

Fifty-one years old, Bill is a friendly, outgoing Texas native who obviously enjoys talking about football more than polyols. His two oldest sons, Jimmy and Mark, were outstanding high school players, and both enrolled at Texas A&M University after considering football scholarships offered by 14 universities.

Bill also played high school football. "But at the little ol' Mickey Mouse school I went to, it wasn't worth mentioning. We had 16 on the team. We was too busy pickin' cotton, plowin', and cuttin' sprouts to play football. We just played whenever we could."

Bill's high school was in the town of Corrigan, named for Pat Corrigan, a genial Irish conductor on the first passenger train to pass through what was then a lumbering camp. (That was in the 1880s. Some 50 years later, Pat's grandson Douglas became famous as "Wrong Way" Corrigan—the 20-year-old pilot who flew the Atlantic Ocean in a $900 monoplane, blaming a faulty compass when he arrived in Ireland instead of Los Angeles, which he claimed he was trying to fly to.)

"I was mostly raised around East Texas. I guess you'd rightly say my home was right in the heart of the sticks—an East Texas hillbilly. We lived in different places, but when I was in high school we lived six miles from town.

"Other times we'd walk a mile to school, sometimes three miles. But walking was nothing then. Everybody walked. We didn't have a car. We went wherever we went on horseback.

"They didn't have school buses then. Come to think of it, my youngest brother [in a family of 11 children] probably rode the school bus, but the rest of us walked.

"We never had to worry much about cold weather. You could go swimming in February. The lowest the temperature ever got was about 20 degrees. We were tough as a boot anyway. Jerked up by the hair of the head.

"Kids were tough then. I bet you that when I was a kid we'd eat things that'd make a dog sick today. When we saw something we wanted, we'd just eat it—berries, stuff like that."

Bill has twice crossed the Atlantic Ocean by ship. "Two pretty good trips overseas and back when I was in the Army during World War II. On the *Queen Mary*, going over, it was five days and nights. We came back on a washtub, a Liberty ship, 18 days and nights."

It was while he was in the Army, stationed in Oklahoma, that he met his wife, Ruth. "I went up there to help set up a camouflage base, just a little patch of woods. She was going to high school.

"When I got out of the Army I thought I'd work for a motor freight company, and I started driving a truck. I was drawing 65 cents an hour. I still got some of my old W-2 forms—$3,100 with overtime.

"Well, anyway, I got to be dock foreman, but couldn't stand that Oklahoma weather. That town, Woodward, got blown away in 1947, blocks of it. I don't know if you've ever been in the panhandle of Oklahoma, but I always figured that was where the Lord finished. He didn't have anything left, and He was tired, so He just throwed it down and quit right there. That's the way it looks.

"It is just exactly the opposite down

here. In the average year the rainfall here is about 50 inches—something like that, 40, 50, 60 inches. Up there it is about 12 to 13 inches, and the wind blows 50 to 60 miles an hour. When they'd see a storm coming, everybody would go in a cave and look out. I just got sick of that place and took off. Everytime I go back up there I get a bad feeling, but my wife didn't know anything else.

"I had put in for a transfer to Houston. I had enough seniority to bump in down here, but I didn't want to just bump in.

"I came down here because I had a brother, Theodore, working at Dow. He's been in the same department ever since he started here 23 years ago—a shift foreman in glycerine production. Synthetic glycerine, you know, is Dow's own baby, they invented that.*

"I started in the mag cells, and worked there until I got laid off when mag [magnesium metal] production was shut down in 1958. I got a job in highway construction and worked there for nine weeks until I was called back.

"That same year I transferred to polyethylene, I started in the bagging room. We

*Broaddus gives Dow a bit too much credit; Shell Chemical was the first producer of synthetic glycerine. Dow, with its own process, was second by a couple of years.

used to have to bag it by hand. Now most of it is shipped in railroad carloads, car after car.

"I never really had a job that I actually liked. I never had one that didn't get to be a routine, never really had one that I really, actually enjoyed. Like when I used to plow, I didn't like it. Here (in polyol production) it's not a bad place to work, it's a lot better than pickin' cotton."

Just what is Bill's job, and how are polyols manufactured? Bill gives the techni-

21

Jackson from a Brady Daguerreotype

General Andrew Jackson

cal terminology a bit of a rural flavor, and here's how it goes.

"There are about 65 different types of VORANOLS [*Voranol* is a Dow trademark for polyols], and some of them are radically different. The rigid stuff is probably the most interesting. The first thing we do is charge the reactor with a batch of sugar. We load it up into a hopper and dump it in there in a vacuum. Then we pull all the air out of the reactor, and then we add propylene oxide. Then we add a catalyst to make it react. Then we heat it to the reaction temperature. It just sits there and you might say 'cooks.'

"Then it goes to an exotherm, which is a fast reaction. Then you cool it so far and then hold the temperature. Then all these molecules do their thing."

And: "The centrifuge is just like a big old milk separator. It flings off the caustic, and it flings off the salt . . . you run the stuff through this filter, and it will filter out water and things you can't even see. When it comes out it's like a syrup . . . the last stripping column takes out the last little bit of hydrocarbon and water. It comes out completely clean.

"It gets to be a routine. But the way I figure it I'm lucky. My wife's the same way. With the six kids, we don't have time to worry about all the poppycock that is going on. It's a rat race, I'll grant you that. But we have things to keep doing, so we don't have time to sit down and concentrate on the rat race. Most of our life has been raising kids."

The Broaddus children are Janie, 23, mother of two herself, whose husband works for Dow; Jimmy, 21, in the Army at Fort Polk, Louisiana, and married to a girl he met in the third grade; Mark, 20, a junior at Texas A&M, engaged to a Lake Jackson girl; Virginia, 16, already the winner of 25 to 30 trophies for achievements in softball and the President's physical fitness program; Clark, 13; and Bonnie, 11.

Though he's only 13, Clark already is 6 feet 1 and weighs 210 pounds—"and he's in shape." Clearly it is the men in the Broaddus family who have the size. While Bill's mother is not quite 5 feet (she now lives in Brazosport), his father was 6 feet 3.

"General Andrew Jackson was a distant cousin on my daddy's side. My mother was a Booth, and with our first child we were going to fix up the family tree and all that stuff. We got diggin' back too far on the Booths. Mixed up in it was ol' what's his name [John Wilkes Booth, assassin of President Abraham Lincoln]. My daddy came from up around Caldwell, and we found a relative was one of the commissioners who started Texas A&M University."

Managing a Little League baseball team, umpiring in Little League, following the boys in football at Brazosport and Brazoswood High Schools, then at Texas A&M, Bill always has kept busy, especially in activities involving youngsters. His wife, Ruth, is a saleswoman at the Montgomery Ward store, and the two of them also drive a school bus route. Their passengers are in the 11 to 13 age group in a special education program.

"There are a lot more kids in special education than there used to be. These kids are just slow learners. Some missed a lot of school because of illness.

"Since I work shifts, Ruth and I just work it out so that one of us can drive. When I'm working in the evenings, I drive in the mornings. She drives it on her lunch period in the afternoon. And when I'm on days she drives before she goes to work and on her lunch period. And when I'm on graveyards [post-midnight], she takes part of the route and I catch it soon as I get home. I meet her at the school house and take it from there."

As we talked we were sitting in a den that had been added to the back of their brick home. "The reason I built this on here was that one of the kids was in a band. I've got it almost soundproofed here, so it will soak up that sound. The kids wanted to practice out there in the garage, and they were disturbing the peace."

On the wall hung a big pennant with one large initial in the center, a "B." I asked if the "B" was for Brazosport or Brazoswood, the

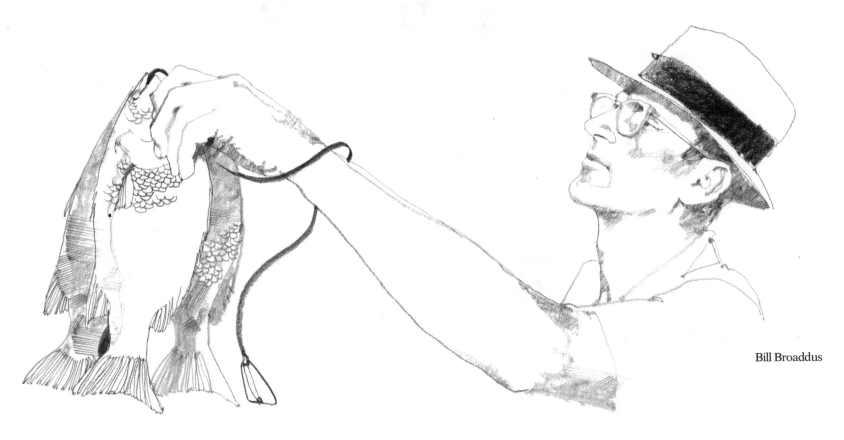

Bill Broaddus

23

two high schools where the older boys had played football, but I was wrong on both counts. The "B," Bill explained, is for Broaddus.

Deep-sea fishing has been another activity of his, though limited because Mark was the only member of the family who shared his dad's interest. "Man, it's a chore to catch fish out there, about 30 miles out. It's work. You get over a hole that's full of 'em, and you just reel 'em up. Once we brought home 600 pounds of red snapper.

"I used to have a boat of my own, lost it in one of the layoffs or strikes. In the first five years I was here we had two strikes and a layoff. For four years we were really struggling."

The Broaddus family lives on Hargett Street, which starts at Main Street and runs to an area that includes the home of the Clute Little League. This has two lighted baseball fields with bleachers and a sign reading "20th Anniversary, 1953-1973." Nearby are the big, new Brazoswood High School, with a flagpole flying both the U.S. and Texas flags and a parking lot with 31 motor bikes, several dozen cars, and six school buses; and the Terrell W. Ogg Elementary School, a colorful structure that combines panels of yellow, blue, reddish-orange, and battleship gray with red bricks.

It's a wooded area, true to the name of the high school. On both sides of Hargett Street, there's a drainage culvert, with concrete tiles running under the gleaming white, oyster-shell driveways. At the Broaddus home were the small old Dodge school bus, a pickup truck, and two cars. On the front lawn there's a water hydrant and a gas light, and on the roof a tall television antenna.

Closer to Main Street the homes are older. Just before Main Street there's the

Kingdom Hall of the Jehovah's Witnesses. A large sign in front lists the services on Sundays, Tuesdays, and Fridays—in both English and Spanish, with separate services on Sundays but combined congregations on the other days.

Then there's the big water tower, with the town's name lettered on the tank, rising above buildings housing the police department and the city offices. In one direction is the U.S. Post Office, newest building on Main Street; down the other way—toward the Dow plant—there's a variety of business houses.

One sign above the sidewalk advertises "Look Beautiful, The Wig Boutique, Wholesale Prices, Specializing in Styling." Another, in red, white, and blue, says "W.C. Thomas, Justice of the Peace, Precinct 6, Marriage Ceremonies Performed."

This part of Brazosport is home for the Broadduses, and they like it here. When the boys were looking at the colleges that wanted them to play football, their parents urged them to pick one close to home.

"They almost went to Oklahoma University. SMU, TCU, Baylor worked on 'em real hard. We went up to Arkansas. Ruth and I had a ball. That was before they passed this rule that they couldn't feed you and take you out as part of the recruiting."

In the summer of 1972, Bill had walked the picket line during a strike. This spring everything looked better. Mark had just arrived home from college. He already had a job working for a contractor in the Dow plant, and he was going to be married in just a couple of weeks. The two families had gotten together to plan a barbecue at the Lone Star Park for the night before the wedding.

Her daddy was going to bring the drinks and the beer. I was invited, and I hoped I'd be in town for the party.

4 | Tremendous Cheek

"I'll tell you the reason for this success...We've been very aggressive in trying to change the European concept of this business."

The English pound sterling, worth about two and a half dollars, was declining in dollar value in the summer of 1973. Five years earlier the pound was worth a bit more, but not much. And Geoff Gaywood was down to his last five pounds on the autumn day in '68 when he drove from London to Rotterdam, crossing the English Channel on a ferry boat from Dover to Calais, France.

Geoff, 25 and "desperate for a job," had high hopes of an offer to join the expanding organization of Dow Europe. But he didn't have time to wait for routine processing of his application.

Besides, he wanted to marry an Israeli girl he'd met while taking a summer course at Munich University in Germany. That was when Geoff had expected to study for a Ph.D. degree in chemical engineering with the help of British government funds earmarked for a development project. Now the project had been abandoned, Geoff wouldn't go for the Ph.D., and jobs were scarce.

So, working on a long shot, he had answered an ad. Dow needed an assistant superintendent to help run a big new naphtha cracker at the Dow production complex in Terneuzen, Holland. Tony Radcliffe, a Terneuzen production superintendent, interviewed Geoff at the Dow office in London.

The production superintendent listened for almost an hour, then told Geoff, "I don't think you know a damn thing about naphtha crackers. But you've got tremendous cheek [that's the British word for boldness], and I'm sure we have a place for you in this organization."

Another interview, about a job in purchasing, yielded a promise that the Dow people would talk about it in Rotterdam.

"Well, I just didn't have enough time for

them to talk about it, so I called and said I was coming to Holland anyway. And there I had one more interview. And thank God I got the job—because that meant my expenses were paid for the trip."

On the summer day when we talked in Switzerland, Geoff was preparing for a business trip to Norway—with no question of whether he'd have enough cash to get home. In 1973, four years after joining Dow, he was now the Dow Europe product marketing manager for molding, rigid, and elastomer urethane chemicals. Describing his responsibilities, sorting out the company's strengths and weaknesses in urethane chemicals, he did no hiding of his confidence that Dow was going to do well in this growing market.

One part of the urethane chemical business is the selling of polyols to customers who produce huge slabs of foam to be cut up for a variety of uses. Geoff described Dow sales to this slab stock market as "a tremendous success story. There's no doubt about it. We've been growing at something like 30 per cent per year in slab stock.

"If you want me to be blunt, I'll tell you the reason for this success. We've been very aggressive. We've been very aggressive in trying to change the European concept of this business."

Changing the European concept meant winning customers away from almost complete reliance on the company that invented urethane chemistry, Bayer of Germany. Bayer sells polyols, and also formulates systems which include the other major raw material, the isocyanates—and even the machinery for production of urethane products.

"To penetrate the European market, we did have to look at Bayer very carefully. And, as with very much of Dow Europe's business, our goal is to penetrate the very big and

profitable markets in Germany and France and Italy and the United Kingdom."

Obviously Geoff relishes his role in market competition against some of the world's leading chemicals manufacturers. He's come a long way from his school days in London—for which his father "made tremendous sacrifices" to provide what Geoff describes as a "most exceptional chance in

Geoff Gaywood

life. Those schools are tremendously well endowed and have wonderful facilities.

"When I left school I went out looking for work in industry because I'd chosen to be a chemical engineer. I was more or less penniless, I wanted some money in my pocket, and I wanted to know what chemical engineering was all about.

"I worked as what they call a section engineer in a towns gas [natural gas] plant near my home, and I worked on a number of different units. This is in a nationalized, state-owned industry, and it was at a time in the U.K. when things were going very badly, even worse than they are now.

"The plant was run in a very stifling way. Every kind of initiative was crushed. Any suggestion that we shouldn't do anything the same way it'd been done for the last 30 years was stamped on very rigorously. It put one ambition in me, and that was to get out of the U.K. as fast as I could. And I went up to the university, Imperial College in London, to study chemical engineering."

Though his entry into the purchasing field when he joined Dow was completely unpremeditated, "It turned out tremendously well for me because it was a very, very stimulating atmosphere. There was a new man running the purchasing business, a guy who knows Dow Chemical very well and who is a very innovative manager, a tremendous motivator, Steve Marshall."

Geoff had a big challenge when he was in purchasing. For a time there was a world-wide shortage of toluene diisocyanate (TDI), the raw material that is combined with polyols to manufacture urethane products. Dow then produced only the polyols. Competitors manufacturing both products were in a better position to supply TDI when a customer coupled this business with an order for polyols. Geoff's job was to negotiate purchases of enough TDI so that Dow Europe also could supply both materials and thus keep from losing polyol customers. Moreover, he had to buy the TDI at prices that would save Dow from losing its shirt in the purchase and resale of a material for which demand exceeded supply.

As a marketing manager, Geoff also faced a substantial challenge. In 1973 his products accounted for only about ten per cent of the company's urethane chemical sales in Europe. Dow had not done as well in selling polyols for molded and rigid urethanes as in the polyols for flexible products.

"The business I have is very new. We have an awful lot to learn. We have comparatively small volume. Right now we are selling two and a half times as much as we were at this time last year. I think that is the right kind of order of magnitude to justify our present program.

"But in rigids we must be constantly reviewing our objectives, constantly deciding on which businesses we really have to put the biggest efforts in. We have to be very self-critical here. We have to be prepared to change the decision we made six months ago if the situation changes, and it does change very quickly."

In uses of rigid urethanes, Europe has two markets of major interest— insulation, with 50 per cent of this business going into refrigerators and growing overall at the rate of 20 per cent a year, and synthetic wood, still quite small but growing at a rapid rate between 40 and 60 per cent a year.

The refrigerator market has been one of frustration for Dow Europe. More efficient than other available insulating materials, urethane foam changed the refrigerator industry by permitting the thin-wall designs prevalent today. Dow, long a supplier of polystyrene foam insulation to the refrigerator industry, was in good position to sell urethane chemicals to the same customers. So it's difficult to measure the Dow vexation in missing most of this business because its technology in rigid urethane foams was lagging.

"We have been trying for six years to break into this business," Geoff said, "and we learned rather bitterly it's a little more sophisticated than we thought it was. We just didn't put enough effort in it at the right time. Meanwhile our competitors have made a lot of money.

"We may have the answer now. There is a lot of Dow development work on the refrigeration business, and once that is settled we will be able to realign our priorities a bit better."

Meanwhile, the development of urethane systems for production of synthetic wood also is demanding sophisticated technology. This is one of the more interesting current activities in the chemical industry. Although the sales volume is small, the rapid annual growth rate attracts attention.

"The reason for the very rapid growth is that Europe's wood resources are simply running out, and plastics are beginning to get over the image of being second-rate replacements for something else. If you can apply those plastics to make something that has virtue because it is being made from plastic, then you can sell—especially in Sweden and Italy, two countries that have furniture makers who are especially innovative.

"The furniture manufacturers are molding bigger and bigger pieces, and these pieces are inevitably slightly imperfect. Somewhere or another there always is a bubble on the surface, which has to be worked by hand afterwards, and this is exactly opposite of the direction the furniture industry wants to go. This means we have to develop better and better products for these applications.

"We are aiming at a particular segment of the furniture market—the fashion end of it, where only a limited number of items will be made. And we are aiming at that segment because this is where urethanes score. The cost of the polyurethane is comparatively high, but the capital investment needed to make a piece is comparatively low. If you only want a few pieces, urethanes score very handily indeed. But in a huge-volume business, hundreds of thousands of pieces, we cannot compete with the cost of other plastics like polystyrene.

"Fortunately the part of the European furniture industry that is growing really rapidly is this fashion-related segment—in Sweden, because that is such a consumer market, and in Italy, because they have such a flair for design. The business is changing almost yearly. Europeans are getting used to throwing their furniture out, which is a complete turnaround, really.

"Urethanes also succeed because they facilitate versatility in design. With urethanes the design is not just a flat top with four legs. You can have a great, sweeping foot to the table. And you can have massive pieces that don't weigh as much as if they were made out of wood—which would just not be practical to make out of wood."

Despite his youth, and his newness in his job as a product marketing manager, Geoff has definite ideas on the business strategy that will best nourish Dow success in the urethane field.

"Our business is enormously fragmented. We have to be very careful not to develop a new product for every single customer. And it isn't a homogeneous market at all. We can go out with a new product that will be enthusiastically accepted by one customer but rejected by another. In Sweden, for instance, we have a very prestigious customer, a well-run organization, that continues to stay with a polyol we thought would go off the market following our introduction of a new product that we thought was better. In this case, it wasn't conservatism; they just think the predecessor product is better. So we are trying to find some common means in which to work. We are trying to bring our business together now and get a program that is more uni-directional.

"Increasing our capacity for urethane production in Europe, and getting a position in isocyanates with Dow production in Texas, will help us. And I must say the new basic chemical production complex at Stade will help us tremendously in Germany, where the urethane market is large and profitable.

"Without European production, we would just have no chance to grow, or even maintain our present market share. Customers are naturally concerned about assurance of supply. Just as in most of the chemical business, we've had continual cycling with shortage and oversupply and prices yo-yo-ing up and down. And of course, your customer forgets the time when he was buying from you at a low price for a long time. As soon as a product gets short and must be allocated, the loyalties get changed around. Everybody is in the same boat.

"The production people at the Terneuzen plant do a fantastic job of turning out product, 'way over and above the designed capacity. We have adequate product now, but we have an expansion coming on at Terneuzen next year to assure our position of adequate availability.

"We will build a new plant at Stade, which will come on to secure our postion. At Tarragona, Spain, we have a new plant that we commissioned earlier this year. We now are a domestic Spanish producer, and that is tremendous for our position as a supplier. That will be a very good investment, no doubt about that one.

"Right now the industry's production capacity in Europe is greater than the market demand, but the situation will change during the next year. The excess capacity definitely will disappear because Europe is getting geared into a boom.

"And this will stabilize the market during the next year. The price decline we've seen over the last couple of years will have to turn around. The industry understands that. They know prices will have to go up because we must pass on some of our big cost increases. We are, for instance, a major consumer of energy for our chlorine production units, and everybody is aware that the cost of energy has been increasing rapidly.

"Our customers don't buy from us because of low price. What has enabled us to win a very hard fight for growth in this industry, really, is excellent technology and first-class raw material position. We really finally secured that with the construction of the basic chemical plants at Stade. We now have salt in the ground in Europe the same way we do in Texas—for producing the chlorine used in propylene oxide. That was vital to our survival in this business.

"We are as well-integrated as any of our competitors. And our strength in production technology gives us the edge. We can weather any storm in the polyol business. We know that, and our competitors know that, and our customers know that.

"As for RS-350, we will continue to have a significant requirement for this production from the United States until we build a plant in Europe, and that is a long way to go from here. We've had shortages of RS-350 here in the past; but to assure availability of the blends made from RS-350 we've found how identical products can be made at Terneuzen.

"I'm confident that in the product shortages that are coming we will be able to put our house in order in terms of getting our returns sorted out and getting our business looking a bit more consistent across the continent. And also that we will be able to grow quite significantly at the expense of the competition."

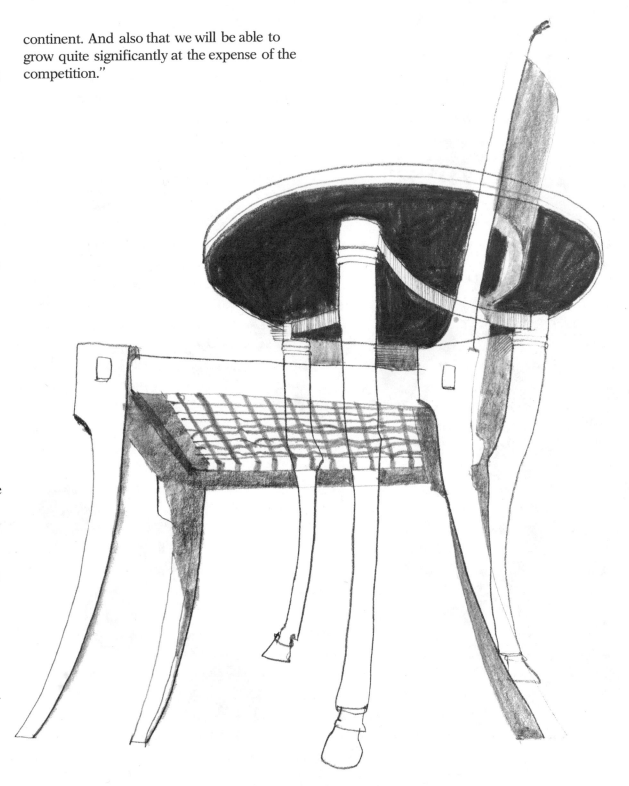

5 | California a No-No

"We were pretty much laughed at—the curiosity of making decorative plaques and stuff like that—but it's now our biggest business for the rigid polyols."

Each of Dow's geographic operating areas—the United States, Europe/Africa, Canada, Latin America, and Pacific—has its own management group for its major businesses. And within each area, the independence of the marketing organizations is limited only by the creativity of research and the availability of product from the manufacturing plants.

However, most of Dow research—certainly the basic research and the development of production technology—is done in the United States. Product development, with close ties to research, also is mainly in the United States. For specific needs, Dow Europe undertakes product development—usually when the project is one that requires close liaison with European customers.

Close communication on market-related product needs is maintained among the Dow areas, with information funneling back to the research department. It's this information flow that keeps Dow researchers sufficiently attuned to the real world to avoid putting too much effort into problems of doubtful market impact.

One of the group leaders in the Dow research organization is Harrell Huff. Harrell, 34, has worked with urethane products since joining Dow in Texas at the age of 21. He's also worked with other products, but even a few minutes of conversation brings out his overriding interest in the growing urethane business. Harrell is in charge of the engineering and semi-commercial group in alkylene oxide derivatives research. The group's work includes research for the production plants, the scaling up of projects from the laboratory to pilot plants, economic studies on production processes, and all the engineering functions in AOD research. [AOD is an abbreviation for alkylene oxide derivatives.]

From Harrell's perspective, the Dow urethane business is one in which "we haven't had any one outstanding product or process. What we have been able to do is come up with something a bit better than the competition.

"Or if they came up with something a bit better than Dow, we could always go them one better the next time. But basically the urethane business all these years has been making flexible foam, and most of that is slab stock. Up until the last two or three years that was done with CP-3000, a standard polyol that has been around since 1960.

"So making CP-3000 better and at lower cost, and keeping the quality up and all this—and it's been refined many times since 1960—that's basically the urethane foam business.

"There are, gosh, 50 different products over at the polyol plant. And a lot of those are used in flexible slabs, or for special cases, or what have you. But still the majority of the business has been slab stock.

"Now it's going the other way. It'll break over pretty soon and be mostly molded. We've carried on the molding technology with new products. We had to have research going in all the product areas all the time—to keep abreast—even though we weren't making much money in those areas. Having had enough foresight to spend the research money, we will come out ahead as the business turns itself around and becomes more molded than slab.

"The rigid area has a lot of potential. As wood gets more expensive, wood replacement will get more attractive, and that's where we are doing our best. That, I think, came about from looking for other uses besides refrigerator insulation.

"We were pretty much laughed at—the curiosity of making decorative plaques and stuff like that—but it's now our biggest business for the rigid polyols. It's making money, and that's more than rigids could say for quite some number of years.

"We got out and tried to get the attention of the right people—the leading furniture manufacturers, the parts manufacturers. Instead of the furniture industry coming to us with a problem, we went out and showed them we had something for them. We do have a good product, and it's designed just for that purpose. The high-priced pieces will have the same density as wood.

"Dow Europe probably is going to finance the research on this. They don't have enough trained manpower to take on the additional work, so they probably will finance it, and we will provide the people to do the work in Texas.

"If our product is accepted in Europe, it won't be very long before it becomes a U.S. product. We want to get Dow Europe a product to compete in Europe, and also get a jump ahead of our competition in the United States. We also can supply the information on the product to Australia, Brazil, and around the countryside, wherever it may be useful.

"The big problem in this particular instance is the equipment. Bayer is the big competitor in Europe. And they manufacture the equipment, the system, everything. They really set their customers up.

"Of course, Bayer is not very strong in the United States. They have a hard time over here selling these complete systems. U.S. business doesn't operate that way."

Harrell graduated from Texas Tech University in 1960, three days before starting at Dow. His wife, Carolyn, is a Freeport native whose father, Pete Gurklis, retired after 43 years with Dow. Gurklis was one of the first Dow men to come to the Gulf Coast

from Michigan to work in building the Texas Division.

Harrell's reasons for joining Dow are straightforward. "'They offered me a job, which was kind of scarce in those days. And they offered me a job in research, which was what I wanted. Dow had what I was looking for, and I stopped looking."

He now recruits some for Dow, particularly at Texas Tech. He hires all the engineers needed in AOD research. Just as he knew what he was looking for in a company, Harrell has ideas on what he looks for in employment candidates.

"I like 'em to have pretty good grades, not too good. I'd rather have a guy who knows he wants to go to work instead of not knowing whether he wants to go to graduate school, or maybe work a year and then go to graduate school.

"I would rather have somebody that is married, and preferably his wife's home is within a hundred miles of here, and all those good things. Marriage is a pretty good settler.

"The way Dow recruits, the Texas Division is almost limited to Texas, Oklahoma, New Mexico, and Arizona. The majority of the interviewees are from Texas because there are more schools, and bigger schools, in Texas. We hire a lot of Texans. But you go talk to the people in the department and find we have a full gamut of the United States. A student may not be from Texas just because he goes to school in Texas.

"We have real hard luck in bringing anybody down here from the East Coast, and West Coast or very far north. California is just about a no-no. People from California want to go back to California. So why fight it when we have plenty to choose from?

"We have some fantastic examples of what can happen when an hourly employee completes the education needed to move up to the professional level. But those guys had the initiative and the incentive; it wasn't anything Dow did for them. They did it on their own.

"The hourly man is part of the union. He works a shift schedule that includes the seven days of the week and the 24 hours of the day. We can't keep changing his schedule to straight evenings or straight days or whatever he needs to do in order to go to school, because then we'd be discriminating against the other men.

"But we will not interfere with arrangements he can make on his own. If he can convince his fellow workers to swap shifts, change, what have you—or take vacation or whatever he wants to do—we will let him do it. We won't interfere with it.

"But when we hire hourly people, that's what we're hiring—operators. If one turns out to be an engineer, chemist, or what have you, great. But between the time he hires in and the time he gets that degree, he is an hourly man just like the next one.

"Now the salaried technicians who have bits and pieces of degrees and have worked their way up, sure, we encourage that. But again the word is 'encourage' for that is what we do. Most of those guys don't have that

degree for a reason.

"The guy who has worked his way up, and finally got his degree, he's better than the one who came in with it. You don't need a master's or a Ph.D. to do a damn good job, to do the best job we got around here.

"So these guys really are sitting pretty. The kids coming out of school need a year or so to catch on, and this guy probably has been here for 10 to 12 years. The day he gets his degree is the day he just bought himself a whole lot more responsibility. He didn't lose stride. He just took off running instead of walking.

"They are jewels, no question about it. It's kind of like the guy who goes off to the Army when he's 18, stays in the Army four or five years, then gets a degree. Now he knew what he was doing when he went back to school. And when you find that kind, they are usually pretty good college graduates. They're older.

Harrell Huff

"For some of them, the Army has instilled too much of its regimentation. Dow Chemical Company doesn't think like the Army, but this guy makes a good leader for people. He may not make the best researcher, but he can lead people fairly well—gets along with all kinds, shapes, and forms. Those are pretty good finds, if you

can find 'em. And we look for 'em."

As for Harrell Huff's own future, he wants to stay with urethane chemicals. The biggest reason is that he thinks "this is the growingest area in The Dow Chemical Company.

"We are going to be number one on the company's profits list in about five years. We've been growing at 20 per cent a year for the last five years, and we don't see anything but 20 per cent for the next five years. That's just with our basic raw materials—not with any of the new projects we've got coming in, not counting the TDI plant that's going to be built here. We think we'll exceed 20 per cent a year, but it's kind of hard to ever forecast anything more than 20 per cent.

"If we maintain our present growth pattern, we'll be number one. If any one of our special projects comes through half as good as we think it will, then we won't have any problems.

"As for the Texas Division research effort, it has been helped by having non-U.S. plants. An expensive part of new technology is research. Even when an area outside the U.S. starts its own research-related groups, such as technical service, there has to be backup, and we are the backup. Being the backup has helped to bring us some money and manpower we wouldn't otherwise have, and this helps build up our critical mass.*

"We're just now nearly to the critical mass needed to afford some luxuries of more people not working solely on making money today. In the last five years most of what we

---

*The term "critical mass" is borrowed from atomic and nuclear science, where it means the smallest amount of fissionable material capable of starting a chain reaction and keeping it going. In business and industry, the term has been borrowed to mean—as Huff does—the size or number of people a work group or organization needs if the work is to move smoothly and without overloading the people involved.

have been able to do is keep up with making money today, and we have. We've also come up with several new project areas that are starting out at zero today and hopefully will grow at a faster rate than the urethane industry.

"We have bettered our position. But in the next five years I think we will accomplish more than in the last five years. We are now big enough to start adding some people. And a lot of that is because the urethane industry worldwide has grown so big we have a bigger base to support ourselves.

"The developing countries, there's no way they can afford a critical mass of 70 people to do urethane work. We're finding you can't do urethane research with two people in a laboratory—or three, or four, or five. It takes like 70 to cover the broad scope of projects we're in. And maybe it will be like 140 people five years from now."

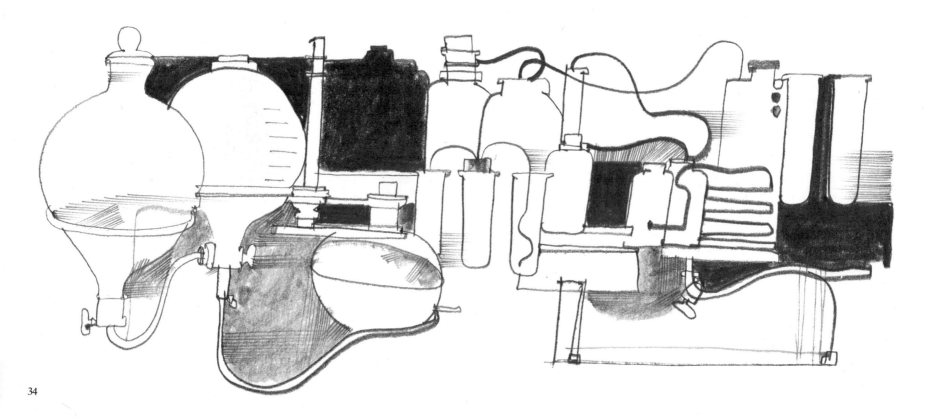

6 | Pancho Villa's Enemies

"I see experience gained on the farm, like working under a tractor and things like that, really paying off here. I love being in a job where you can use everything."

"It's a hot project right now. You can usually tell how hot a project is by the number of little presentations you're asked to give. And it's pretty hot when a little two-year Dow chemist like me can get before a vice president of Dow with a presentation."

No matter how hot the project—development of a new plastic with high use potential in the auto industry—there were other reasons for the big smile of Fred Martinez III. In just 12 days he was going to marry the kindergarten teacher at A. P. Beutel Elementary School in Lake Jackson. And, for the first time in 16 years, the Martinez family would be together—his father, who went to school for just three years; his mother, the first Mexican-American to attend Rotan High School on the plains of West Texas; his oldest brother, Bobby, an M.D. in Houston; Marie, married to a Ph.D. working for a chemical company; Kathy, a mathematician with the National Security Agency in Washington; Johnny, writing his Ph.D. economics dissertation at the University of Oklahoma; and all the others in a family of 11 children.

"My mother is overjoyed. She just can't believe it."

Fred, 26, is in the third generation of a family that began moving to Texas several decades before Dow's 1940 arrival on the Gulf Coast. Dow was looking for abundant raw materials for chemical products, and for the fuel needed to produce energy for processing. The Martinezes were looking for peace and quiet.

"In the early 1900s, during all those revolutionary times, my granddaddy evidently was on the wrong side down in Mexico. My dad told me that my grandmother's father and two or three of his brothers were hung by Pancho Villa. So my granddaddy and my grandmother, with my oldest uncle, got just as far away from Mexico as they could.

That's how they ended 'way up north of Abilene."

That's some of the background of Fred III, a Texan who especially loved his days in college. College was the University of Texas, also attended by four sisters and four brothers—counting Dr. Bobby at the University's Medical branch in Galveston after three years at Notre Dame.

"I went to another university for one year, a university with 16,000 students. But it wasn't my idea of college, even though I did come from a little bitty high school. There were only ten in my high school graduation class.

"My brothers and sisters went to Austin, and I wanted to go to there, to the University of Texas. So eventually I did. The first two years—boy, did I study. I was scared. I'd get in there and see all these guys around me. I had to prove to myself I was up to these guys.

"I didn't have a very good high school background. I was doing almost twice the work they were because most of them came from big high schools, and they had unbelievable preparatory courses. This was the first time I ever had seen some of this stuff. And I finally proved that, heck, I was in their league. And then, shoot, I decided there was a little more to college than that.

"I helped myself out by working in a girls' dorm. I worked in there all three years for my food. It was the biggest dorm on the Texas campus. It was where all the rich girls stayed. It spoiled me, it really did.

"I got to meet every one of them, and I did this for three years. So if I wanted to impress someone, or inflate my ego, I could walk across the campus, and it'd be, 'Hi, Fred,' 'Hi, Fred,' 'How are you doing, Fred?' It was a captive market.

"I credit my working in that dorm for a

Fred Martinez III

37

lot. You know I used to be a real, real shy individual. I wasn't sure of myself, but I worked in that dorm, and I loved it."

There were differences between Rotan, his home town, and Austin. Fred remembers Bobby going to the barber shop and being told, "Bobby, I can't cut your hair. I'd lose all my business."

"When I was a little boy I knew the meaning of the word 'prejudice.' In the area where we lived the general idea was—but it's changed now—'Aw, you're a dirty Mexican. I don't want anything to do with you.'

"The last time I really had a serious encounter was back in Rotan. I was dating this little girl, and her parents were new-rich. Oh, her mother didn't like our dating. I got called a lot of dirty things, and from then on everything else was mild.

"Up at Austin, for all practical purposes, I had no problems. I think once when my roommate was getting me a blind date the girl said, 'Sure, who is it?' When he said 'Fred Martinez,' she changed her mind. I said, 'Well, that's fine, no big problem, there are plenty of other girls. There are people I don't want anything to do with, so it's her prerogative not to have anything to do with me. It's her tough luck.'

"I met her later, and she sure was friendly, but I was sure snobby.

"Here I've heard, maybe a few little references. Like 'those dirty Mexicans,' and then, 'Oh, I'm sorry,' after they've heard your name. But it wasn't any problem.

"I know Linda, my little fiancee—her last name is Schmidt—was told by one person in particular, 'Now, Linda, you sure you want to go through with this? You're from two entirely different cultures, and this and that. I don't think you should.'

"Linda came home and said, 'I know what I want to do.' It's none of their business

really, and Linda was kind of hurt.

"Nowadays, being of Latin descent actually is a great advantage. I always thought of it as a liability when I was a little boy. It's easy for things I do to get recognized. Maybe that's not fair, and I hope it's not the reason that things I do get recognized. I don't want to be here just because my last name is Martinez.

"It bothers me when a job applicant comes through and I hear, 'He's an engineer, and he's Mexican. We've got to have him.' I hope that's not the reason I'm here. That's about the only thing that worries me. Shoot, I realize there is prejudice everywhere in everybody. If they want to be that way, that's their problem."

In high school, Fred competed in track as a hurdler and middle-distance runner. He also participated in slide-rule competition—a slide rule being an engineer's basic tool for solving mathematical problems. In statewide competition, Fred took second place and won a $4,000 scholarship to any state university in Texas, $1,000 a year.

"In slide rule it's a matter of speed and accuracy. You'd have a slide rule, and you'd have a booklet of problems. They'd say 'Go' and you'd have 30 minutes to do as many as you could and as accurately as you could. It took extreme practice, and you had to develop your own ways of working problems and keeping all sorts of things in your head at the same time. I practiced a lot, and my coach

branching out and doing a lot of computer science."

Today Fred is working on a new urethane chemicals system. He describes this as "so fast-reacting we have a problem of how to evaluate it on a lab scale to see just what we've got here. So I got together with our engineer, and we designed a little mixing unit that is helping to find what properties we get, how is our processing, and other questions like that.

"I see where a lot of my old experience gained on the farm, working under a tractor and things like that, is really paying off here. I'm using as much or more of the skill I

took me up to other high schools, and I'd learn from these guys.

"My dad would say, 'Fred, don't you think you are spending too much time on this?' He didn't say that after I got my scholarship.

"In the state competition I committed two sins. I went blank twice because I was so nervous, and lost by five or ten points. That was a shatter."

Fred's first two years at Dow were not exciting. Bored, he looked for a challenge by helping program other people's problems into a computer.

"I have a real good math background, and I've taken a few courses in computer science. Consequently, if someday I want to

do something different, I'll brush up on my computer science. I've done programs for guys around here, and I just love that, really do. I love the challenge of someone presenting me with a problem, a useful problem, and then turning around and breaking it down into logical steps, writing 'em down."

Fred started in the department he's in now, alkylene oxide derivatives research. Those first two years he worked on fire retardants and flexible foams.

"I didn't enjoy fire retardancy. It was a pressing issue, but it was set up so that everything I did was 'Bake at 2,000 degrees' or something like that—strictly evaluation, without too much room to get down to studying the whys. That was when I started

picked up at home up on top of a windmill or whatever. Plus you've got the schooling to explain it mechanically or chemically. I love being in a job like this where you can use everything.

"This new system looks great for the auto industry—not only because it reacts so fast but because it looks good for bumpers, side shields, fenders, and things like that. Pressure has been put on the car makers to make things that will withstand the five-mile-per-hour impact without totally tearing up everything. If you've got a flexible front end, or energy-absorption unit, that's what they're after.

"The market potential is just unbelievable."

7 | Construction People

"Raise a tower—you got something sitting there that you can look at. It's not where you work for a year and don't know if you accomplished anything or not."

It was a Monday morning and, for the moment at least, Jerry Powell was relaxed. Jerry, superintendent of the Texas Division's brand-new Walter Roush Ethylene Plant, had been responsible for the start-up of the plant—one of the world's largest and most costly petrochemical complexes.

In this glistening maze of pipelines and equipment, Jerry produces two basic materials extensively used for manufacture of plastics and chemicals—ethylene and propylene. The feedstocks are ethane and propane, by-products of petroleum production, piped in from the Texas oil and gas fields as liquefied petroleum gases.

The Roush Plant's capacity for its main product, ethylene, equals the combined capacity of the two naphtha crackers at the Dow Europe complex in Terneuzen, Holland. Some of the ethylene produced, and a substantial amount of the propylene, ends up in the polyols sold by Dow for the manufacture of urethane products.

This complex, in addition to size, is notable for utilization of Dow's "total energy concept," generating its own steam to run the big compressors, and recycling cooling water from its own cooling tower. Actually, the massive nine-cell cooling tower is more prominent on the flat landscape than the production plant itself. But that's not unusual in the Texas Division, which in many instances saves money on process cooling by recycling fresh water rather than fighting corrosion from the more abundant salt water that could be used in a one-pass cooling arrangement.

The big new plant was known as Light Hydrocarbon 7 during construction, then renamed to honor Walter Roush. Now retired from Dow, Roush in his career years was the key individual in the company's emergence as the world's largest ethylene producer and recognized leader in ethylene technology.

At the peak of construction, some 700 people worked on the building of the Roush Plant. The work was carried out under four major contracts, with U.S. Contractors of Lake Jackson the successful bidder on three of the contracts. And now a number of the men who had helped build the plant were working a few blocks away on the modernization of an older Texas Division light hydrocarbon unit.

There was, for instance, Jim Mobley, 32, project superintendent, who had followed a brother to Texas because there wasn't much work in the Missouri Ozarks town where he grew up. And Pat Burns, also 32, who quit high school after the 10th grade in Galveston, Texas, and went to work for his uncle as a rigger's helper. And Lon Whiddon, 60, a tobacco salesman out of El Dorado, Arkansas, when he joined the Marines during World War II.

In Doniphan, Missouri, there's not much to hold a teenager graduating from high school—no industry and not many jobs. So, like Jim Mobley, most teenagers do leave Doniphan; and most go to St. Louis, 175 miles north.

Jim "had a brother in Port Lavaca, Texas, working in construction, and he more or less brought me with him. My brother went back north, but I enjoyed it real well and ended up staying.

"I started working for a contractor here in the Dow plant as a painter's helper, which is about as low as you can start in the construction industry, and I worked up to foreman. I was making good money for a young fellow, but I wasn't happy. So I quit after four years and went back to school at Wharton [Texas] Junior College."

But Jim never stopped working completely. Though he earned an associate degree at Wharton and attended the University of Houston full time for a year, studying for a degree in management, Jim also was in the plant part time. For a year and a half he helped prepare bid estimates for a contractor. He was an assistant purchasing agent for a year, then went into the field as assistant superintendent, then maintenance superintendent, and now project superintendent.

During these ten busy years, he was president of the Lake Jackson Junior Chamber of Commerce the year the Lake Jackson group was voted the outstanding club in Texas. He also had found a wife, Shary, and now they have two children—a son and a daughter.

Slim, trim, pipe-smoking, white shirt unbuttoned at the neck, Jim talked enthusiastically about the business and technical aspects of the construction industry. It was obvious that his varied background—combining field work, business-type assignments, and school—had provided him experience helpful in successfully heading up a force of 125 men on a project costing tens of millions of dollars.

Looking to the future, Jim "would like to stay in the construction business but eventually in a bit different capacity—where I don't have to worry about the work day and night. I started pretty far down the line. My parents were pretty poor. They were good people, but they couldn't send me to college."

When Jim mentions worrying, he's talking about the responsibility of the project superintendent to keep the job on schedule. Missing the completion date costs penalties in the construction contract, while meeting the date can make long hours and overtime premiums necessary.

"The part I really enjoy the most is seeing something work after you have been building it, like Light Hydrocarbon 7. It tickled me to death to see that come up as well as it has, and to know we were part of it.

"In the construction phase it is interesting just to see something going. Raise a tower—you got something sitting there that you can look at. It is work where you can see what you are doing. It's not the type where you work for a year and don't know if you accomplished anything or not."

Except for six months on a contract at another Texas petrochemical plant, all of Jim's work has been in the Dow Texas Division. But those six months provide some comparisons. At Dow there is less "leeway in the specifications," the people are "more safety conscious," and Dow has its "own engineering department and staff to do engineering work and to supervise the work in the field."

The fact that Dow does its own engineering is one reason a small construction company can land a big job in an industry where the majors operate worldwide. "The big contractors are not much interested unless they do the engineering. They make as much money, probably more, on the engineering as they do on the construction."

But there was nothing small in the construction of the Roush Plant.

"That compressor unit is fantastic. It's something you wouldn't believe. Fantastic. Biggest compressors I've ever seen—and I'll probably never see them that big again in my life. One of those trains is 88 feet long from end to end, all rotating equipment. It was something to put that in—really interesting, quite a challenge."

The Roush Plant was the first big job for U.S. Contractors, an open-shop contractor.

However, most of the management people had previous experience with Monical & Powell, a company that had done many jobs at Dow and elsewhere in the area with unionized work crews.

"A lot of the people on this job had never belonged to a union. They had lived here all their lives, but had to drive to Houston or somewhere else to get work. Now they are able to work here. Most of them were new to U.S. Contractors, and that made my job harder. But I had a real good nucleus—

Jim Mobley

42

my foremen— and in every craft I had people as good as I've ever worked with."

The 90-member Lake Jackson Junior Chamber of Commerce (Jaycees), one of Jim's major interests, believes in community involvement. As one project, in the neighboring community of Clute, the Jaycees had finished the construction of a home "for a Mexican-American fellow who got an arm cut off in an accident with a tractor lawn mower. Before that, he'd already had one foot partly cut off. This is the type of project Jaycees thrive on, what they like to do. We worked evenings for two weeks—building, painting, and putting in the electrical wiring.

"Another project, lighter, but a lot of work, was publishing a directory of all the people in Lake Jackson. We sold ads to pay for it and made a profit of about $800, or about ten cents for every man-hour we'd worked on it. We did everything except the printing. And at about the same time we had the annual Easter egg hunt, cooking, dyeing, and hiding 10,000 eggs."

Pat Burns is one of Jim's foremen—a foreman for rigging and operating heavy equipment. His first construction job was working for his uncle, also a rigging foreman, building an oil refinery on one of Texas' biggest ranches, the King Ranch. He started just after his 18th birthday.

Earlier Pat had worked on a shrimp boat. Catching shrimp has long been big business on the Gulf Coast, out of the ports of Galveston and Freeport.That's what brought Pat to Freeport, where he met his wife, Mary Ellen, and they were married about the time he quit high school.

"My stepfather was in shrimping just when they were really making a killing, but then it started tapering off. My father-in-law and his brother had a diesel shop, and they bought a shrimp boat. Eventually they had to pay a hundred dollars to give it away, to sign it over to someone else.

"They'd get a captain on there, and he'd be—well, you know. They'd run up a big grocery bill on the boat. You can go in and charge all your groceries to the boat, and that's the way they usually did. And then when you come in and make a settlement with the fish house, the boat will get probably 60 per cent and the crew 40. And the crew splits that up. That's the way it usually works. Anyway, that's the way it was for my father-in-law—and they went in the hole. I've always figured that if you're going to have a shrimp boat, you better run the thing yourself or forget about it."

Pat looks at being the foreman of a rigging crew about the same way. "You've got to get out there and get with it. You've got to get involved in it if you want anything done the way you want to do it. You've got to show everybody how you want to do it, or nobody knows but you.

"The construction business started booming here in about 1967, and that's why I stayed. I've never had any problem getting

Pat Burns

Lon Whiddon

43

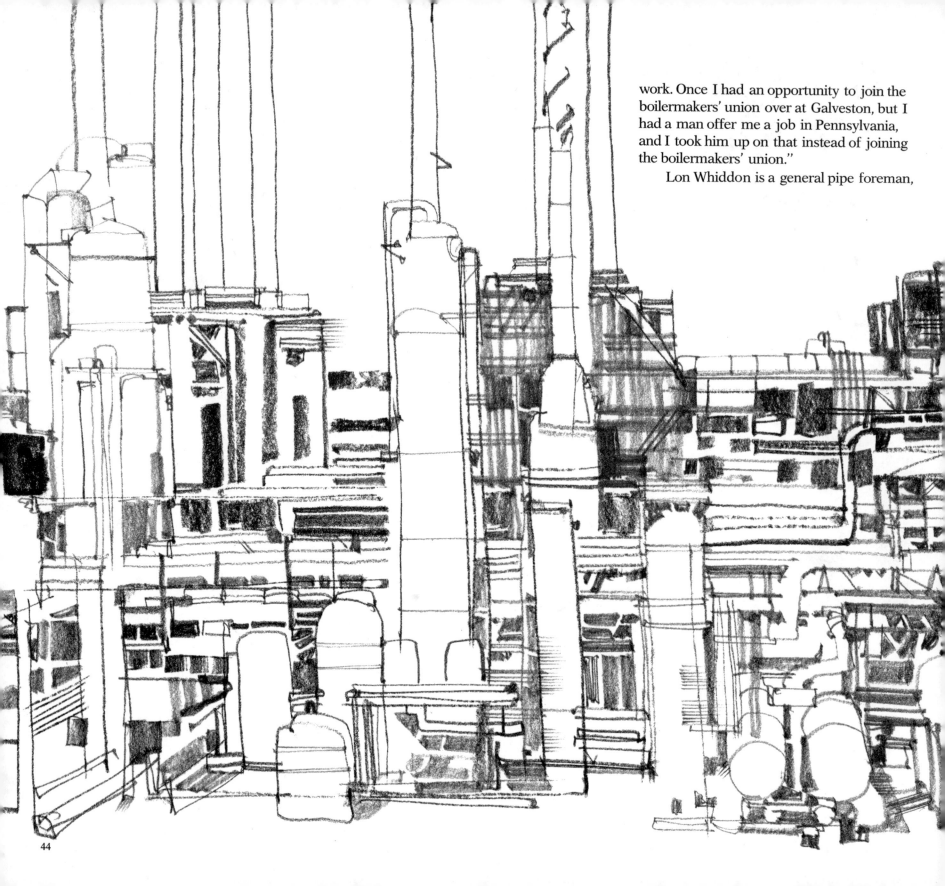

work. Once I had an opportunity to join the boilermakers' union over at Galveston, but I had a man offer me a job in Pennsylvania, and I took him up on that instead of joining the boilermakers' union."

Lon Whiddon is a general pipe foreman,

44

and he had up to 30 pipefitters and welders working for him during construction of the Roush Plant. Lon figures he'll retire in two years, when he's 62, and move to his weekend home at Lake Buchanan, a five-hour drive from Lake Jackson.

"Fishing? Oh, yes sir, that's my only vice. I get up there to the lake every two weeks on the weekends during spring, summer, and fall. My wife would go up there tomorrow if she could. It's beautiful country up in the hills."

Back in the 1930s, Lon "had a little confectionery in El Dorado, Arkansas, and I got talking to a man who needed a tobacco salesman, and I said I'd try it. Back there you just looked for a job, period, and you took what you could get."

In 1942, he joined the Marine Corps, where he was an instrument technician in an airfield service squadron. After the war, he worked briefly in selling office supplies, but turned to construction for one basic reason: The work paid well. And he'd known lean paydays in El Dorado—where he unloaded box cars, dug ditches, and "everything else" after finishing high school during the depression.

At 6 feet and 205 pounds, Lon looks the part of a construction foreman. His formula for a good foreman is "to know your business and have the ability to get along with your crew. Occasionally, when you go to reduce your crew, then you have to cull them. That's the hard part, you know. If a man doesn't produce, you have to let him go. You can't be soft-hearted about it."

But what Lon—ditch-digger, tobacco salesman, pipe foreman—enjoys most in life is "my home, my wife, our two boys, and two girls [he also has eight grandchildren]. I enjoy my home most of all. It's a pleasure to go home everyday."

Almost as an afterthought, Lon adds: "In the early 1940s and 1950s, if you followed construction, that automatically made you a thug. In the small towns they wanted your money, but they didn't want to associate with you. They thought of construction workers as uneducated people, dropouts. But that has changed. There are a lot of well-educated people in the business."

Maybe Lon was thinking of Jim Mobley. Or of one of his own sons, a graduate civil engineer.

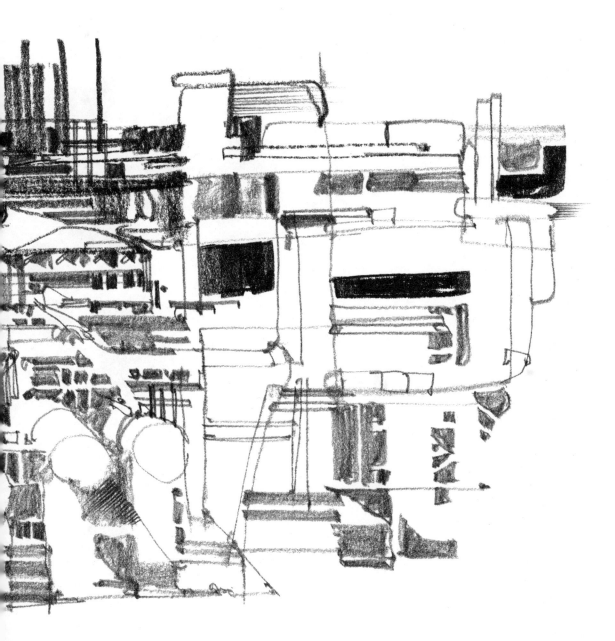

8 | Charter Member

"I said...'I don't know anything about the chemical business. But you're going to have to get things on a more sure basis.'"

In 1933, at the depth of the depression, many Oklahomans were packing up and leaving the dusty wheat lands to look for work in California. But Dolph Wood, a teenager in Checotah, Oklahoma, didn't go west.

Dolph went south. And his trip was only remotely connected with looking for a job. He was following a girl who had sung in his church while visiting friends in Checotah.

"I couldn't keep my eyes off that girl. I thought she was beautiful. She looked innocent. And she sang in the song service. Now I just couldn't get my mind off of her. So I asked where she lived, and just the minute I got free in Oklahoma I came down here to Freeport—and that was the main object, to see this girl. Some months later we were married."

That was when Dolph was 19. He and his wife, Gladys, have lived near Freeport all of the last 40 years except one—when Dolph went to California in a roundabout route to getting a job with Dow in Freeport. Before going to Santa Cruz Dolph worked for Freeport Sulphur, then the major industry in Brazosport.

"Freeport Sulphur put me to firing boilers, and in 1942 I still couldn't see anything bigger than firing boilers and working shift work. It was then, in 1942, that Dow started to blossom good. I wanted to work for Dow, but Freeport Sulphur scolded Dow and told them 'not to hire our key men.' That kind of aggravated me because I couldn't grow any more with the Freeport Sulphur Company.

"So a Dow personnel man told me that if I'd go somewhere else and go to work, they could hire me without any bad relations. And so I went to California and stayed a year, working as an equipment maintenance man in a food cannery at Santa Cruz, then came back and went to work for Dow in 1943.

"I don't like California. It don't miss me, and I'm a Texan. Too much competition in that state. Stand in line for everything. Bumper to bumper. The highways wouldn't accommodate the traffic that was there in 1942."

Dolph left Dow after four years, "during a lull," to go into construction work as a pipe fitter and pipe welder. But he's spent most of his working time in the Dow complex. "I've worked on almost every plant in the Texas Division. I can name on one hand the plants I didn't help build."

For the last eight years, Dolph has worked for Key Associates, a Freeport contractor that during my visit to the polyol production plant was making changes in the piping for pumping polyols into railroad tank cars.

At 58, Dolph Wood is balding, a short man of sturdy build. In his sun glasses and clean gray work clothes he looks as though he might have just stepped off the laundry truck he drove from time to time while working shifts for Freeport Sulphur. It was in delivering laundry that he came to know Dr. Willard Dow, then the Dow president.

"Dr. Willard Dow was a personal friend of mine. He came here in 1939. I'd met him and took care of his laundry problems, and he began to question me. He said this company was going to come in, and would our facilities grow to take in all the demands that the Dow company was going to have? I said no, I didn't believe so—because the people that owned it was well up in years, and they was already looking for a buyer. And I suggested he put in his own laundry, and that's what he did. But I talked to him on many an occasion and handled his personal laundry."

Dolph also knew and admired immensely Dr. A. P. Beutel, founder and long-time general manager of the Texas Division. Two events in particular brought him to Beutel's attention: Dolph was one of the three men who organized the first union in the Texas Division; and a number of years later his son cracked up an airplane on the Beutel farm.

"And I worked partners to Levi Leathers on research all during the war. He and I was the team that worked together researching the vinyl chloride unit. He later became general manager of the Texas Division [and now a Dow vice president], but at that time he was just a chemist. And he and I were a chemist and fitter working together in setting up our pilot plant. I worked for him 18 months."

Dolph now lives in Jones Creek, where he built his home in 1940. One of his sons, Tommy, also a pipe fitter and pipe welder, is a foreman with the same company Dolph works for. His daughter, Kay, lives next door to Dolph in Jones Creek.

"I have the privilege of enjoying my five children, three boys and two girls, every day. This is a lovely place to raise a family. It really is considered the religious belt of the whole United States, right here in the southern part. Well, Texas in general is just good people. I'm not saying it is the only place you find good people. But as far as the standards and the morality, it is high here.

"In the South, people are more religious to worship God, the Creator. There is more deep-seated religion than in other states—and that's good because you don't have as much crime, as much hooking and crooking and thieving. You meet your fellow man, and you trust him. You're sad when you find one you can't trust. I've been away from home five months and never locked my doors, with all my furnishings here, and come back and there wouldn't be one thing bothered. Many places you can't do that.

Dolph Wood

"Without a doubt as the world turns we have dropped a lot of our standards, but I still say it is the best place I have found to live, and I've been over about 32 states. Pennsylvania would be my second choice for living—in an area with the Amish people.

"You never hear of any case here, hardly, where we have a racial problem in our schools. The simple reason is that we don't oppress them, and everyone's got work. We've got a colored boy working with us, and we love him like a brother. We don't fight with one another in the South. We help one another.

"Now I understand there's some smart alecks in every place. You've got some white people that are smart alecks, just trouble-makers. And you've got a few of the colored people that is, too. But basically we get along, never have any trouble."

Dolph is really a man of many interests, including fishing and flying his own airplane.

"I took flying lessons in Victoria, Texas. How I came to do it was that a man wrecked an airplane with a good engine in it. It couldn't be repaired economically, so I built the plane myself, worked on it 18 months. I put a new body on it, new wings, and a new prop, and I've been flying it since 1966. I built it in my backyard and flew it right out of the cow pasture."

The plane has a 330-horsepower engine, is 35 feet long, and 35 feet in wing span. That's the same plane his son ground-looped into A. P. Beutel's backyard. Dolph was hurrying to get some equipment to move the plane off Beutel's property, until Dr. Beutel told him: "Don't you worry. Be careful and don't take a chance of damaging your property till the plane is ready to move. Get out of here, boy."

On Brazosport fishing, Dolph's views are as definite as on most other subjects.

"Before Dow came, I used to go floundering up and down this river, and I've had as high as 40 flounders in one night's catch—just picking 'em up bedding down along the river bank. After Dow was here about five years, you couldn't catch any more fish in that river. They drained these Dorr tanks and put the lime, thick lime, on the river beds until there wasn't any bait left for the fish to feed on. We used to catch tarpon up and down that New River. Take a speedboat, troll and catch tarpon. But you can't do that any more.

"We complained about it a number of times. I've seen a number of things that cause fish kills. But it became clear to all industry in about 1967 that you better stop polluting our water. And I find Dow has made great strides in cleaning up the river. We're catching fish inland now in places where for 10 to 12 years we never saw any."

When he was a teenager in Oklahoma, Dolph was an auto mechanic. From cars to his airplane, he always has enjoyed mechanical work. "My dad always said, 'If you want something done real bad, do it yourself,' and I just took him at his word." He jumped at the chance to become a pipe fitter and pipe welder when he joined Dow.

"That was the greatest thing Dow did for the crafts, that trainee program. I got every phase of pipe fitting. The greatest thing that ever happened to me was what Dow contributed to my knowledge of pipe fitting.

"I've taught at least 25 people how to weld. But that's not like the Dow trainee program because we got every phase of pipe fitting during 18 months in the trainee program. If I'd had my choice, I'd gone through another 18 months.

"When I first came here they didn't have any engineering to speak of. There were no blueprints for the big addition to Chlorine 1 in Plant A. But we knew what we wanted. They set me up and told me to install all those meters and the necessary piping, and I had to pick my own route."

It was about this time that Dolph added another interest, organizing a union in the Texas Division.

"I was a charter member of the Pipe Fitters Local Union 390. I'm one of the 'guilty parties' that organized Dow in the first place. I'm one of three. What brought it about was the dragline operator that was my helper on that addition to Chlorine 1. This man, my helper, had helped build the big canal ditches. He was a dragline operator, but he got sick of that ditchdigging and said he wanted to be a pipe fitter. He was an older man than me, but he didn't even know how to put a pipe wrench on a piece of pipe.

"I had to school him—and he was drawing more wages than me. His was based on how much he had made as a dragline operator. He was digging ditches—running this big, huge equipment day and night, and mosquitoes eating him up—and he got sick of it, and he came down here and said, 'You've got to give me as good a paying job.'

"The only thing they could offer him was fitting pipe. And yet, he didn't know anything about fitting pipe. Honestly, I had to nod my head to show him which way to turn a pipe wrench.

"It was difficult putting in a line with no more training than I had at that time, but we got it in—at least 25 different instruments to

set, and running the pipe to the cells, and what have you. That was quite a tax on me. But it'd been fine if I'd had somebody who knew a little bit about it, too.

"Then I'd say, 'That man is drawing more wages than I'm drawing. It's not fair.' I said, 'This company needs to be leveled out, it's unbalanced.' And I said we'd never have loyalty in this craft if we don't get things on more of an even keel. And I still believe that today.

"You can't have a man drawing $1.17 an hour and another 95 cents, when the 95 cents man was the one who knew more about the work—was the leadoff man. You can't get any harmony out of a job, you can't get any loyalty, and you don't get any production either.

"I was bold enough to tell the people in authority about this. They resented it and said, 'We don't want people telling us how to run our business.' I said, 'I don't want to tell you how to run your business. I don't know anything about the chemical business. But you're going to have to get things on a more sure basis.

" 'You are going to have to have one price for pipe fitters, one price for operators. You need a set scale. And I don't know any better way than to take a union contract and read it over, and let's see what it's going to take.' In a short time we brought it to a vote, and it didn't take very long either.

"I'm a union man and no doubt always will be. I think there is power in a union, and great results can come from it that are good.

I believe they hold the standard of life higher, conditions better.

"And I also know there has been some people that got their feelings hurt because Dow is now hiring more non-union contractors than union. But, you know, time just changes as it goes on. One will be in power a while, and then another. It was time for a change, time for a cleaning-up.

"If you give a man too much power, he'll hang himself. And I think that was just about the situation we had met—a union that got power-happy and they weren't producing like they should. It was time for a change, and I've got no resentment. I enjoy fellowship with the other fellows, and I know that they got to live, too. I'm not trying to take the bread off nobody's table."

9 | Squeezing the Barrel

"We have, I think, very interesting possibilities for a new process. An 'interesting possibility,' incidentally, is one you probably are going to flush."

Propylene oxide—often spoken of as P.O.—is not one of the world's most precious materials. It's not like gold or platinum, and it costs only a fraction of the price for Scotch whisky—ten cents a pound in 1973. But in late 1973 it became precious if you were running a plant making the polyols used in urethane products.

The *Bow Elm*, a Norwegian tanker chartered by Dow, had to wait at Brazosport a couple of days, and then dodge a hurricane, before the Texas Division had enough material to load a million dollars' worth of propylene oxide for the Dow Latin American polyol plant in Brazil. When the *Bow Elm* reached Guaruja 13 days after leaving Brazosport, the Brazilian polyol plant was down to less than a week's supply of its critical raw material.

Producing the P.O. in Texas—and helping to keep other Dow plants doing the same in Louisiana, Canada, Holland, and Germany—is the responsibility of John Barton, 46, a native Texan. His job as a general superintendent covers the production of propylene oxide and propylene glycol. Besides the volume of output, John is responsible for safety, quality, the motivation of his people, and protection of the environment. He also has a worldwide responsibility for the technical side of the business.

John is cut from the same cloth as a number of other Texas Division people who have stepped into Dow's upper echelon. He appears almost uncomfortable in tie and coat. The Texans tend to offices more spacious than elsewhere in Dow, but from the clutter of blueprints and technical material you get the feeling John would be more at home out in one of the plants where he has been involved with production since 1950.

John's P.O. plants are tightly linked to the plants making polyols for urethane products. At Plant B, there's a pipeline for pumping the P.O. to the polyol plant. At Plant A, there's a pipeline that moves the P.O. to the dock for shipment to Brazil and Australia.

"The urethanes certainly have been the cause of the big demand for P.O. Probably half, maybe 60 per cent, of the total oxide in the world is used in some form of polyglycol. Maybe even more than that."

On the other hand, it was a big capacity for producing propylene oxide that thrust Dow so strongly into the urethane field in the 1960s. This capacity became available when the company adopted a new process for making ethylene oxide [E.O.]—thereby freeing up existing E.O. plants for a switch to P.O.

"As a producer of oxides, we have a certain advantageous position in the manufacture of polyols. Actually it puts us in a business where we might not otherwise be. Right now there are only three manufacturers of P.O. in the United States. Without the basic oxides position, we would have a tough row to hoe in the polyols. Our profit margin certainly would be less, and our overall market position would be substantially less.

"This year there is a worldwide shortage of P.O. We're squeezing the barrel. We'll probably be about seven to eight per cent short of what we need to take care of our present business. In a year or two we should catch up, be in a more favorable producing position for taking care of the polyol market both in Dow and with other customers.

"We have two major authorizations in the mill plus a number of de-bottlenecking operations to overcome the shortage. We're planning to improve our position worldwide by expansions here and in Louisiana, Latin America, and Europe. And we think that through 1979 we will be able to sell all we can make."

In view of the high demand for chemicals and plastics derived from petroleum, the next question was whether making propylene oxide is the most profitable way for Dow to use its available supplies of petroleum and energy.

"If you look at the alternative products, I think it certainly would be competitive with the other uses for propylene—certainly for propylene going into the polyols. From the energy standpoint the unit returns are equal to or better than those on the other products. Yes, it is a good place to put our energy and our propylene."

John was the man to ask questions on two other subjects: Environmental impact—since P.O. process wastes have the reputation of being a real problem—and how the Dow process for propylene oxide stacks up against the newer process of a competitor.

"What we call the T.O.C., [the total organic carbon] in our effluent has been reduced 95 per cent in the last five years. We intend, and we've got the technology, to get it down by 98 per cent. And actually we think we can get the T.O.C. very close to zero. Three or four years ago this would have been a dream. But we think we can reduce the total waste load from a chlorohydrin oxide plant something like 99 per cent.

"The first 90 per cent reduction probably netted us a profit of two to three million dollars. We'll have to pay for the last ten per cent. But even after we pay for what we're projecting in the best operating facilities, we will have made money overall."

As new propylene oxide plants are built, as the total business grows, the incentive increases for improvements in any phase of the process.

"We have, I think, very interesting possibilities for a new process. An 'interesting possibility,' incidentally, is one you probably are going to flush. Research people, when

they refer to something as 'interesting,' usually mean they are doing it without regard to the costs that were suggested.

"We have other ways to make P.O. Our concern is that the process must be competitive with both our chlorohydrin process and

John Barton

Salt is "mined" by pumping water into underground salt deposits—it is dissolved and pumped back to the surface as brine.

the process of our competitor—and this means using the economics that we face for the cost of energy and raw materials and, certainly, capital."

For some people, the chlorohydrin process means using chlorine and water to hypochlorinate propylene, and then taking an alkaline solution like lime or caustic soda to hydrolyze it into crude P.O. And then the crude is distilled to get finished P.O.

"Quite frankly, if you buy chlorine and buy lime and buy propylene, the chlorohydrin process is not a real good process. In Dow, we don't look at it as making oxide from chlorine and caustic and propylene. We are making it from salt and power and propylene. In other words, our total technology includes our ability to make chlorine and caustic.

"So if you look at our total process, we mine salt, send it through the chlorine cells and make chlorine and caustic, buy propylene, and then go from there. We also make propylene from LPGs (liquefied petroleum gases)—but we don't consider that part of our oxide technology, because we could probably sell all the propylene we make without upgrading it into other products. We plug in the propylene at its purchased value in the economics for making propylene oxide.

"The secret to the chlorohydrin process is how to make chlorine and caustic and maintain a real good energy position and a capital position."

In effect, John was saying Dow's success in propylene oxide is based on keeping out front in the technology for making chlorine and caustic soda, plus being able to buy or generate relatively low-cost electricity for getting caustic and chlorine from a virtually unlimited supply of salt. And, all the while, staying profitable enough to finance huge investments in the required production plants.

Fifteen years ago, John would have spent almost all his time in Texas in his job as a production superintendent. And that might have suited him fine. He was born in Corpus Christi, graduated from the University of Texas in 1950, and he and his wife Darlene have two daughters, Karen and Kimberly. Today, his worldwide responsibilities take about a third of his time and include visits to the other P.O. plants, especially the newer ones. The newest is at Stade, Germany; another is being built in Salvador, Brazil.

Nevertheless, what John finds most interesting is seeing the continual improvement in the production process.

"I mean the real live improvement. Five years ago you thought you were doing as well as you could. Right now, boy, we may not see how we can do any better. But if you apply the same effort, there's goodies to be gotten out of the process.

"I think the approach to the pollution problem is a good example. The 95 per cent reduction is in real numbers, and you can see the impact on the environment—I mean the favorable impact—and it is real satisfying to be a part of this kind of thing.

"And also to try new ways to get even higher efficiency, raw material efficiency. To take these numbers—and what I like to talk about are real numbers—how much energy did it take five years ago to make a pound of P.O., and how much does it take now.

"There are things that can be done, especially if you have a bunch of good people working with you. One of the satisfying things on this job is to have people working for you that know more about it than you do. What's really disturbing is if you feel like you know more about it than the guys working for you."

10 | The Country Club

"We've really come a long way here on computers and air conditioning. Everything runs better, don't give you near as much trouble."

When Dow dug into historical records in connection with its 75th anniversary, several families were found to have had four generations as employees of the company in Midland, Michigan, where the company was begun by Dr. Herbert H. Dow in 1897. The Texas Division, much younger, sprouting on the Gulf Coast in 1940, already has families who have been with Dow for three generations. And appropriately, since polyols for urethane products are the offspring of propylene oxide, there's an operator in the polyol plant who is the son of a long-time operator in one of the P.O. plants.

There's a lot of other Dow history in the Texas plants now manufacturing propylene oxide.

The first Texas Division job for Earle Barnes was assistant superintendent of a plant producing oxides and glycols. That was in 1941, a year after Barnes started with Dow in Midland. He went on to become general manager of the Texas Division and is now president of Dow U.S.A.

As assistant general manager of the Texas Division for 23 years and, later, manager of technology administration for all of Dow, Walter Roush built a career that in the early years included many hours in the control room of an oxide-glycol plant. He is described by a veteran operator as "knowing everything that was going on all the time. He'd call at night—and you had better give the right answer because he knew everything that was going on."

Jim Means, who became general manager of the Louisiana Division, was in charge of the Texas oxide-glycol operations for many years.

E.E. (Buddy) Zwahr and Robert Welch both have been with Dow since 1942. Zwahr is an operator in the P.O. plant at Plant A, and Welch at Plant B. Zwahr's father worked

Buddy Zwahr and Robert Welch

in magnesium production during World War II. Zwahr's oldest son is a welder in the boiler shop, and a daughter is in the accounting department. Welch is the P.O. operator who has a son that is an operator in the polyol plant.

Zwahr lives in Jones Creek, where he bought three acres in 1946. He now lives in his third home on this property, having built new houses in 1953 and 1955. Welch also lives in Jones Creek, where he grows pecan trees on an acre and a half.

Zwahr, 54, and Welch, 57, are examples of men who sank their roots in Brazosport after moving into the area at the time Dow started building. They also typify the many professional chemical operators who have helped and seen Dow and Brazosport grow more, perhaps, than anyone could have

guessed back in those early years.

Buddy's father "has been gone a year, but he used to come back here every year. We'd just drive around, and he'd notice himself the changes in just a year's time. He'd notice where a new plant had been built, like the Salt Grass power plant, the Oyster Creek Division. He'd notice a lot of things. Where we used to go fishing, now they've got plants.

"When they first started this plant up in 1948, I was a helper working a relief job here and at EDC [ethylene dichloride]. The way it is now, some of these new operators wouldn't believe the way it was at that time. If some of the new operators came in here the way it used to be, they probably would walk out. They call it the country club now because it's been improved so much. Last year we got air conditioning.

"There always has been a little improvement from one superintendent to the next. Things always have gotten a little better, modernized equipment and everything. It's a lot easier to operate, a lot easier to control. Getting better equipment helps a whole lot. Like we've got two big hydrolyzers that we run all this stuff through, and we used to have seven small ones.

"Now we have instruments that tell right off where a problem is, and we can get on it right away. We used to have to go by pressure and temperature and things like that. Now we have caustic analyzers, chlorine analyzers, and things like that.

"We have a problem if Light Hydrocarbons feeds us some poor gas, or the caustic gets weak, or something like that. As long as we get good caustic and good chlorine and good propylene, it runs all right.

"This place has been shut down two or three times, but not during the last 12 years. We've had cutbacks during recessions, and there were times when it looked pretty shaky. I've gotten bumped back a couple of times, to second-class operator and back to utility. Jim [Means] was here then, and he said 'you can't do anything but come back up, just hang in there.' And I'm glad I stayed."

Buddy's home, before Brazosport, was at Damon, Texas—in Brazoria County, like Brazosport is—but he came to Dow by the way of Florida. "My dad and I were working for a seismograph outfit in an oil field. When Dow started building, there was plenty of work here. And when they started rationing gasoline during the war we came back home.

"When I went to Jones Creek, there wasn't anything, just a store. We were living in an apartment in Freeport, and the kids were getting into the street, and I had a chance to buy a house with three acres of land. So we thought we'd get a little air and a place for the kids to play where they weren't in the street.

"I bought the three acres in 1946. Tore the old house down and built another house in 1953. Then I sold it and built another house in 1955. My dad, he was a carpenter most of his life, and he left Dow after the war. He and I built the houses.

"Working on shifts gives you daylight hours at home. I've had a chance to get off shifts, but I like being off during the week. We work six days, then off two, then work six evenings and off two, then six graveyards and off two. Then every six weeks you work five days. When you start on Tuesday, you work through Saturday, then you get a long weekend off. Everybody gets a long weekend every six or seven weeks."

Buddy has seven children. Besides the two who work for Dow, one is in high school, one in the Marines, and three live in Houston.

Robert Welch was working in a Texas sawmill town, Diboll, when he moved to Brazosport. "I was a night watchman at a box factory, and I was hunting a better job. Earlier I had worked in a government job at Apple Springs, where I met my wife.

"Working at Dow has been my life. I enjoy it, and I encouraged my older son, Michael, to become an operator. The other boy likes being an electrician. I was just bragging the other day: He's 23 years old, and he's a journeyman electrician. He works for an electrical company in Houston, and he's graduating from the electrical school this week. He said the other day that when he gets out of this school he's going to come home. He'd like to come back. He loves home.

"My first job at Dow was working in the mag cells for three years during the war. I was at Plant A for 15 years, and I've worked in glycols for 27 years. Jim Means was the superintendent when I was in glycols at Plant A. He was just a gem of a fellow.

"Things got slack there, in 1957, I believe, and they needed an operator over here. This plant has run pretty steady except for a week when they changed over from ethylene oxide to P.O. in 1972—after they built all that new part for E.O. in the Louisiana Division.

"We've really come a long way here on computers and air conditioning. Everything runs better, don't give you near as much trouble. We're still growing. They're converting two glycol stills into oxide stills now. And they're engineering for a new hydrolyzer. We don't keep the product here very long. It's gone as quick as it hits the tank."

Like Bill Broaddus, the Welches are natives of East Texas. "We'll go over to East Texas to see my wife's folks on vacations, but most of my time is spent here repairing the two houses. The old place is in Freeport where my son lives, and every year there's something to replace or repair—a roof, a garage.

"We have a wonderful home in Jones Creek, an acre and a half with lots of pecans and garden. My wife went to school this last year, and they made her a beauty operator. I'm building her a shop there at the house. With all the children gone, she wanted something to do. She keeps busy with her flowers and lots of company. We're going to stay here the rest of our time."

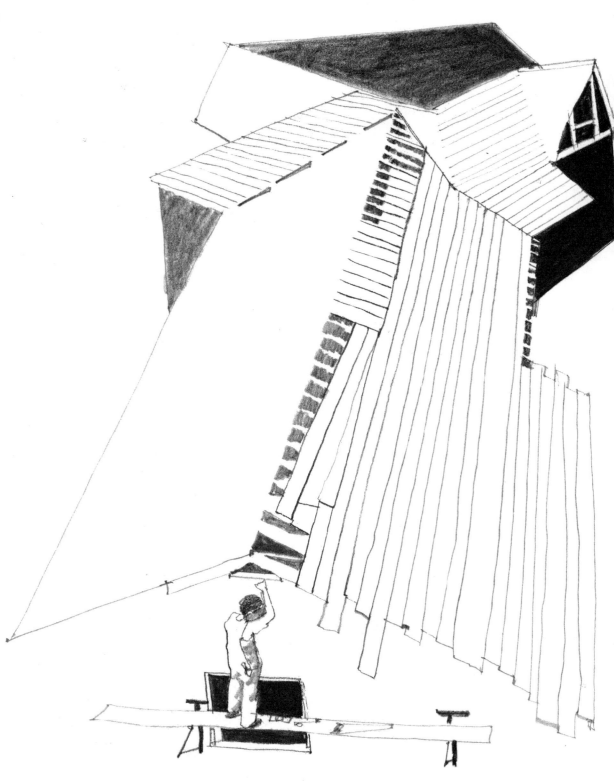

11 | More Human

"It's my living, you know, and I haven't done anything except on ships. All our family in Norway have some connection with ships. So we are raised to like them."

Elfrida Morsund

Though her home is in Reipaa, Norway, near the Arctic Circle, Elfrida Morsund never has been to Sweden. The slender, blue-eyed blonde hasn't even seen much of Norway. Yet here she was on the bridge of a ship tied up at Guaruja, Brazil. And she had been to Japan, Australia, Holland, Canada, Peru, and—in the United States—to New Orleans, Houston, Jacksonville, Disney World, and Brazosport.

Elfrida is a radio operator. She's also the mother of a nine-month-old boy, Brian, and

wife of the cook, Harald, on the same tanker on which she has been sailing for most of two years.

Elfrida was one of three women on the *Bow Elm,* the other two working in the galley, and she's among 500 women radio operators in the Norwegian merchant navy. Would she recommend sailing as a career, especially for a girl? Definitely not.

"No more, if I don't have to," she said of sailing. And she was hoping her savings would make it possible to stay at home in Reipaa when she returned in about a month.

For a Norwegian at least, it had been too hot for her to enjoy her visit to Disney World in mid-July. And though she'd been on Bourbon Street in New Orleans, it was the shopping that she had liked the most. "Women," said Captain Nils Veivag, "are the same the world over."

Like Elfrida and many other Norwegians, Captain Veivag is from a family of sailors. He has worked aboard ships ever since he was a 15-year-old deck boy on a passenger ship traveling the fjords. In appearance, he would be difficult to pick out of a group of businessmen, and in this respect he was not like the Norwegian sailors I had met previously in this venture.

In the very first days of my visit to Brazosport I had gone down to the Dow docks to see a Norwegian crew bring in a small tanker, the *Stainless Trader.* The tanker was to load liquid chemicals, including polyols, for Colombia on the north side of South America. It was 1:30 a.m. and the Dow ship *Leland I. Doan* had not yet departed for the East Coast. The *Stainless Trader* was at anchor in the Gulf, waiting for space.

Bob Metcalf was the Texas Division marine supervisor on duty. Bob was on a metal platform outside a small office, foot propped on a railing. As we stood and talked,

Bob kept a close watch on all that was going on below, at a dock where many flammable liquids are handled in large volumes. He reminded me of a baseball manager, the Walter Alston type, standing at the front of the dugout silently observing the players at batting practice and infield drills before a game.

"We generally have problems only on a ship's first trip here," Bob said. "After several trips they get to know what we expect."

Fifty-four years old, Bob has worked in the Texas Division longer than any of its other 6,000 people. He started just one week before his 21st birthday, and he's not a native Texan; he came from Michigan.

"I worked for Midland Paper and McCandless, delivering paper and supplies to the Dow plant and filling up the cigarette and candy machines. Beutel lived just four houses down the street, and when I heard about the new plant in Texas I asked my dad if he'd talk with him about a job for me."

Beutel was Dr. A. P. Beutel, the pioneer who built the Dow Gulf Coast operations, first in Texas, then in Louisiana, from the bare ground up. Beutel started with Dow as an engineering draftsman in 1916, and retired from the board of directors in 1971 at the age of 79.

And now, on a brisk spring night, at a site that was little more than mud when he arrived in 1940, Bob was supervising the loading of products for Dow's worldwide business. Another tanker was parked just around the bend, preparing to sail later in the morning, and a freighter was anchored several hundred yards away at the dry-cargo dock.

Finally the *Leland I. Doan* was cast loose, departing at 2:30 a.m., and the *Stainless Trader* eased up to the dock 90 minutes later. The officers were young Scandinavians—tall, tanned, blond with darker beards, and they looked ready for yacht races.

Bob boarded the tanker, where he and the captain reviewed their papers to make sure they had the same information about the products to be pumped into the ship's tanks and to check what had recently been carried in those tanks. Then Bob climbed down to inspect each tank and make sure they were clean, with no chance of product contamination when the fresh chemicals were pumped in. The tanks were spotless—unlike those on the ship just around the bend, sent back to sea unloaded twice because the tanks weren't clean when it docked.

Weeks later, talking with Captain Veivag at Guaruja, I also recalled four Norwegian sailors who sat on the other side of a hook-shaped bar in Rotterdam. That was after I had crossed the Atlantic on the *Bilderdyk*. I'd never been in Rotterdam before, but after two weeks aboard ship I felt a kinship with seagoing people. Despite the reputation that has accrued to the waterfront in New York, I thought of the harbor bars as some of the friendliest spots in town—people happy to be ashore after long voyages.

What a picture those four Norwegians made! Two were big hulks of men with beards and long, clean, straggly hair on top—as though it had been whipped by wind and sun—and in short-sleeved shirts revealing arms heavily tattooed. Next was a thin man, clean-shaven, middle-aged, appearing worried for some reason, as if he'd just had a letter saying his wife was going off with someone else. And the fourth could easily have been Paladin, the good-guy righter-of-wrongs in that old Western series.

But now the port was Guaruja on a dismal day, with rain falling on the windows of the forecastle deck, and neither the comely radio operator nor the captain looking

anything like a gnarled veteran of the sea. Appearances can be deceiving. Starting in 1960, Captain Veivag had for seven years been master of a ship sailing around the world on a regular route from Rotterdam to the U.S. Gulf Coast, Panama, Japan, the Far East, South Africa, and back to Rotterdam.

From his boyhood on Asky Island, four miles and 15 minutes by ferry from the city of Bergen, the captain has been on the water—including 18 months in the Norwegian Navy. His father was a sailor; his two brothers are on ships; and the older of his two sons, 19-year-old Beoern, is a deckhand on a tanker owned by the same company that operates the *Bow Elm*.

"Most of the people who live near the coast do fishing," the captain explained, "and when you are a small kid you are in a boat, fishing. There are lots of island people who have to use a boat to go anywhere. It's my living, you know, and I haven't done anything except on ships. All our family in Norway have some connection with ships. So we are raised to like them."

Asky, one of dozens of islands along the Norwegian coast, has 15,000 residents and industry, too. A boat is the only means of reaching the mainland. Though the inland lakes freeze in the winter, ice is a rarity on

Bob Metcalf

61

Captain Nils Veivag

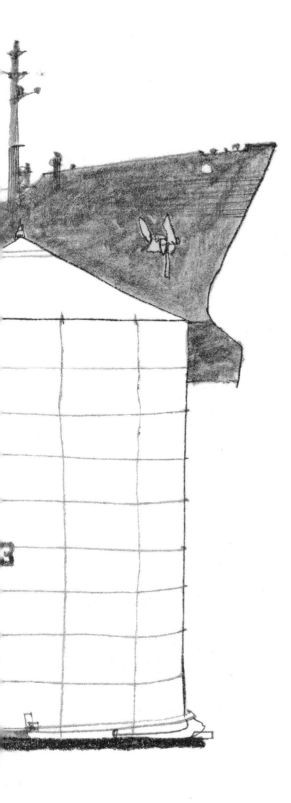

the waters around Asky, which are warmed by the Gulf Stream.

When he regularly sailed around the world (so many times he knows not the total), the captain worked for another company. His vessel was a ship that carried products in containers—big boxes about 20 to 30 feet long.

In joining the Odfjell line he changed to a different type of ship, and he started as the first officer on the *Bow Elm* when it was new in 1971. Odfjell specializes in small, specially-equipped tankers for moving chemical liquids and gases—tankers small in comparison to the supertankers that carry 250,000 tons or more, but larger than the *Stainless Trader*.

The *Bow Elm* is 411 feet in length, and its deadweight limit—that's the maximum for cargo, fuel, supplies, and people—is 8,587 metric tons. It is one of only two ships built to meet U.S. Coast Guard rules for carrying ethylene oxide, which require two sets of cooling systems outside the pressurized tanks, each system fully capable of refrigerating this extremely flammable material. The *Bow Elm* and the *Hardanger*, also owned by Odfjell, were designed specifically to meet Dow's needs.

It had been a 13-day voyage for the *Bow Elm* from Brazosport to Guaruja. In taking on the chemicals it was half loaded when Hurricane Delilah changed course and headed for Brazosport. The ship stopped loading and sailed 30 miles off the coast, waiting 24 hours till the winds blew through Brazosport and Galveston.

Captain Veivag had rejoined the *Bow Elm* in Montreal, Canada, flying from Bergen to relieve a captain going on vacation. The ship then sailed to Norfolk, Virginia, to pick up a cargo for Peru, and came back through the Panama Canal to Brazosport. From Guaruja it traveled with empty tanks to Puerto Rico to load another company's chemicals for delivery to Rotterdam.

Asked his favorite port, the captain said, "No matter where you go in the world, you always think of home, that's the favorite port." Pressed for a second choice, he said "It must be similar to home, like nature, like the North—and the closest I can come to that is Canada with its bays, woods, snow, and ice." The captain has four children, and he noted that "ships are now being built with family cabins so when the officers have a chance, they can have their families with them."

The *Bow Elm* carries a complement of 24 men and women, about a dozen fewer people than ships of this type needed ten years ago. One of the reasons is instrumentation that makes most jobs easier. The engine room, for example, is manned only from 8 a.m. to 5 p.m.—and has automatic alarms in case of a problem during the night.

What does the captain believe is the biggest difference between being the master of a ship now and 20 years ago? Not the instrumentation, or the navigational aids, but the relationship between the captain and others on the vessel.

"It is more of a family now. The whole ship is more of a family because we are working together, all of us. It's not like before when the captain—he was standing there, telling you what to do.

"These days we discuss, honestly, together, get the opinions about problems, and you say OK. After a while, if you can't come close, you still have the captain to make the decision.

"Before, it was more cold. It used to be: 'You have to.' But now you can discuss and say, 'OK, let's do it that way.' It's better now, more human."

12 | Island of Guaruja

"Here you are more free. In Sao Paulo you are more like a machine; here you can be more human."

If "Island of Guaruja" has a glamorous, far-off sound, it's well-deserved. Vacationers on the small Brazilian island have included King Olav of Norway, the King of Nepal, movie star Kirk Douglas, Bettina the model and friend of Aly Khan, and novelist Francoise Sagan. This is where the jet set of Sao Paulo spends its summers.

Apartment buildings overlook the beach on a small bay at one end of the island, giving an effect of Miami Beach in miniature. Most of the apartments are occupied only a few months of the year. So the sidewalk cafes and the avenue along the beach are largely deserted in the autumn, winter, and spring.

Even in winter, temperatures stay in the 50s or above. But days and days of rain and fog keep the beaches bare. The rain-swept, empty streets build an aura of remoteness—even though Latin America's largest city, Sao Paulo, is only 60 miles away.

On another side of the island is Dow's largest Latin America terminal for importing and storing liquid chemicals, and also a production complex. The complex—the only manufacturing industry on the island—is directly across the Pouca Saude River from Santos, Latin America's largest port, and downriver from the heavy industrial operations at Cubatao. Most of Guaruja is marshy, loaded with banana trees, making for a general economic appearance in striking contrast to both the island's beach resorts and the Santos skyline of modern business and apartment buildings.

It was in 1971 that Dow completed Brazil's first waterfront facilities for bulk storage of liquid chemicals. Previously, such shipments had to be trucked from ships to inland tanks. For the future, this Dow operation—close to the most industrialized area of Latin America, but lacking sources of salt

and petroleum for manufacturing petrochemicals—probably will develop more as a terminal than as a production complex. It is at Salvador, to the north, that Dow has started building a plant to produce basic chemicals.

Guaruja, as a terminal, is already a busy place. There are 17 large storage tanks, and about 20 ship arrivals a year bring in—from the Gulf Coast of Texas—large volumes of caustic soda, propylene glycol, chlorinated solvents, styrene, carbon tetrachloride, propylene oxide, and diethylene glycol.

The first plant at Guaruja was the joint-venture Propenasa plant for manufacturing VORANOL polyols from imported raw materials, built in 1972 and already being expanded. Next came a Dow plant for production of styrene-butadiene latex. And a third plant is under construction for producing STYRON polystyrene.

The site manager is German Posada, a native of Colombia who joined Dow in 1964 in his home country. He holds a bachelor's degree in chemical engineering from the National University of Colombia and a master's from Case Western Reserve University in Cleveland, Ohio. The superintendent of the Propenasa polyol plant is John Berner, a Swiss born in Budapest, Hungary, where his father was a diplomat during World War II. John received his bachelor's degree at the University of Pennsylvania and his master's at Pennsylvania State University, both in chemical engineering.

Besides a Colombian and a Swiss, there are natives of China and Chile among the 100 or so Dow people at the site. But the majority are Brazilians, with all but a dozen or so being from the Guaruja-Santos-Cubatao area.

Among the Brazilians working on the polyol expansion is Jose Julio Ruivo, a 33-year-old native of Cubatao. Three generations

of his father's family grew bananas. Jose has worked on the banana plantations—but only because that was the work available, not with any intention of being a farmer.

"All my family used to be banana planters. They used to have a farm close to Santos, and I lived there until I went to Sao Paulo to study engineering. My father, his brothers and sisters, they have a big piece of land between Sao Paulo and Santos that was a banana plantation.

"Now this land probably will be divided into lots for houses and things like that. But in the time my grandfather was a farmer this land had no value. Actually, it has a lot of value, but in that time, no, it was used only for a banana plantation. Because I studied in the morning, I used to have some jobs in the afternoon that related to farming.

"I prayed for this type of job that I now have in a manufacturing plant. Mainly this kind of job, with some of the more difficult things. Like on this project. Although the project is small, we have only a few people—and I believe in this project we have to put more of ourselves than the things that are written in the books.

"On a big project, you have no opportunity to do something different from the things that are written in the books or specifications. Even after we have started working in the plant, something may have to be changed, and we may have to make some deviations. A small project is good for that.

"If we all together arrive at a conclusion that this is the best thing to do, we go ahead. We are not tied to some massive structure. We know that what we have to do is to make an expansion of this plant—and we have a lot of opportunity to find the proper way."

Jose graduated as a project engineer from the University of Sao Paulo in 1965, and worked five years in a Cubatao plant producing chlorine and caustic soda before starting with Dow. While working in Cubatao he was married, and he and his wife Maria have two children, Luiz, 5, and Liliana, 3.

In Cubatao, Jose has seen his hometown become one of the most polluted in the world, both the air and the water. "When I started to have some idea about things, say when I was eight years, something like that—we had only a paper plant, hydroelectric plants, and the banana farms. I believe we now have the most important basic, heavy industries in Brazil. But the municipal services and the related things did not grow together with the industry.

"They are faced with a pollution problem because of the plants. The government did not foresee that they must take care with some things. Sometimes it is impossible to breathe. It's chlorine and a lot of things together. And those big plants keep expanding."

I remembered how pointedly German Posada had commented that the nearby river, the Pouca Saude—meaning Little Health, or Poor Health—had its name long before Dow built its first plant at Guaruja.

When Jose joined Dow in 1970, the company had just purchased a polystyrene production plant in Sao Paulo. It was there he met and worked for Posada, who had transferred from a Dow polystyrene operation in Colombia to become superintendent. Now, asked what he'd like to do following completion of the polyol expansion, Jose said:

"Mainly I believe it is better to say what I do not want to do—and it is that I do not want to do purely maintenance work. During my last five months in Sao Paulo, I ran a small project in the polystyrene plant that gave me some project experience. After working six years in maintenance with a

previous company and now with Dow, I feel that I can do more than be tied to only maintenance. I would like to have a general responsibility over a lot of services—like small engineering projects, preventive maintenance, supply stores, purchasing. Or a general service department to serve a site like this that has small plants.

"But if it's to decide what I want in the future, it is the general responsibility of, let's say, a total plant—from project to start-up to running the plant for some time. And the other thing, when it is running normally, to start again.

"I don't feel satisfied when the job doesn't present some different things. If it is running normally, I start looking for another thing. Like in the polystyrene plant, when things came to be routine, no problems, I

told my manager, 'I believe you could do the job with a young boy. And he probably would have more motivation than myself in this type of job.' Now I am here on this project because of that."

The process engineer on the polyol expansion, 26-year-old Victor Yang, was born in Shanghai, China, as was his wife Yvonne. Both have been in Brazil since they were children, and they have a two-month-old son, Emerson, who was born in Santos.

Victor's family left China at the time of the communist takeover, when he was a year old. They spent eight years in Hong Kong, then moved to Sao Paulo. Victor's brother and two sisters all live in Sao Paulo, where his father is a builder of small homes.

Victor is a chemical engineering graduate of the Massachusetts Institute of

Technology. In his senior year he turned down a job with Dow in Texas because he wanted to go back to Brazil.

"I would like to continue in Brazil, but I wouldn't mind traveling, a foreign assignment, so long as Brazil remained the home base. I grew up here, maybe that's the reason. I'm more fluent with the language, the customs.

"If I had a chance to travel, I'd perhaps choose China as one of my stops, but that doesn't mean it would be my first choice. Right now, that would be Europe as the place to visit, more to see in a short time."

It was now six months since Victor had started working on the polyol expansion. "I went first to the Dow Latin America headquarters in Coral Gables, then to Louisiana and Texas. Henry Bell was the site manager here before German Posada, and he got the expansion started before going back to the Louisiana Division. So I went to Louisiana to pick up what he had started, then we went to Texas for technology discussions, and then back to Louisiana so I could work with him. We got the engineering package up to a certain stage where we could continue here in Brazil.

"The thing that struck me very much about the United States was the uniformity throughout the country. By that I mean if you travel anywhere in the United States you can go to the same hotel, eat the same kind of food, meet the same people in terms of clothing and everything. Things like that you don't see in Brazil; if you travel 60 miles away from a big city, you can see a completely different lifestyle. In the United States, people's housing, cars, and highways—and even some cities—look the same or close to the same to someone who is not familiar with them.

"As far as my impression of the Ameri-

Jose Julio Ruivo

67

Victor Yang

can educational system, as compared to my experience here, I think that at the college level the U.S. education is much more flexible. From a student's point of view, he is much more independent, has more options open to him. And he has to mature faster.

"At most colleges in the States one has several options for electives. You have the basic core courses, but aside from that you usually have 50 per cent of your time for electives, which can be almost anything.

"And this, at least a few years ago when I was here, was very rare in the [Brazilian] universities because the curriculum is very strict. If one chooses to go into, say, chemical engineering, he has to spend five years in a curriculum that somebody dictated 10 or 15 years ago. There is very little choice as far as elective courses.

"This is maybe because of the facilities at U.S. universities, the size of the bigger universities. They are very well equipped for buildings, lab equipment, and so forth."

A Brazilian native, Sergio Petrovcic, 24, is the man described by John Berner—the polyol plant superintendent—as being "in charge of the day-to-day work." Sergio started as a shift coordinator in 1972. He has a degree in industrial chemistry. Now he's studying business administration at the university in Santos, and plans to go into chemical engineering in another year.

Sergio grew up in a small town 40 miles from Sao Paulo. He and his parents, five sisters, and one brother now live in Santos. And in just three months he was going to marry a Santos girl.

What Sergio finds "fascinating" about his job is the variety of problems. The evening when the *Bow Elm* arrived, the plant supply of propylene oxide was barely sufficient to maintain production for five or six more days. Sergio had been at the dock at 7 p.m. to meet the tanker, and to work through the night with Norberto Garcia, supervisor of the terminal and the quality control laboratory.

When he's not at the plant, Sergio carries a radio-activated beeper so that he can be reached at any time. For one thing, telephones are erratic in Guaruja and Santos; the day we were talking there had been no phone service in or out of the plant. Someone said you could expect that whenever it rained.

Martha Rodrigues, the secretary in the production office who translated for our conversation, thought there had been rain every day of the six weeks she had been working for Dow. Martha, born in Sao Paulo, has lived in Santos since 1960 and formerly worked in the office of a coffee exporter. Divorced, she lives with her mother and daughters Stella, 11, and Ana Cristina, 8.

Almost all the Dow secretaries I met in Latin America and Europe speak and write English. And Martha was delighted at the opportunity to converse in English; she hadn't used the language much on her previous job. She's also an avid reader, and was just finishing *Jonathan Livingston Seagull.*

In Martha's 14 years in Santos, the area has "changed so fast that it is impossible to describe. There was only one apartment building in Guaruja 15 years ago, and the island was much more beautiful then. Now, during the vacation season it is crowded."

Martha likes to travel. "The south part of Brazil is very nice, and Bahia [north of Santos] is beautiful. I would like to be in Amazonia [the big undeveloped region in the central part of Brazil, including lands along the Amazon River]. It is just beginning."

But she prefers the Santos area to Sao Paulo. "It is easier to live here, and it is more pleasant. Sao Paulo is bigger and there is more choice of schools. But here you are more free. In Sao Paulo you are more like a machine; here you can be more human."

"More human," those were the same words used by the Norwegian ship captain, and they were words I heard elsewhere.

German Posada's secretary, 21-year-old Jocely Derito Pavao, also is a traveler—just recently returned from Missoula, Montana. Jocely flew to the States with a group visiting New York, Miami, the John F. Kennedy Space Center, and Denver. But she then went on to Montana to see a friend who had married a U.S. law student.

Her friend had attended high school in Janesville, Wisconsin, for a year. And, in the two hours just before she boarded an airplane to return to Brazil, she met the college student she later married. They corresponded. He visited Brazil. They were married in Brazil. And now he is a lawyer in Missoula.

Jocely was enthused about visiting a part of the United States she wouldn't have seen on the tour. And she recalled: "There are only two gates at the airport in Missoula, Montana." I agreed it wasn't like New York, that it's probably a rarity to see even two airliners in Missoula at the same time.

Continuing to study at the university in Santos, taking a course in journalism, Jocely started with Dow when she was 20, as secretary to the accounting manager. Her parents are lifelong residents of Santos, and a brother, Jair, 19, is studying medicine in Sao Paulo.

"Now we have much more factories and industry and pollution in Santos. Most of the young people tend to go to Sao Paulo, where the jobs are the best paid in Brazil. But it is much easier to make friends here than in Rio or Sao Paulo. Santos is a small city. We know everybody."

Jocely is, of course, Brazilian. Andras Ariztia is Chilean, and he has found that "friends are very difficult for a stranger to get here in Brazil." He has lived in Brazil for two years, leaving Chile because he didn't like the policies brought in by the Communist Party when it was voted into power.

A Dow employee since 1969, Andras was in charge of maintenance at the company's Chilean plants when he left, a year before they were taken over by the government.

"Nothing had happened to the plants when I left Chile. But it was on the way to happening because the government said that they were going to take the plants over. This was just words that were in the air.

"The first factor that was very strong in my deciding to go out of Chile concerned education. They had a program that they would teach communism and socialism and take religion out of school. Another factor was that they made a law in the Congress that nobody could go out of the country if they did not pay some big amount of money. They were talking about $10,000 at the time.

"And another fact was that, in the enterprises they had taken over by this time, they had put in charge persons who had no knowledge at all of the industry. They were just people that were political. So industry was taken away to be handed over to the political persons instead of to the people capable of getting the business to progress.

"Since I've been in Brazil, I know—from one of the instrument men who came here to work with us in Guaruja—that the polyethylene plant was not working at all. And the PVC [polyvinyl chloride] plant was at less than five per cent of the capacity because of lack of technology.

"I am glad I left because the situation is worse day by day—unless today. Today,

Martha Rodrigues

Allende was taken out. It was on the radio. German Posada told me. This is good news."

That was how, midway in my conversation with a Chilean, I learned of the revolution in his home country. Later it was reported President Salvador Allende had been killed, the military taking control of the government. For the rest of my stay in Brazil, this was the headline story in Brazilian newspapers.

Ariztia grew up on a farm near Santiago where his father raised corn. He was in the United States eight months for training in the maintenance of electrical equipment and instrumentation. In Houston, Midland, and Freeport, he found things "a lot different, and the life much easier, more facilities to live the life," than he had known in Chile.

"I liked the United States very much. I got a very good impression all the time I was there. But my English was poor, like now.

"When I was at the university in Chile, the books in Spanish were very expensive, and I had no money to purchase them unless in English. They were one-fourth of the price if I purchased in English. I studied English to learn how to read it and understand it. That was, I'd say, the beginning.

"When I really began to speak English was in General Electric. That was my first job after I went out of the university. These were, I'd say, the big chances I had to learn English before I went to the United States. In school we studied English more than ten years, but this was a very poor course, teaching only how to read it, and nothing at all on speaking it."

With Andras, now living in Santos, are his wife Nora and children Carolina, 4, Andras, 2, and Maria Cristina, eight months. His family finds a lot of similarities between Chile and Brazil.

"My wife likes it very much. The only thing that we wish to have is friends. Brazilians are very, very difficult to make friends. They are close to one another. Friends are very difficult for a stranger to get here in Brazil."

John Berner, 28, first reached Brazil when his father, the Swiss diplomat, was assigned there. John went to school in Switzerland, Uruguay, and Brazil—and then to college in the United States.

"Selecting a college was a very strange process. I didn't have any idea about American universities. I had never been to the United States. I'd heard about some of the universities like Harvard, the big universities.

"I went to the consulate in Sao Paulo, and they have a book on universities. I opened pages and picked at random three that had chemical engineering. And I wrote to the three. They were Ohio State, the University of Pennsylvania, and I don't even remember the other one. I picked the University of Pennsylvania because of it being in Philadelphia. It seemed like a historical city, an interesting city close to Boston and New York.

"When I started my graduate work I went to Columbia, in New York. About a month and a half after I arrived, the 'war at Columbia' broke out—the student protests—so I left Columbia real fast. When you are on a scholarship and so on, you can't waste your time. It wasn't really an academic environment, so I transferred to Penn State."

John has been with the Brazilian polyol project ever since he joined Dow on the first day of 1969. He worked and trained in the polyol plant in Texas, then transferred to Sao Paulo for the detailed engineering, and then to the plant site at Guaruja.

"For professional experience, this has been fantastic. I couldn't have asked for anything better. It is very rare to get a chance

to follow a project from zero, from the time it is born on a piece of paper until it starts producing material. This is a very rewarding experience—interviewing and hiring our people, being involved in the purchasing, and following up with the contractors. It's an opportunity that doesn't present itself very often.

"In hiring even for the unskilled jobs, like drumming, we prefer to get people with a bit higher intelligence, like college students, because this gives us a chance to promote people from within. For example, from the people who started here as drummers one is already an operator, one is a lab analyst. As need arises, we are constantly promoting them.

"Now with the STYRON polystyrene plant starting up, they are interviewing our people and giving them a chance to move up. This would not be possible if we restricted ourselves to people that just meet the need for that job. This is very well looked upon by the people themselves. Dow is one of very few companies here that does this—that takes, very seriously, this promoting from within."

His father having been in Swiss government work, and he having lived in several countries—including Brazil both before and after the 1964 revolution—seemed to make John a good choice for comment on the current Brazilian situation.

"There is a dictatorship in effect here, but it's not the typical kind of dictatorship that people would usually associate with Latin American countries. It's a dictatorship that at that time was a necessity because the country was in complete chaos, anarchy, in 1964, when the military regime took over.

"And they really set the country on its right foot. The growth Brazil has experienced is almost unparalleled anywhere in the world. It has a growth rate between 10 and 12 per cent per year of its gross national product, which is very, very high—surpassed, I think, only by Japan.

"As an individual living here, not involved in politics, you don't feel the fact that you are living in a dictatorship. Some articles in the newspapers are censored. They don't allow criticism of the regime, or they allow mild criticism but nothing overt. It tends to a very quiet existence."

By "quiet," John didn't mean dull—at least for a young superintendent of a plant manufacturing relatively new products. Less than a year since he married his wife Paolo, taking a 40-day honeymoon in the United States and Mexico, here he was—managing a plant that he had seen started on a piece of paper, and already in the busy process of expansion.

"The project is extremely interesting because of the fact that it is not a pat process. As of now, it still is a little bit of magic and mystery and art. It is not one of those big plants where you just produce tons and tons of material. It still has quite a lot of excitement to it and unknown factors. We discover new things practically every day about polyol processing."

At the Guaruja plant, small compared with Dow plants in the United States, I talked with people who had lived or studied in eight different countries—and not an American among them. It was one evening at the Delphin Hotel at the seaside in Guaruja that I met an American, traveling with a woman he introduced with a laugh as "my nurse, because the doctors said I needed to go away for a vacation after having sort of a stroke."

I was awaiting dinner, and there was no one else in the dining room. Shortly after my new friend arrived, he heard me speaking English to the waiter, and invited me to share their table. He was the jovial sort; we both enjoyed the Brazilian wine; and by his own admission he was an athlete of considerable achievement in the 1940s—basketball, football, track, and baseball. I knew the newspaper in the town where he attended high school—the *Pantagraph* in Bloomington, Illinois—which I presume recorded his athletic feats. And my wife had been at school in Nashville, Tennessee, at the same time he was at Vanderbilt University.

That old saying about a small world came to mind as we jointly recalled a number of sports highlights from the 1940s and 1950s. (I was reminded, too, of my experience at a sidewalk cafe in Milan, Italy, two months previously—having considerable difficulty in trying to order half a grapefruit, when a couple came to my rescue. He was from Indiana, his wife was a beautiful Italian, and in two weeks—even before I would be home—he was going to be in Midland because he was a Dow customer, in the furniture business.)

My friend in Guaruja, reminiscing about sports, could have continued all weekend. But beyond sports, I learned not much more than that he'd "made a lot of money in real estate in the U.S." Of myself, I said I was gathering material for a book, and he laughed with a good-natured, disbelieving, "Sure." Then: "How do I know but what you're with the CIA or the FBI or whatever?" he asked.

He never told me where he lives. So, after this book is printed, I'll mail him a copy through the Vanderbilt alumni office. Maybe then he'll believe I was indeed working on a book—and I didn't have anything to do with the revolution in Chile, either. On second thought, I'd better ask the Vanderbilt alumni office for his business address. He had a nurse. Maybe he has a wife.

13 | Youngest on the Board

"We won't have nationals for nationals' sake... We'll fill a job with the best-qualified Dow performer we've got anyplace."

Dave Schornstein first heard about urethane chemicals as a Dow salesman in Boston in 1954. That makes Dave a rarity—one of the few Dow people associated with this business, even tangentially, for 20 years. And Dave's interest in urethanes has heightened since he became general manager of Dow Latin America in 1969.

At 45, Dave is the youngest member of the board of directors of The Dow Chemical Company. His youth has advantage. Managing the big geographical area of Latin America, from Mexico to Argentina, requires stamina and strong legs and a hardy stomach—and he's fit for the task. Dave is 6 feet 2, athletic-looking, and as sun-tanned as you'd expect for a man who finds his favorite recreation in sailing, gets to the golf course occasionally, and has his office in Coral Gables, Florida.

I talked with him the afternoon before he was named to the board of directors, and he gave no hint of his pending appointment. What he did talk about was how Dow became such an active entry in the urethane business, and how the company is growing and prospering in Latin America.

"The first time I heard about urethanes was in Boston when Jim Leenhouts [from Technical Service and Development] made a trip out there. Jim was talking about urethanes, and because Jim was talking about them, so were a few customers. These were the very beginning stages, and I remember writing to a couple TDI [toluene diisocyanate] manufacturers for literature on the types of reactions that could be run and what the stuff would do. And I remember reading that and then coupling it with our own polypropylene glycols.

"At that time, Leenhouts was claiming this was one of the real promising growth areas for oxides. But there's a large difference between sales and potential. And we really were just starting. I think TS&D had been working on it for a couple of years.

"In 1955 I came back to Midland as an assistant product sales manager, and one of the responsibilities I had was the oxides. The P.O.-glycerine series of oxides was kept by Roger Zoccolillo [later general manager of Dow Italy, when Dow's urethane business started to flourish in that country], and I had the E.O. We used to cover for each other, so I went back and forth—E.O.[ethylene oxide] and P.O.[propylene oxide]—and kept up with the urethane business.

"In the early '60s, flexible foam was coming on like 'Gangbusters.' Because it looked like a large potential for P.O., we started to do some work. There were some people ahead of us in development, so we were trying to play catch-up and also do a little innovating. We started increasing the applications research then going on, plus the straight research for developing products, so we could build a position in that growing market.

"As we got more involved, the business continued to overshoot forecasts, which is unusual. And it kept growing much faster than people were forecasting. So we kept increasing our commitment.

"Dow had a unique position in propylene oxide. We were sitting with literally oodles and oodles of capacity that we could convert from ethylene oxide—much more than our P.O. competitors would even dream about building. The original process for making E.O. was the same chlorohydrin process as for P.O. But during the 1950s many of our E.O. competitors were putting in direct-oxidation plants for E.O. rather than the chlorohydrin process.

"The economics of the chlorohydrin process are based on chlorine. With Dow's strength in chlorine production, our economics were different from those of competitors who either purchased chlorine or had a chlorine position not nearly as strong as ours. All the Dow E.O. and P.O. expansions in the '50s, mostly for E.O., were with the chlorohydrin process.

"So we had a large chlorohydrin base. We had plants which could be converted to P.O. when, eventually, we elected to go into direct oxidation for E.O. production. Instead of building new chlorohydrin plants for P.O., we'd build a direct-oxidation plant for E.O. and switch that chlorohydrin capacity to P.O.

"That was a hidden strength. It made decisions hard for competitors investing new money in a P.O. process that might become obsolete. In the '60s a lot of people around the world were trying to develop alternative processes to make P.O. Any new P.O. producer had to guess whether, if he used the chlorohydrin process, his technology was going to be good or not. Dow, with all the chlorohydrin plants and the strong position in chlorine, held a unique advantage.

"One of our goals in new product development, particularly with specialized products, is to develop a family of products open to constant innovation and improvement of the individual products. You try for a series of products, and then constantly upgrade that product mix in terms of value to the customers. The polyols for urethane products fit this approach perfectly.

"You can have protection by patents. But there is no protection like thinking faster and better and quicker than the other guy—and innovating new products. Your best position is based on a continually changing mix of new products.

"We were trying to do that in polystyrene products. We were shifting from general-purpose resins to upgraded, high-

impact types. Our latex development certainly has been a story of continuous product innovation, always a step or two ahead of competitors. And we wanted to do the same thing in urethanes—develop a series of products with each one better for particular applications.

"And we had two purposes. First, to have products which, in the customer's plant, performed better than our competitors' products. And second, there were certain new applications coming up where unique products would allow us to expand our markets.

"The products standard to us then wouldn't do for the new applications, so we'd work to develop one that would. When you are out-innovating competitors with specialized products, you can price those products on a value basis. That's a much better position than if you are selling a commodity chemical. In the case of propylene oxide, the alternative is selling industrial-grade propylene glycol and propylene oxide itself in a commodity-type market. But there you are offering the customer nothing unique, nothing that does a better job for him than anything else he can buy.

"There was a real growing market in the early 1960s for flexible-foam seating in furniture and also—tied in with safety—foam was just coming in in automobiles. Besides flexible-foam seating for comfort, you had padded dashboards, padded visors. Prospects in the transportation markets looked tremendous. It was one of those times when a lot of markets —sizable markets—had promise. The ultimate needs got into astronomical figures that were large in the early '60s, although they'd be common today.

"Every year until 1969 we overshot our sales plan and our profit plan. Yet when we made those plans—a year in advance, or five

Dave Schornstein

years in some cases—we were accused of being wild-eyed optimists. When you continually keep overshooting those types of forecasts, it's hard to be a pessimist.

"I know that in Latin America we have fulfilled or overshot every forecast we made on the VORANOL products back in '67, '68, '69 for Brazil and Argentina. In Brazil's case, the first plant was supposed to hold us for two or three years. It started up last November, and we're already in a hurry-up expansion. And we're really becoming short of capacity right now.

"We've had a real good market in Argentina over the years. In fact we'd like to build a VORANOL plant there. Selling product from outside, we have about 50 per cent of the market. And that market, in spite of Argentina's economic problems over the past two to three years, has continued to grow. It hasn't surpassed expectations, but it has lived up to them.

"We would have liked to put a plant for VORANOL products in Venezuela, and we had a permit for that at one time. But then the government would allow us to own only 30 per cent of the plant. And since this is unique technology, we didn't want to invest that uniqueness in a minority position. Somebody else is planning a polyol plant there now, and the next best thing for us is to sell P.O. to them.

"The overall Dow business in Latin America has grown quite readily, and from the profit standpoint we've improved the quality of our business tremendously. We've had to adapt to changing conditions in the business environment, but the results show we are one of the fastest growing parts of Dow. Since 1970 our sales goal has been an increase of 17 to 18 per cent a year; and now sales are gaining 20 per cent a year, and profits 25 per cent.

"Ninety-nine per cent of our hiring for Latin America is in the countries where we do business. The people running Dow operations in Latin America in 15 years will be people we're hiring today. As an example, in 1970 we started up a $35 million complex in Chile, and after the first year there were only two non-Chileans in that operation. One was Budd Venable, an American, who was half-time general manager for Chile and half-time for Argentina, and the other was the manager of the Petrodow plant, Alfonso Suarez, a Colombian.

"Most companies with operations in Latin America do not interchange people between countries very much. We were surprised at that. We started doing it around '69 or '70—like sending a Colombian to Chile, or a Colombian to Brazil, or an Argentinian to Brazil. Each year we have increased the number of people moved around. In almost every case they've been a success. But we've only transferred our good people, and good people do well anywhere.

"We won't have nationals for nationals' sake. We're developing the philosophy that we'll fill a job with the best-qualified Dow performer we've got anyplace. And within our Latin American organization we are developing many highly-qualified Dow performers.

"There are many misunderstandings about Latin America. Many people in the U.S. tend to lump it all together, see it as a glittering generality. But there is as much

"Being different, they present varying degrees of business risk. With the flood of investment money coming into Brazil—from the U.S., from Europe, from Japan—I can hardly think many people regard Brazil as an unstable situation. It's receiving more investment money from outside than most major nations, particularly among the developing countries.

"On the other hand, there isn't much going into Peru. Right at the moment there isn't a whole lot of investment money going into Argentina from Europe or elsewhere. There are differences, and I think they are evaluated that way.

"I think our job is to understand the varying environments we're in and to understand everything that Dow has, and find places where the needs of the countries meet our own needs as a company. Where the two match, let's do it—provided the risk posed by the political and social situation is commensurate with the potential profit.

"It isn't all that dangerous. What you really do is keep your eye on the fundamentals and learn how to scramble. If you do that—and stay loose and flexible, and adapt, and know how to live under those circumstances—you may not get much sleep at night, but you can do quite well business-wise.

"Dow people, in general, tend to be more flexible and more creative compared with many people our competitors have. Thrown into an environment where this pays off, the differences they can create in a short time are magnified much more than in a stable situation like the U.S. or certain parts of Europe.

"As a sidelight, we seem to start doing better when it appears that a country has a stability problem. Let something start to look the least bit shaky on the surface, or be

reported that way in the foreign press, and our competitors—the ones who aren't really part and parcel of the country—run out of there. If you're in a country, and a part of it, you obviously can do better when you have less competition than when you have more.

"The hardest decisions for me were in deciding to go ahead in Argentina on what was to be the very large Bahia Blanca project and then, about a year later, having to decide it wasn't the right thing because changes had occurred in that country's business environment.

"The tough decisions are in sorting things out—making sure you are doing the right thing at the right place at any one time. The computer doesn't help you. No amount of data will really help you. It gets down to weighing all the odds in that human mental computer, your mind.

"Another extremely difficult situation was our position in Chile. We were operating under a Marxist government—something with which we as a company had no experience. We were committed to fulfill a contract with the previous government as long as the current government recognized the contract. We had built up a beautiful organization of outstanding people.

"Then, as the situation started to turn, and the government got hostile and requisitioned our facilities, we had the questions: How should we react with that government? What should we do with our people? Deciding what to do under those circumstances isn't easy. A lot of us lost a lot of sleep over that one.

"The things that are the most difficult are the things that don't go well. In the things that go well, you may have moments of doubt when making or being involved in decisions. But then you don't remember those decisions as being difficult."

difference between any two countries in Latin America, between Argentina and Brazil, for example, as between Germany and Italy—which people in the U.S. accept as being quite different.

"And just as the United States is different from England, even though we share a common heritage, so do the South American countries differ. Each country, though generally founded on the basis of Spanish law and a Spanish or Portuguese heritage, has had 200 to 300 years of individual evolution.

14 | Love and Illness

"Everybody is watching each other...to see who comes out first. The race is on, and we're running it."

"That is where my love and illness started, when I took the job of technical salesman in Argentina for one group of products, basically the VORANOL products."

This was Marcelo Restano, an Argentine, the 29-year-old product sales manager in Brazil for oxides and derivatives, including the polyols for urethane products.

"I say 'illness' because you speak with anybody who handles the VORANOL products and it's something that gets into your blood. You never get it out of your system again. You can ask people like Dave Schornstein—he was involved in oxides and the VORANOL products; ask Gerry Pearson, he was involved in oxides and VORANOL products before he came to South America. [He was then the Dow general manager for Brazil.*] Somehow everybody comes back to that line of products."

Supposedly Brazilians and Argentinians do not mix well, but Marcelo was a distinct success in his first year in Brazil. His relationship with the VORANOL products goes back six years. His association with the United States started in 1959 when, at 16, he went to Annapolis, Maryland, as an exchange student sponsored by American Field Service.

"For a year, I did nothing but study and give speeches and meet people and have people meet me. I went to high school in Annapolis and graduated. That was the least important thing I did. The basic reason for my going was to help gain more of an understanding between nations, between people, between cultures. With this objective in mind, which was an American Field Service objective, I got in touch with many people—Rotary Clubs, Elks, Jaycees and so forth—in

*About a year after this conversation, Pearson transferred from Brazil to become director of product research for Dow Chemical U.S.A.

the Annapolis area. I think my first speech was to the AAUW, the American Association of University Women.

"When I returned to Buenos Aires I kept on working for American Field Service, which kept me in contact with trade associations, and other groups. As soon as I graduated from the university, my natural interest was to go into an American company—basically because it was something I liked, something I felt comfortable with, something I felt part of.

"I joined Dow without knowing much of the commercial aspects of chemistry. My background is technical, and for me the commercial part was something that would allow me to be in contact with people.

"Because Dow in Argentina was growing very fast at that time, in 1967, I was an inside salesman for only six months. Usually the inside sales job would have been for one or two years. But there was a need for much more development of personnel so I went to field sales.

"I stayed as a salesman for one year, more or less, then I took the job of technical salesman, which is more specialized toward one group of products. That is where I got involved with the VORANOL products.

"In 1970 I was offered the opportunity to go to the States—to the Dow Latin America headquarters in Coral Gables as a trainee for a year and a half—and come back to Argentina for a big plant, a big investment that was going to be taking place now, in 1973, if everything had gone OK. Unfortunately, that did not happen. When the project was dissolved, I had a bundle of experience and knowledge that I had been acquiring for six or eight months, and I was offered the job of product manager in Coral Gables."

When his temporary visa to the U.S. expired in 1972, he transferred to Sao Paulo.

"I like to see myself as one typical international Dow citizen. I'm an Argentine, but I've been out of Argentina for three years, ten per cent of my life already. Things are changing in Argentina. I won't say I don't want to go there, no; I always want to go. And I think that is the place I would most like to live in the whole world. But I like Dow, and I think the possibility of Dow sending me back to Argentina is not all that big."

Marcelo's parents and grandparents were born in Argentina. He speaks Spanish, English, Portuguese, Italian, and a bit of French. "Marcelo is a very Italian name, although it is Argentine. No one looks at me in Argentina as an Italian; but outside Argentina I've become used to the fact that 'OK, I'm an Italian.' Italian is a very strong culture in Argentina, very strong. To the point where the food is basically Italian, and our Spanish slang is based on Italian.

"I attended the National University of Buenos Aires, which I think is the largest in the world in number of students, about 200,000. I have a license that is something similar to a master's degree, after seven and a half years of pure chemistry. That's when I decided not to go into the lab for the rest of my life. I wanted to go more toward the people side of my profession.

"Chemistry is all that I studied. I did not study humanities. I did not study history or language. This began in high school, something like 15 subjects per year—chemistry, math, physics for seven and a half years. It should have been six and a half years. It took me a bit longer because I got married and started working. By the way, I met my wife (Elsa) at the university. She also has a license, a master's in chemistry."

Marcelo describes the Dow involvement in the urethane market in Latin America as very intense once it started, though Bayer has been in the market a longer period of time. "If you multiply the period of time in the market times the intensity in the market, Dow is number one. Dow is by far the smartest, the most aggressive. Dow knows how to get what it wants much better than any other company.

"We know how to do business in the large sense. Look around. Wherever Dow is located, we have selected that share of the market we want. We fight there—and usually get it. The rest of it, we don't get because we don't have the products or the people to go after that share of the business. So I think we are much smarter than anybody else.

"In Brazil, all the urethane markets for polyols are interesting because we have protection in the form of tariffs on imported products. And that is because it benefits Brazil to have these products manufactured in Brazil. That means if we want to get into the rigid applications for VORANOL products we can. We have the plant. And we want to. And we're going after this market.

"Traditionally, we have not been very strong throughout the world in the rigid urethane area. Bayer has been the strongest. In Brazil we have a plant and an organization clearly established for going after this market. We haven't gone after it so far, but we will.

"One of the biggest potential applications is in insulation for refrigerators. Urethanes in refrigerators is practically non-existent here. But it is going to grow like crazy, and we're ready for it. In Europe, Bayer is tremendously strong competition. But here, there is still time to win the race— and we have everything in our favor.

"A million refrigeration units per year are manufactured in Brazil. This business is growing at the rate of 15 per cent a year, and of these units fewer than ten per cent are being insulated with urethane. Only one manufacturer is using urethane, and he is not applying urethane to each unit.

"That means the present urethane share of the total potential market is very small. Everybody is watching each other to see what they are doing, to see who comes out first. The race is on, and we're running it. We are alert. We are watching. Any Dow success elsewhere in the world may be a success here, because we are going to borrow it and try to implement it here.

"One thing I've learned is that situations change so quickly. Today I'm going to be here, tomorrow maybe Midland or Zurich. Basically, if I had my druthers, I'd like an assignment in Europe."

Marcelo Restano

[In 1974, Restano was appointed product sales manager for chemicals and designed products in Mexico.]

In addition to studying and working in the United States, Marcelo has visited Europe twice—once as a tourist and once, for Dow, to learn about the urethane business as it exists there. But living in the United States is something he remembers fondly.

"My experience at Annapolis was tremendous. I lived with a family, and I still visit, call, and correspond with them. When I was living in Coral Gables, I went to see them very often. It was a very nice experience living with them, and I understand now they are going to Argentina and live with my parents for a month or so."

While Marcelo's "love and illness" with the VORANOL products began in 1967, the stage was set by his scholarship from the American Field Service. That organization started during World War I as a volunteer ambulance service in France. The exchange scholarships were initiated after World War II.

"AFS has no strings attached to it whatsoever—commercial, political, social, religious, nothing. It was started by a group of medics. They wanted to do something for world peace and understanding."

That's what started Marcelo toward becoming "one typical international Dow citizen."

15 | Black Markets

"It was like driving down into a cloud, like an airplane dipping into an ocean of milk...the peaks of hills and mountains jutting above the thick fog."

The American in the adjacent seat on the Varig airliner explained: "In the United States you can say whatever you want, but you can do only what the law allows. In Brazil, it's just the opposite: You can do about whatever you want, but there's censorship."

Another American noted how Brazilian newspapers make censorship obvious by leaving blank space on a page when a deletion has been ordered. But some indication of the infrequency of censorship is that during three weeks in Brazil I never saw a blank space. I don't read Portuguese, but a newspaper in almost any language can be figured out for the weather report, what's happening on the stock market, and whether Billie Jean King or Bobby Riggs won the tennis match.

I also was told the income tax situation in Brazil is far different from what it was in the recent past. The country does collect the tax, and has a system for preventing evasions. In what may seem an oddity, the government proudly describes the income tax system in a publication designed to attract industry.

Currency exchange rates are inescapably a subject of interest to any foreign traveler. Perhaps less so today than 20 years ago when, in many countries, official rates and black-market rates were far apart. And certainly the changing rates commanded attention of American tourists early in the summer of 1973 when, in Central Europe, the dollar was slipping in value almost daily.

I recalled how in 1955, in the back room of a tobacco shop near the waterfront in Istanbul, I cashed a traveler's check for almost twice as many Turkish kurus as I would have received at a bank. But on the same trip, I was more cautious in Yugoslavia—never having been in a communist country before. On the train to Belgrade, the dining-car steward asked if I wanted to change some dollars, but I declined.

And at the largest hotel in Belgrade, the young man carrying my bags up the stairs to the third floor—because the elevator didn't work—inquired if I wanted to change some

money. And I declined. Next day, when I asked the local Yugoslav correspondent for The Associated Press about the advisability of such transactions, he said I had done well. The bellhop was an informer for the police.

For my 1973 travels, I adopted the simple rule of changing money at banks whenever possible, because they usually offered better exchange rates than the hotels. This, of course, is completely legal; the hotels collect what amounts to a service fee that's a bit higher than the banks charge. Besides, every tourist guide I've read advises that travelers always receive a bit better transaction at banks than at hotels. Still, I've never figured out why traveler's checks are worth more than cash in some countries, while in other countries it's just the opposite.

In Sao Paulo, however, I found there continue to be exceptions to every rule. The hotel gave more cruzeiros for dollars than the bank—and this in a bank 45 per cent owned by Dow. The lesson is not that Dow is necessarily a high-priced company to do bank business with, but that the economic rules aren't quite the same in Brazil as elsewhere.

This seemed confirmed when the hotel was quite agreeable to accepting my personal checks—but asked that the space for the name of the payee be left blank. When the canceled checks came home with my monthly statement I found the checks had not been cashed in Brazil, but in New York. One was paid to an individual, the other to a company. Whether this had anything to do with exchange rates, income tax laws, or limitations on profits that can be legally taken out of Brazil, I don't know. But I have my suspicions. (You needn't be suspicious of Mr. Hilton; my hotel wasn't part of an American chain.)

In Rio de Janeiro, a plastics salesman told me he could retire for life if he could sell his polystyrene and other petroleum-based plastics at the black-market prices rather than the government-controlled prices. For Dow, it is a serious responsibility to see that plastic resins are sold only to ethical customers rather than to those who might resell on the black market.

Sao Paulo also provided my first encounter with a rent-a-car agency which, despite all the advertising on worldwide acceptability, wouldn't accept its own credit card. Driving a rented car in heavy rain while en route from Guaruja to the airport at Sao Paulo, I was just starting up the mountain road from Santos when the windshield wiper on the driver's side quit working.

To get a windshield wiper motor repaired at seven in the morning, I figured, was beyond hope. So I drove carefully. And slowly. And I missed my flight. Now, at the airport at last and returning the car, my main concern was to pay up—by credit card or otherwise—and move on.

As the clerk figured the charges, I told him what a difficult trip it had been and how the faulty wiper caused me to miss my flight to Recife—and those flights don't leave every hour, or every two hours. But I didn't get a word of sympathy. The clerk just explained how anxious he was to return to Los Angeles—as soon as he could move without fouling up his pending divorce.

Actually, my problems had started before the wiper quit. In Guaruja I had been detoured to a ferry and an unfamiliar road through Santos because the highway I had previously traveled was closed. Whether it was because of flood, a rockslide, an accident, or some other reason, I'll never know. But the new route kept me busy looking for the signs to make the correct turns.

En route to Guaruja on the four-lane divided highway known as "the spectacular Via Anchieta," I was detained 45 minutes. A big truck had skidded sideways and, wedged across a bridge, completely blocked traffic in one direction. There was no way to cross over to the other half of the highway. My car was 13th in the double row of vehicles behind the truck; at the rate the traffic was moving, the accident must have happened within two minutes before I stopped.

A Brazilian magazine describes this highway as one on which "the capacity already has been reached." That's an honest statement. It's also the reason the new Rodovia do Imigrante highway to Santos is under construction. Hundreds of trucks, cars, and buses were backed up on the old road before traffic started moving again. As tightly as the truck was wedged, I was surprised to see it freed and swung around to clear one lane in only 45 minutes.

The description of this highway as "spectacular" is probably no exaggeration.

But for me it was like driving down into a cloud, like an airplane dipping into an ocean of milk. It was an unusual experience to see the peaks of hills and mountains jutting above the thick fog. Franco Moraes, a Paulista (native of Sao Paulo) and supervisor of traffic operations for Dow Brazil, said there have been tremendous vehicle pile ups on this road, and I can believe that.

Except when I was in a car, or crossing a street, I regarded safety as no problem in Sao Paulo. I've never seen so many policemen. There seemed to be little requirement for their services except for one who was writing a traffic ticket. And perhaps at the airports, where carry-on bags and clothing are thoroughly checked by the police, and all luggage is inspected by customs officials if the flight is from another country. Departing on any flight, domestic or international, requires a show of appropriate identification, either a passport or a Brazilian identification card.

One departure, from the airport in Rio, produced considerable confusion. I couldn't understand the questions in Portuguese, but the problem seemed to be a discrepancy between the number of passengers checked in at the ticket counter and the number waiting to board. The woman standing next to me suggested that perhaps the gate attendant wasn't aware the police had diverted two women after finding handguns in their clothing.

After I returned to the United States, I happened to read a news story describing Brazil's crackdown on "pre-teenage criminals" involved in robberies and murders. It might have seemed incredible except for an incident in Rio. I was having a late-evening snack at a sidewalk cafe—yes, there are a lot of those in the warmer countries—when a youngster asked to shine my shoes. I said no,

because the hotel provided overnight shine service on shoes left outside my room door. But he was insistent, pleading "just one cruzeiro" in English.

So I said OK. By the time he finished, he had been joined by a couple of friends. When I pulled out my money clip—because a cruzeiro, worth 16 cents, is in paper—his friends asked if I had any American dollars. From a table 25 feet away came a warning from an English-speaking patron: "Be careful—they'll grab your wallet and run." And a Portuguese-speaking man at the same table got up and shooed the boys away. Had those boys grabbed my money clip, what little chance would I have had for catching them as they darted away into the dark?

16 | Opting for Opportunity

"Sure, I'm not making the top decisions...But with the products I handle, my opinions are taken real seriously."

Ladislau Lancsarics

Hideki Kato

Hideki Kato and Ladislau Lancsarics are Brazilians—sons of immigrant parents who, looking for new opportunities, moved to Brazil in the 1930s. Both studied in the United States, both are chemical engineers, both joined Dow within a six-month period, and both work at encouraging the appropriate use of VORANOL polyols. Hideki, 29, provides technical services; Ladislau, 36, is in field sales. Their parents came to Brazil from countries half a world apart, Hideki's from Japan and Ladislau's from Hungary.

In 1938, when Hideki's parents moved to Brazil, "Japan was not economically in a very good situation, and the government was offering opportunity abroad. In looking for a better opportunity in their life somehow, my parents heard about Brazil, and in those times they had ships full of Japanese families that would like to start a new life in a new country. There was some restriction like they should work at least two years in agriculture, then they could do something else."

When Hideki was in his first year at the university in the State of Parana, he also set a goal for himself—to go to the United States to get his master's degree.

"You always think you should be above average, and just getting your degree here in Brazil nowadays is not anything. Let's say it doesn't make you different from the others. Nowadays, a degree is very easy to get because many people work during the day and go to school in the evening. Five, six, seven years ago, that was very difficult.

"And I said, 'Well, I think I would have a much better future if I could go to a foreign country.' First I thought about Japan; then I made up my mind to go to the U.S. In my first year at the university I started studying English by myself and going to English school. When I finished college I had a very good knowledge of the language—mainly because the books I used were 80 to 90 per cent English books, American, and many others.

"The only way I could go away to graduate school was by getting a scholarship. When I was in my fourth year at the university I started writing letters all over the world. I wrote to many universities because I knew they had money from various interests and industries in the U.S. that grant scholarships for students in graduate school.

"But the way I was successful was through the church. I am Episcopalian, and my church gave me a scholarship to the U.S.

Before I finished, I also received a scholarship from the University of Akron, where I was studying."

Before going to Akron, Hideki thought that earning a scholarship might be the most difficult part of his effort. But he still had a long way to go.

"In Akron, I felt completely lost. Even though my background in English was not too bad, I could not understand Americans speaking. I also had a lot of trouble with food—completely different—and also the way of living, the way of thinking. Now, there is no difference. Two and a half years is enough time to get to know people, know how they live, get to know their feelings. Now I can go to the U.S. and it's just like going to another state in Brazil."

Hideki wanted to return to Brazil, but he hoped to first work in the U.S. as a trainee for a year.

"At that time, late 1970, the market for jobs in the U.S. was very, very bad—even for an American. Dow wrote and said they could not give me a job in the U.S., but I should go back to Brazil and try to get a job there. That would be much easier.

"When I came back, many of my friends also were looking for jobs, and they told me it was not going to be very easy. It was April then, and most of the companies had hired the people they wanted, since the school year runs from March to December. But I did not have any trouble—mainly, I think, because I had a master's degree. I think Dow hired me to work with urethanes, but I really didn't know until after I started my job."

In Dow Brazil, the function of Technical Service and Development is concentrated on problem solving and the promotion of applications for existing products.

"We are dependent on technology from the U.S. and Europe. We do not have the manpower or a facility here in Brazil for developing new applications or new polyols. But in the future we will be equipped for formulation modifications and product development, because the market is not the same in Brazil as in the U.S.

"Chris Loefgren is the TS&D group manager for urethane chemicals here. He's from Switzerland, and I believe he knows the most about urethanes of anybody in Dow. Together we take care of Brazil and Argentina. The markets are very similar in flexible foam in these two countries."

For many of the Brazilian customer plants that Hideki visits, from Porto Alegre in the south to Recife in the north, the start-up of the polyol plant at Guaruja was welcome news.

"Many, many customers in Brazil feel safer when their raw material is made here in Brazil. They don't have to worry about importing it, don't have to worry about being short of material, don't have to worry about, let's say, planning for a long time. Because if they run out of material today, they can give us a call—and then two days later, maybe one day later, they will have a tank truck of raw material."

Hideki is in a field of work where he'd like to stay for the next few years.

"I think our department is going to grow. We soon will have four men in our group, and I really think we all are going to have an opportunity to grow with the company within this department."

And that's what it was all about when his parents moved to Brazil, and when Hideki went to the United States for graduate study—economic opportunity.

Ladislau Lancsarics started with Dow in late 1970, shortly before Hideki, when Jesse Vargas from the TS&D group in Texas was providing tech service for Latin America urethane customers. Ladislau has worked full time on the sale of VORANOL products since the start of 1973.

"I started here when Dow was putting its feet on the ground in urethane chemicals. It is an interesting field because the urethane industry is developing together with the country.

"When you have more need for sophisticated materials, materials that can help produce new goods, and people are able to buy more mattresses, get more foam in the cars, more foam in the furniture—you see why there's a growth rate of 20 to 25 per cent in individual areas. The automobile industry will develop, and it will support lots of production of flexible foam, mostly molded parts—cold molding, hot molding, all types of molding.

"In Brazil there are four large-sized urethane manufacturers, five or six medium-sized, ten smaller companies with some potential, and others who are just backyard operators. I have some pride in the development of urethane chemicals here in Brazil because I have seen this business grow almost ten-fold in three years.

"I know from other companies, and from working in sales for the last eight or nine years, Dow Chemical is completely different from any other American company located in Brazil—the type of organization it has, the opportunities it gives to develop with the company. And also the opportunity the company gives that your point of view, your ideas, are also taken into consideration.

"That just wasn't a part of it at the last company I worked at. You were not asked, or your opinions considered. It wasn't like it is in Dow. Here, we participate in mostly everything that's going on.

"Sure, I'm not making the top decisions about how much money we spend in Brazil, or what the investments are going to be. But with the products I handle, my opinions are taken real seriously. Many times I tell my friends who complain about some situation at Dow that they should go to the other companies and see how it is.

"My original interest was in plastics. My father has sold products in Brazil for several American companies, products all made in the States. Fifteen or 16 years ago, I decided why not go into chemical engineering. There was no school here in Brazil for chemical engineering, and I had friends at Lamar State College of Technology in Beaumont, Texas. They were all tennis players [as was Ladislau]. At one time, Lamar State College had six tennis players from Brazil—and the best tennis team in all of the United States. It beat all the big schools in California.

"I decided to go where I knew somebody. For me, it was very good because it was a small school and I was more of a person than a number. I received very good attention, and it was easier for me to develop.

"Technical support has been one of the big reasons for Dow's growth in Brazil; also, our direct and straightforward way of doing business. We have been consistent with our sales policy concerning price and other activities.

"Among those who are well-established, who know their business and have a good technical background, Dow is highly-rated. We try to develop a good quality of finished products—though you cannot control this, because any customer can do what it wants to make its own products. In Brazil, there are a lot of people looking for new ideas, new businesses, new products. We are interested in developing large-volume business with selected customers who can really give the end-use products a good quality."

17 | An Awakening Giant

"The largest portion of the Brazilian budget is for education... Not even the movie houses or theaters attract masses like the colleges do."

"**B**razil, as a land, is different things to different people. To most it's Rio, the land of carnival, beaches, and beautiful girls.

"In the Hollywood version, it may be boa constrictors, man-eating *piranhas*, or wild Indians.

"To others it is a backward land where the rancher and the fisherman eke out a meager existence, or the *favellas* [slums] of the city.

"Brazil is all of these but more, much more. The real Brazil today is a vibrant, awakening giant. The hustle and bustle of the big cities, crowded ports, growing industry, a flourishing agricultural economy."

That's how Gerry Pearson started his report to the Dow board of directors in 1973. Gerry, general manager of Dow operations in Brazil, is 6 feet 4½ and boyish-looking at 40.

Gerry had an extensive background in the oxides business when he went to Latin America in 1970 as Dow general manager in Argentina. He moved from Argentina to Brazil in 1971.

With Dow since 1955, he managed U.S. marketing of organic chemicals, including oxides and polyols, in 1968 and 1969. He then became U.S. business manager for oxides and derivatives and monomers.

In Sao Paulo I discussed the economic outlook for Brazil, and its potential as a growing market for Dow, with both Gerry and Peter Meier—a Swiss who had just transferred to Brazil as marketing manager. [In 1974, Pearson was appointed director of product research for Dow Chemical U.S.A., and Meier was named general manager in Brazil.] Peter worked in Venezuela, Colombia, and Ecuador for four years before joining Dow in Switzerland in 1954. Later I talked in Rio with General Golbery do Couto e Silva, president of Dow Quimica S.A.

Gerry spent most of his life in Michigan before transferring to Latin America—where he rejoined Dave Schornstein, his old boss from prior years in the organic chemicals department of Dow U.S.A. A graduate of Michigan State University, he started with Dow as a salesman in Cleveland and Pittsburgh, then moved to Midland in 1961.

"Today in Brazil, there's a significant problem in the distribution of wealth between the very wealthy and the very poor—which really is being promoted continuously when the government adjusts all wages by a fixed percentage. The executive making $3,000 or $4,000 a month, and the worker getting $50 a month, each get the same percentage increase under the government regulations.

"This specific point was taken to the Minister of Industry by the American Chamber of Commerce for Brazil in conjunction with a couple of European chambers. The government leaders were asked: 'Is this practical? Why not make it the same percentage up to x level, say $800 a month, and then taper off above that?'

"They said their interest is in creating a capital market in Brazil, and that the only way to do that is to give the higher-income people more money to invest in the country. Basically, this is working. The savings rate in Brazil today is 20 per cent of the gross national product, one of the top three or four of the world in this regard. Japan is running about 23 per cent; the U.S., 17 or 18 per cent. And in an inflationary economy, Brazil's 20 per cent is quite an accomplishment. So they are developing a capital base.

"I think the Brazilians have been very pragmatic about their whole approach to development and what they are trying to accomplish. And since 1964, they usually have finished up their five-year programs in about three and a half to four years.

"They have been able to accomplish what they set out to do. They have raised real income. For the worker making $50 a month, income has come up in the last ten years—his real disposable income has increased. But the income of the executive making $4,000 a month has increased faster. So they have this problem, which the government recognizes as a problem.

"The income tax system is one way to reduce income differences, except today there is no capital gains tax in Brazil. So those with the $4,000 income have been able to invest in stocks and companies and other things, make a lot of money out of it, and have no tax on the gains.

"That does create more of a capital base—one of the government's objectives. They have been pretty straightforward in saying, 'Look, our objective is creating a capital base, which means we are going to distort the income situation for a time.' They also have made it very pointed that they are going to bring it back in line some time in the future.

"As for development—in the automotive industry, Brazil is fourth in the world today; in petrochemical production, about 10th. Industrially, the country is pushing ahead quite well. But I think the most fantastic potential for the next 10 to 15 years is in agriculture. This is developing, but not as fast as the industrial side.

"Forty-two to 44 per cent of Brazil's agriculture is in the State of Sao Paulo where, oddly enough, all the industry is concentrated. The agriculture in Sao Paulo is pretty modern. They use insecticides, herbicides, fertilizers. In the fertilizer industry, plants built in 1969 and '70 were anticipated to have enough capacity for the next decade, but demand for fertilizer already equals capacity.

"As Brazil develops the cattle industry

over the next several years, I think agriculture will really boom. This can grow at a tremendous rate. Ten years ago Brazil was about 15th in the world in sugar production; today it is number one in cane sugar. In soybeans, Brazil wasn't even rated four or five years ago; today it is second to the U.S., and expects to pass the U.S. within five years.

"We see the Brazilian political situation as being stable through 1979, through the term of the new president taking office in 1974. Brazil has been working toward the development of political systems. During this next five years, I think there will be a lot more progress.

"Brazil's history has been turbulent at times. Since its independence, in 1822, it has existed under monarchies, dictatorships, and several tries at a republican form of government—with the result of little democratic tradition. The last try at a republican system led Brazil to a new low in early 1964.

"Inflation was running at an annual rate of 144 per cent, and interest rates rose to six per cent per month. The labor unions had become completely controlled by communists, and the country was paralyzed by a series of strikes. At one point more than a hundred ships sat in Brazilian ports, waiting to be unloaded. In Sao Paulo alone, there were 392 strikes in one year. The anticipated 1964 federal budget deficit was double the budgeted revenue.

"The military took control of the government in March, 1964, and they still have very strong control. I think they will maintain it as long as they feel they need to, which is both good and bad. So far it has been good, but these things are like walking a tightrope. You can fall if you are not careful.

"I think agriculture is the real key to the success of Brazil, and the agrovet [agricul-

ture-veterinary] area has very interesting opportunities for Dow. We think we can triple our agricultural sales in the next five years with just the products we already know will be available—without any of the new products we hope to have. For example, we have few fungicide products today, and Brazil offers a huge potential for such products to combat coffee rust and things like that.

"In the plastics and chemicals businesses, you either build plants here, or you will be out of the market."

When I talked with Peter Meier, it was only the second day he had been on his new job as marketing manager for Brazil. But,

like Gerry Pearson, he had charts showing forecasts for both increased sales from Dow production in Brazil and in imports from the United States.

"I am convinced the current boom in Brazil can continue. In another, let's say ten years or so, this country will be among the most developed of the world. They are undergoing development very similar to what Germany went through after the war. I think Brazil is the next economic miracle—if they can maintain political stability, and continue

putting emphasis on education and economic growth. Together with a fair measure of social justice, these seem to be their top priorities.

"The largest portion of the Brazilian budget is for education. Even 20 years ago I was convinced that the biggest problem in Latin America was the lack of education. You don't see any other city in all of Latin America where people are going to school at night as they are here in Sao Paulo. Not even the movie houses or theaters attract masses like the colleges do."

Peter remembers well when he first became associated with the VORANOL products in a significant way. "In 1966, when I became the chemicals marketing manager for Europe, I wasn't told very much what my duties were going to be—as is quite usual for Dow Europe. But Zoltan Merszei [president of Dow Europe] took time to single out one situation. It happened to be the VORANOL products.

"This I remember quite clearly, as if it were today. It was in September of the year I took on the job. He said, 'Look, we have this plant for VORANOL products at Terneuzen,

Gerry Pearson

and it's losing money hand over fist. I hope you can turn that situation around and show that this is a profitable business. But I want you to know that you don't have much time. If we don't show by April that this is profitable, we are going to get out. We are going to shut the plant down.'

"By following some of the old marketing rules—analyze the situation, set your priorities, set your goals, and marshal your resources behind the plan—we turned the situation around. We were making money by April. I remember we cut down our list of customers to about half or even less. We also cut down the number of products we were selling, and we actually reduced total sales.

"We were selling less but making a profit. And from then on, we never went backward. It was up in volume and up in profits.

"Another very important aspect was working with Dow U.S.A. in setting up a worldwide strategy for propylene oxide. At that time we were running ethylene oxide plants on the chlorohydrin process. We had just proved out our direct-oxidation process for ethylene oxide. And we figured it would not take very long for Dow to be in a strong position in propylene oxide—the world leader in fact—by building direct-oxidation plants for ethylene oxide and converting the ethylene-oxide chlorohydrin plants to propylene oxide.

"At the time, Gerry Pearson was the U.S. oxides sales manager, working for Dave Schornstein, and I would really say the strategy for propylene oxide was the key to our success in the VORANOL products today. With a spirit of very close cooperation between Europe and the U.S., we had the means to really take the leadership. And we spent a lot of time trying to understand our position and mapping out the strategy."

In transferring to South America, Peter

brought his wife Susan back to the continent where they first moved two weeks after they were married, in 1950, but had not seen since joining Dow in 1954. Both are from Basel, Switzerland, but they met while in college in Manchester, England. Peter was 24 when a Swiss chemical manufacturer assigned him to Caracas, Venezuela.

"My wife just loved it. I guess the early years of marriage are always especially happy times, a time we always have good memories about. But apart from being quite far away from home, the necessity of mastering some unusual situations—difficulties and what have you—was a strong component in fostering some lasting bonds. This is an ideal situation under which a marriage can start."

Besides anticipating that the Brazilian economy will continue to boom, Peter expects exceptional growth for Dow sales, and for VORANOL products in particular.

"The VORANOL products account for a pretty large chunk of our sales in Brazil. Almost 20 per cent of our current sales is in the polyols, and next year this business should almost double and account for a strong quarter of our 1974 sales volume.

"It is a very, very good situation—unusually good. Today, of course, the problem is mainly of getting supplies, the oxides from the U.S., not a sales problem. This should add to our responsibility to make sure we keep doing the things to give us a satisfactory business when the going gets rougher—which it surely will.

"I don't think we can expect to forever be without competition in the local manufacture of polyols. And, obviously, there are going to be new developments in the urethane field. We have to make sure that we continue to be pioneers in urethane applications."

18 | He Rode Buffaloes

"They had no mattresses in this region, nothing. All the time they used hammocks. Because of this, I thought this foam mattress would be a good product..."

If a ship were to sail due north from Recife, Brazil, it would pass closer to London, England, than to New York. Recife is on the eastern nose of South America. During World War II it was the site of a hospital for American soldiers wounded in Africa. It is closer to the Ivory Coast of Africa than it is to Buenos Aires, Argentina, or Caracas, Venezuela, or any other large city in Latin America outside Brazil.

The adjacent city of Olinda is a century older than Recife. Olinda was founded by the Portuguese, who sought protection by living on the hill overlooking the ocean. Recife, sprawling at the foot of the hill and divided by waterways, was settled by the Dutch, who found the lowlands more like home.

Olinda is the home of the offices of the Duarte brothers, Hilton and Aecio. They own a company, Sintequimica, that produces textile dyes, and for 17 years they also have served as Dow sales agents in the north of Brazil. Also in Olinda, on the hilltop, is the Mercido Riberia—an open square where, in the city's early days, slaves from Africa were sold.

Recife is a delightful place—at least when it is not raining. Although Aecio Duarte said the annual rainfall is substantial, in four days I saw only a few minutes of rain. From summer to winter the average daily temperature varies only five to ten degrees, with highs usually in the 80s.

It's a city of a million people. Downtown traffic is congested, especially at the bridges leading to the island site of the international airport and to the beach where a visitor can see the reason for the city's name. *Recife* is the Portuguese word for "reef," and the reef is clearly visible when the tide is out.

For relaxation, for viewing the sights at the beach, this is Brazil at its best, even more enjoyable than Copacabana Beach in Rio.

But it is a poorer area. There are more beggars than in Sao Paulo or Rio. There are more people sleeping in flower beds and on sidewalks.

There was one scene I particularly remember. It was a warm Sunday evening, and a small plaza was crowded with people looking at the goods for sale on benches—paintings, wood carvings, leather purses, belts, wallets, crocheted table cloths. Vendors were offering popcorn for 20 centavos, three U.S. cents. In the plaza, coming from a small church overflowing with people, singing could be heard. And in front of the church, lying in the lane of flowers, a man slept soundly.

Leaving the Miramar Hotel, where a four-piece ensemble provides dinner music, you can walk past shacks that have television sets but no indoor plumbing. Or stroll by the villas fronting on the ocean but gradually giving way to apartment buildings. Recife—despite its location far to the east—is on the same time as the rest of Brazil. It's daylight at 5 a.m. and dark at 5 p.m. And one morning, sticking out of an apartment window for airing, there was a mattress readily identified as one made by Piraspuma do Nordeste, a subsidiary of Piramides Brasilia—Sami Koudsi's company. It was easily identified because of the distinctive, colorful patterns of cloth Piraspuma uses to cover these urethane foam products.

Piraspuma's current line of mattresses was introduced to Recife at a country club preview. The Piraspuma general manager, Juarez Correia de Araujo, isn't lacking in imagination. He had the cloth for six different mattress-cover patterns fashioned into bare-shoulder evening gowns that 12 girls modeled at the party.

Juarez has been with Piramides since 1970, starting as a sales agent. Previously, he sold medical supplies for an American company in an area running from Salvador on the coast to Manaus deep in the interior—cities almost 2,000 miles apart.

"I used to be out on trips of up to 90 days. Manaus has an airport, but you had to use all kinds of transportation to get to the small towns. I rode horses, and I rode buffaloes. You didn't have any choice; it was horrible. Now, it is different. But I like sales work. If I were asked to do it again, to sell in the interior, I would do it.

"I know very well the situation in this entire region, even the small towns, so it was easy for me to introduce a new product. They had no mattresses in this region, nothing. All the time they used hammocks. Because of this I thought this foam mattress would be a good product in a completely new market.

"But people had the idea the foam mattresses would not sell because the foam would be very hot. So we had to prove to them that it is refreshing to sleep on, that you can move from one side to the other (which isn't easy in a hammock), and it is not hot."

Piraspuma was not the first urethane foam producer to make mattresses in the northeast; Trorion was there first. But the Piramides subsidiary built a plant—without encouragement from the government, despite a big program to attract industry to the northeast. The Sudene development agency simply didn't believe the market would be large enough to support two foam producers.

In 1971, Juarez was selected as the Piramides "Agent of the Year" and the plaque presented to him is proudly displayed in his office, behind a desk with phones in green, red, and beige. And then, in 1972, he was named general manager of the Piraspuma plant being opened in Recife.

ESPUMAS

COLCHÕES

PiraSpuma

INDUSTRIAIS

Juarez Correia de Araujo and Aecio Duarte

The VORANOL polyols for the Piraspuma plant are hauled 1,700 miles from Guaruja in tank trucks. The plant produces mattresses for double beds, single beds, and cribs, and also sells the foam in many shapes—from big buns to fabricated parts. Some of the latter are cut and laminated with heavier-density foam for the areas of greater wear, such as the front edges in the cushioning of truck seats.

The Recife plant also sells foam to other mattress makers. Some is shipped as far as Manaus, transported by water since the Amazon is navigable for oceangoing ships to Manaus and beyond. This plant also supplies another Piramides subsidiary, Piraspuma de Bahia, which makes mattresses in a plant opened at Salvador in 1973.

In the Recife plant there are 95 employees, most of whom live nearby, many of whom have not studied beyond the third grade. Says Juarez:

"Education is a problem of the region. But the people are intelligent, very intuitive, and they learn the work quickly. We started with a nucleus of people from Sao Paulo, but they were needed for only a limited period. Some of them were originally from this region, and they stayed; some others went to Salvador to help start the plant there."

In addition to the factory workers, the two Piramides subsidiaries have 11 salesmen in the northeast. At first all worked out of Recife; now three are headquartered at Salvador. All have cars. The government is building thousands of miles of highway to help develop the northeast, and no longer is it necessary to travel by horse or buffalo.

One needn't look far in Recife to find the urethane products of both Piraspuma and Trorion. The padding on the deck chairs at the hotel carried the label of Trorion, but Juarez pointed out that foam from Piraspuma also was used inside the hotel lobby.

The neighborhood supermarket sold not only food, along clean, brightly-lighted aisles, but more miscellaneous products than most U.S. supermarkets—and including pillows made by both Piraspuma and Trorion. A plain foam pillow in a plastic wrapper sold for 8.8 cruzeiros ($1.44); those with cloth covers were tagged at 15.5 cruzeiros ($2.54).

The information on the labels and wrappers was in Portuguese—except for the pillows that Piraspuma sells without covers, which had the word "topless" in large letters.

"Everybody knows what 'topless' means; it's the same in English or Portuguese," Juarez explained.

"All that was necessary to start the sale of the foam products was a seller. But it is important for the seller to believe in the thing he is selling.

"The products are very, very good, very useful. And the company is very good, so it was easy to convince the people of this. I am very fond of the company because the management thought I could do the best job of managing in the northeast.

"I also think the company is very human. The management people are not only businessmen, but they are human and give enthusiasm to the people who work for the company. And I think this is not only on the surface. Whenever they come to Recife they are very easy to work with. They are human, they are happy."

I think the only question I neglected to ask Juarez was what happens at his home when someone shouts "Ana." His wife is Ana Maria, and his daughters are Ana Cristina, 17; Ana de Fatima, 14; and Ana Claudia, 11.

19 | Two Doubles Three Singles

"I want to be in a big city like Paris or Rome...They have a cultural background. In the United States, no; and in Brazil, they don't have it either."

The hero of "Around the World in 80 Days" has me beat. I spent 88 days on the road (and on the water) following urethane chemicals, including 63 days outside the United States, and I didn't circle the world.

All through the venture, my greatest curiosity was for who would be next in the chain of buyers—in Europe and Latin America—of the products that began with the chemicals I was following from Texas. With a little selectivity here and there, the outcome could have been rigged or semi-rigged—but then it wouldn't have been so interesting. I wanted the progression to be spontaneous. From step to step, company to company, city to city, I did not know—nor want to know—where I would be going next.

I tried to follow a typical path, not necessarily tracking the largest customers but staying in the mainstream of the business. This meant resisting the temptation to pick out the most glamorous or most unusual applications and sales. I learned, for instance, that among the buyers of bathroom furniture manufactured with components molded in urethane were a movie actress in Italy and a sheik in Kuwait. Either one would have been interesting to talk to, but neither would be a typical end-product consumer.

There was more adventure too, when I was talking with people who had no direct dealings with Dow. Some hadn't ever heard of the company. And in Italy the furniture makers were skeptical of my motives. They suspected that I really was after information and pictures of their latest designs—so these could be passed on to U.S. manufacturers who would copy the designs, sell more products, and buy more chemicals from Dow.

In Recife, I had the good fortune to have an interpreter who not only translated well but had an interesting background herself. This was Leda Sobre, who works half days as a secretary for the Dow sales agent, Sintequimica, and the other half for a French-Brazilian group building a hospital. In the evenings she gives language lessons, for which she is well qualified—speaking Portuguese, English, French, Italian, and Spanish.

Leda has been to Europe six times, but never to the United States. And if she were to travel abroad again, she still would want to go to Europe and not to the United States.

"I have nothing against the United States, but the United States is a new country, everything is new there. I don't want to go to the United States to see industry, because I can go to Sao Paulo and see it. I don't care about it. I want to be in a big city like Paris or Rome. These cities have lots of different things to do because they are older. They have a cultural background. In the United States, no; and in Brazil, they don't have it either."

I found her comments especially interesting because I often heard Europeans say they hoped some day to visit the United States.

"I started studying Spanish because I like the language. It sounds very beautiful. I was 18. At the same time I was getting into the university, so I was doing both things.

"While I was finishing my course at the university I also was finishing my course in Spanish. My last year at the university, I applied at the Institute of Spanish Culture. So I got a scholarship, and when I finished my course at the university, I went to Spain.

"I was on the scholarship for six months, and I stayed one year. I did everything I could to earn money; I baby sat, I served in a bar. I went to employment agencies, but at the time it was harder than now to find work because I spoke only Portuguese and Spanish.

"After one year I came back and started working for the Institute of Spanish Culture here, teaching, and at the same time I started studying English. When I finished my course in English I applied for a position with AID, the United States Agency for International Development. I started as a typist because I didn't understand English very well.

"After two and a half years I was getting better and better. So then I went to work for another company, an American-Brazilian venture for the construction of a highway in Bahia. I worked four years till the end of the contract. After that the company was dissolved. My English was good.

"By then I was studying Italian, and I think Italian is the most beautiful language in the world. I love it. I was so full of enthusiasm that I went to Bahia with an amateur theater group to make a presentation in Italian. I told the lady in charge I wanted to go to Italy. She got a very good impression. One year later, when I had finished my contract with the American-Brazilian venture, I got my scholarship.

"I studied in Perugia, in central Italy, a beautiful place, very old, medieval. I spent one year traveling around Italy. I loved it very much. I made a lot of good friendships.

Leda Sobre

99

Everywhere I met people. I ate with them in their homes. I learned Italian very well.

"After that I came back to Brazil, and I studied French. Then I went back to Italy to Rome, then to Perugia to see my friends. Then I decided to go to France.

"I stayed in France, then I went to North Africa. At that time I was writing for *O Globo*, the newspaper in Rio. I was writing about tourism. I was taking notes and pictures every place I went in Africa.

"Finally, in 1971, I married a French boy. We stayed in France another year. Then we came to Recife, and I started working as soon as I arrived. There is a lot of work to do here in the translation of technical material. And I like this part of Brazil, though it is easier to get much money in Sao Paulo and Rio because they have lots more industry. You can choose your job, because they look for bilingual and trilingual secretaries.

"Really, though, I am not happy here because I'm without any prospect to learn something new. I want to learn Deutsch [German]. I am going to try to get a scholarship to go to Germany. I have a plan. I always have a plan, but it is not so easy now that we are three with my little boy, Serge, who is a year and a half old."

So it was that Leda and I went looking for a business place called Soplasticos, on the Rua Direita in downtown Recife. Juarez Correia de Araujo had given us the name of this company as one that sold many Piraspuma mattresses.

We thought Soplasticos would be a wholesale company—one that bought mattresses in volume from Piraspuma and sold to retail stores—and that then we would go on to a department store. But this was a retail area in the fullest sense of the word. We found Soplasticos on a narrow street of stores and open-air vendors with tables of

merchandise, sandals, dresses, socks, and underwear. It was like a Middle Eastern bazaar, or a shopping scene in the *medina* (shopping quarter) of a city in the Arab part of Africa.

Among the items sold by Soplasticos are mattresses, pillows, yard goods, and some foam-filled furniture. Even before we met the manager, we spotted a young woman toward the back of the store discussing mattresses with a saleslady. She was exactly the person we were hoping to find—a buyer of a mattress manufactured by Piraspuma, made with urethane foam, made with polyols produced at the Propenasa plant in Guaruja, made with propylene oxide produced by

Dow in Texas.

Dilma Santos Lins, sunglasses pushed atop her sun-bleached, ash-blond hair, was buying the mattress because she planned to be married the following spring—most likely in May, the popular month for weddings in Brazil. The mattress would go into storage at home until the wedding. Leda explained that buying household goods in advance of a marriage is not unusual in Brazil.

Dilma lives on the Avenida Boa Viagem (Good Voyage Avenue), facing the beach on a street lined with palms. She was born to Brazilian parents in Recife, has lived there all her life, and is the third of six children, the other five all being boys. Her father owns a

Dilma Santos Lins

sugar mill. Her fiance is going to school, but he also is working.

"He works in a coffee-processing plant that is owned by his father with other partners. He plans to continue in the business and build another plant in this state, but in another city.

"After the wedding, I plan to continue at the university and then work. But when children arrive, I know that it would be difficult to work, and then I will become a mother."

The price of the mattress was 230 cruzeiros (about $38). I asked Dilma why she had selected this store for her purchase, since this shopping area seemed a bit unusual for one who lived on the Boa Viagem and whose father owns a sugar mill. It was a store she had been in many times, she explained, because the owners are good friends of her family. From manager Albani Rio Lima, we learned this was one of six Soplasticos stores—there being two more in Recife, two in Campina Grande, and one in Caruaru.

But plans for a wedding were not the only excitement in Dilma's life. In a week she was flying to London with a British couple, also friends of her family, on an excursion promoted by British Caledonian Airways for a new non-stop service between Recife and London. They would visit friends of the British couple, and Dilma had been excused from the university for two weeks.

If there was any chance she anticipated falling in love with Europe, like Leda, it was not indicated. Dilma speaks only Portuguese. Before she left to continue shopping, in her purple slacks and black-and-white checkerboard shirt, the store had sold another mattress to another buyer. As Leda and I walked away, a delivery boy headed up the street with five mattresses—two doubles and three singles.

20 | The General

"I will speak candidly...People were thinking Dow always talks, talks, talks but never spends money to build. Now this is disappearing."

Rio de Janeiro had two attractions for me—the city itself, with its tremendous Copacabana Beach, and General Golbery do Couto e Silva, who became the president of Dow Quimica S.A., or "Dow Brazil," in 1968. The 62-year-old general, after retiring from the Army in 1961, figured in events bringing the military to power in 1964 and subsequently served in the cabinet of President Castelo Branco.

Discussion of virtually any facet of Brazilian life almost automatically goes back to the 1964 coup, and the events preceding it. For the General, those events started in 1961. That was when the government of President Joao Goulart took office, and Golbery retired from the Army. That also is when he was promoted to the rank of general.

But now, almost ten years after the revolution, what interested me most was the Brazil of today. Certainly two aspects of continuing controversy are the reports that in Brazil "the rich are getting richer and the poor are getting poorer," and the censorship of the press. The General says, in essence, that part of the first statement is false and that the second is true. But he anticipates the censorship will diminish and then be abolished.

The question of censorship lends itself to a shorter answer, so let's take that first.

"I think it is important to the country to have it [censorship] during critical periods. But it is important to change that as soon as possible, in order to get another type of relationship with the press—to give them liberty, but to expect from them responsibility.

"I believe it is good not to have censorship, but to ask for responsibility, and I think we are going to have that. This is very important, because there is no way to make censorship work well. Censorship grows by leaps. And each time the censorship grows,

the authority goes to people less qualified to make decisions."

The General is just as adamant in contending that, since 1967, economic conditions have improved for both the poor and the rich—more for the rich than the poor, but that overall the country has achieved tremendous gains through successfully promoting the accumulation of savings for investments needed to create jobs and develop Brazil's resources.

"We have that kind of comment ['the poor are getting poorer'] in all the articles we read about Brazil, but this is not really true. The basis for that was a study made by an economist who gave it to Mr. [Robert] McNamara at the World Bank.

"This was based on two censuses, in 1960 and in 1970, giving indications about the wages, the incomes, and so on. Between those two years we had a big inflation, until 1964. After that we had a depression, a short time of stability, then another depression.

"And now, from 1967, a boom. With the big declines we had before 1967, you know that a comparison of the years 1960 and 1970 does not give a good indication of what is happening now.

"If you take a good look at the numbers, you will see that the poor people are better off now than they were before. The rich people are much better off than the poor people, this is correct. All people improved, but really the rich people improved more than the poor people. There is some sense in that because first we need to have savings in order to invest.

"We are investing in Brazil now 20 per cent of the gross national product each year. Twenty per cent, it is a good mark. I know the Japanese put more than that in investment. But we put 20 per cent from savings within the country. Foreign capital represents

2 per cent, and we invested last year a total of 22 per cent.

"The foreign-capital participation is small, but it is critical because this makes the growth rate increase. This is a very important point. The foreign capital comes to Brazil with technology also, another important point.

"The government is very interested in giving indirect benefits to all the people. The government prefers not to put more money in the poor people's pockets, but more opportunity in education, sanitation, and so on. The indirect benefits are helping the poor people more than the rich, because the rich are not going to lack for these things anyway.

"I think Brazil is really a very good window shop for the liberal, the free-enterprise regime. There has been necessarily some jealousy by other countries in South America. But I hope that within a few years this jealousy will change to the idea of using the same mode of capitalistic development we have in Brazil, because all the other experiments they are making have bad results.

"It is of interest to Brazil, this large-sized country, to have well-developed neighbors also, not poor neighbors. Poor neighbors are not good neighbors."

I talked with the General late on a Friday afternoon, after 6 p.m., after he had participated in a hastily-called meeting on how to cope with a good customer whom the Dow salesman suspected—but didn't know for sure—was reselling purchased plastic materials on the black market. It had been a long and busy day, but it was plain the General thrived on activity.

"All days are busy. I think this is good. Dow offers to anyone in Dow a lot of different problems. We have technical problems, we have political problems, problems

with the relationship with the government, and we have problems with people.

"I enjoy it very much. It is really a very exciting experience—especially because I am working now in Dow, and Dow has a lot of experience to give us in a country like this. And really I have been in the government many years, and we needed to see the problems from both sides of the hill.

"Now I have been outside the government, and I have a better knowledge of the problems than I was able to have when I was in the government. And really I suppose that in working for Dow, I am really working for my country. Because Dow is helping the country, too.

"Dow, I believe, is doing a very good job in recruitment of people. The problem in Dow is really not in bringing people, young people to the company, to train them and so on. The problem Dow has is to keep people in the company. Brazil's economy is in a very impressive boom, and the people who are capable are in a sellers' market. They come to Dow, they are trained. They go to the United States, they come back and receive many, many proposals for much more money. Really it is not easy sometimes to keep the people. But I am happy. Training people is one way of helping the country."

In appearance, General Golbery is not exactly what most people would expect in a South American general. He's a trim 5 feet 6½ inches and his office is small—two chairs for visitors, a single pink carnation on his desk, and a miniature Brazilian flag in a holder with the date May 27, 1971, a souvenir from the dedication of the Dow terminal at Guaruja.

The General reads and speaks a half-dozen languages, including the Italian he learned while a captain with a Brazilian unit in Italy during World War II. He is familiar with the United States, from military training at Fort Riley, Kansas, and his later visits to Dow headquarters in Midland.

By almost anyone's appraisal, 1964 was a turning point in Brazilian history, the year of a revolution with little or no bloodshed. For the General, 1961 was of great significance because that was when—retired from the Army—he became associated with a civilian group prominent in both the political and economic planning that preceded and followed the revolution.

"I was retired from the Army at the same time I became a general. The reason was a political reason, really.

"In 1961 we had a new president in Brazil, elected by a large majority, Janio Quadros. He hastened the feeling of a great lot of expectations because of the good government record he had made in the State of Sao Paulo.

"After seven months, there was some problem with the Congress. These questions never were explained, but he resigned as president. And the next president was Joao Goulart. He was a well-known man from the south of Brazil, from the State of Rio Grande do Sul, and he had been labor minister in one of the two Getulio Vargas governments.

"At that time he showed his tendency to the left. He really was not a communist, we knew that. He was a demagogue who talked that way to get support from the syndicates and from the labor people. And he also used many leftists and communists.

"When Quadros went out, some people in the armed forces took a position against the inauguration of the Joao Goulart government. We were most sure that the Joao Goulart government would inaugurate a period of instability, inflation, leftism, and so on.

"And we tried to block the rise of Joao Goulart in the government. But we were unable to do that. There was some division in the armed forces, and there was danger of a civil war.

"In Brazil we like very much to try to find some way to bypass a problem, and luckily we were able to do it at that time. The agreement was to change the form of the government. In Brazil we had then, and have now, a democratic government by constitution. But we have a strong executive, like the United States. At that time we agreed to have a parliamentary regime—hoping by that way Joao Goulart would be more conservative, and he would agree more or less to be like the Queen in England. And all the danger in his leftist support would be held down.

"Joao Goulart became president on September 7, and at that time I asked for my retirement because I was very concerned about the future. I was more or less sure that the Joao Goulart government would represent a bad future for the country.

"As I had many friends in the Army, they asked me to stay. They took my resignation and put it in a drawer. In the end, they agreed with my decision to go out. It took two months for my resignation to be accepted. I went out on November 7.

"I joined a civilian organization that was created at that time by friends of mine. Its name was the Social and Economic Research Institute. This organization was financed by an entrepreneur and by people in Rio and Sao Paulo in industry and trade—people also concerned about the future.

"The Institute was really a facade for the observation of the political situation and the organization of a front to block any attempt from the government to go more and more to the left. This was really the idea.

"We made some important economic studies about the agrarian reform, the tax laws, and so on. But the main idea was to organize a front, civilian and military. I went to the Institute to be a liaison man between the military people and the civilians from all the sectors of society, but especially industry and trade, the doctors, the engineers, and so on.

"Some time after the inauguration, Joao Goulart held a plebiscite. And he made very good use of propaganda to ask the people if the parliamentary form of government should remain, or the constitution should return to the presidential type of government. And the plebiscite was favorable to him. He returned to the presidential type of government.

"Each day the communists were taking more and more control of the situation. We hoped to prepare a good election because time was going by, and it seemed there really was no sense in making a move. The election would be in less than two years. We thought it was better to wait until the end of the government's term, and to use the new election to put in a good manager.

"But really the inflation was very high. We had in the third quarter of 1964 an inflation of about 85 per cent. This made a projection for the year of, more or less, 140 per cent. That was a large instability.

"It was impossible to remain watching such a situation till the end of the government. And there was a revolution in 1964. The Social and Economic Research Institute provided the focal point for communications between civilians and the military."

I asked the General if development policies successfully pursued by other countries, Japan and West Germany, for instance, had been helpful in laying the groundwork for Brazil's boom of the past six or seven years.

"We looked at many countries. We looked at Japan, which has had a very strong development, a high gross national product and so on. But the conditions were very different and, really, the biggest problem we had was having to start from a very bad inflationary situation. And it was inflation that you are unable to think about—because in the United States the people are very upset when the inflation is above five or six per cent. We had 85 per cent in one quarter. We could not plan, we could not do anything.

"I believe that for this problem there was an original solution taken in Brazil. The IMF, the International Monetary Fund, they didn't believe in our solution; but the solution we took gave good results. Last year the inflation was, more or less, 15 per cent; and this year it will be 12 per cent.

"Our solution was a gradualist approach—in order to make the country able to live with inflation and, at the same time, to continue working. The people in the IMF didn't believe in the gradualist approach."

The Brazilian government contends the IMF was urging "shock treatment that would have forced a freeze on prices and salaries, a sharp increase in the cost of basic services and elimination of other government subsidies, drastic restrictions on credit, and a reduction of public investment." Brazilians

feel this approach would have "cured the illness through a complete breakdown of the economy and consequent social upheaval."

The General said: "There were many measures to cope with inflation, not just one, but I will emphasize the monetary correction. In an inflationary situation there is really a fight between all classes of the people and between the syndicates. [Both manufacturing associations and labor unions are known as "syndicates" in Brazil.]

"Each one wants to have more than the other. There is a fight. This makes the inflation each day grow more and more. We put in Brazil this 'monetary correction,' to allow a fixed percentage of inflation each year—but to all things at the same time, and only one time, each year. The syndicates were not fighting one another, and the debtors were not gaining against the creditors. This was a very important move that we made.

"Another, similar to that, was control of wage rates. Wages were allowed to go up only at the same time each year and only by the amount of inflation we expected that year, plus a little percentage for the increase in productivity. There was social peace. There were no strikes, nothing. And at the same time there was not a constant pushing pressure.

"Another traditional remedy we took was not to have a deficit in the government budget. Brazil has had deficits at all times in its life. Now we have a nominal deficit of less than one per cent of the gross national product."

Today, the General views Brazil as being in a position to continue its domestic gains and also to help alleviate some of the shortages plaguing other parts of the world. He has no doubts that the growth of Dow in Brazil will be beneficial for both the company and the country.

"I believe Brazil has a very large potential for agriculture and livestock. We have a very good potential to raise cattle for export, and we will do that in the next few years. For agriculture also, we have a very good opportunity to expand our exports. The farmers respond very well to some incentives, especially in prices.

"We have some problems in transportation, especially in order to export, but this will be solved in three years more or less. Our potential for food, I think, is no problem. We have agriculture, the raising of cattle, and also fishing. We have a good potential in shrimping and in fishing. I think we will be able to export in all of these."

The General believes Brazil is in an excellent position for generating electrical energy, but that it has not found an answer to the petroleum shortage.

"The problem of energy is much more difficult than food for Brazil, because we haven't found very good oil fields. We have some oil in Bahia, but the quantity is small. I hope that perhaps we will be finding the jackpot in the Amazon area. I believe in that. But this takes a lot of risk capital. And it takes six to eight years to develop a field. The problem is not easy for us.

"On the question of coal, we have a lot of coal, but it is not good coal. There is too much ash, and to some extent there is a sulphur problem. Now we are improving the technology for gasification of the coal for use in iron-reduction plants. We are doing some work about taking the sulphur from coal.

"But we have a very good and large deposit of shale oil—in Sao Paulo, Parana, and the south of Brazil. We have a very good pilot plant. And if the price of oil goes up a good bit, it will become economical to use that shale, but now it is not economical.

"We also have a very good source of

hydroelectric energy. And we are using that with very, very good plants. We are impounding water resources for the hydroelectric plants. The hydroelectric energy will be sufficient, surely, until the last years of the 1980s.

"We also have to take a look at nuclear energy. We are looking at that more from the standpoint of technology. We have a plant in Sao Paulo, but the objective is more to train, to take notice of the several types of nuclear plants in order to choose the best one. We are doing that, and Brazil for many, many years will be in a very good position for electrical power in terms of both quantity and price."

General Golbery had been president of Dow Brazil for six years. During that period he believes the company has made substantial progress while, at the same time, the country itself has been advancing.

"I will speak candidly. Dow for some time had a bad image in Brazil. The problem was that Dow had a reputation of working in Brazil like a commercial trader. There was some talk, I don't know by whom, that Dow would put a soda ash plant in Brazil. This

General Golbery do Couto e Silva

was I don't know how many years ago.

"But Dow didn't put a plant in Brazil. There were not good conditions for doing that. As time passed and there was no plant, the idea grew that Dow was only maneuvering to block other companies from building the plant in Brazil and, in the meantime, to import caustic soda and to have the profits from that. This was the problem we had.

"By now, as we have plants, the image is changing, and they know we have a very good investment in Brazil. People were thinking Dow always talks, talks, talks but never spends money to build. Now this is disappearing.

"When I retire from Dow I would be very happy to feel that my efforts had helped. I believe that with the plants in the south and the northeast, the good terminals, and all that, Dow will continue to expand because it will have the base to grow."

In early 1974, General Golbery retired from Dow Quimica S.A. to accept an appointment in the Brazilian government.

21 | Kidnappings Terrorism

"When we will begin to work and to be serious is the difficult thing to establish. I hope that with this election we can begin going that way."

A "patriot" is defined by one dictionary as a person who loves and loyally supports his country. General Golbery is a Brazilian patriot. Hugo Vivern, 27-year-old salesman of VORANOL products in Buenos Aires, is an Argentine patriot.

Though Buenos Aires wasn't on the route of the propylene oxide and VORANOL products traveling from Brazosport to Recife, I took advantage of a weekend to visit Argentina. I wanted to hear about multinational business in another Latin America country. A common sin in the United States, Dave Schornstein had warned, is to think Latin America is all basically the same when actually there are major differences between countries. Argentina in 1973 had to be viewed as an unusual situation because of the many ransom kidnappings and the extortions from foreign companies through terrorism.

My visit was on the Sunday preceding the election that returned Juan Peron to the presidency. Campaign posters advocating the election of Juan and Isabel Peron were everywhere, even in the immigration and customs facilities at the airport. And just as many political messages were painted on buildings. I tried to identify the opposing candidates, but the only name I saw on placards and graffiti was Peron.

The young Dow salesman wished I had more time to spend in his country and to follow a VORANOL product to an end user in Argentina. It was obvious that Hugo, a 1969 chemical engineering graduate of the University of La Plata, has great pride in this country where he has lived not only in Buenos Aires but from the north to the south, the east to the west.

"My father is in the Army, and he has lived in a lot of different places. I remember I have lived in 19 different houses. I was born in the north, in Misiones, which borders on both Brazil and Paraguay. Then I came to Buenos Aires. When I was five years old I went to live in Comodoro Rivadavia in the south, where all the petroleum is. Then I returned to B.A.; then I went to Mendoza in the west; then I lived in Rio Cuarto in the interior. And I studied in La Plata.

"We have been, during the last 50 years, one of the most advanced countries in Latin America. For instance, we've had subways since 1920. It would be interesting if you could do some walking in B.A.—because I'm sure you would be surprised by the kind of city we have, the kind of country we have, and the kind of people we have.

"For business investment, I really am very confident that we have to grow. Argentina's only problem has been not very good government and politics. There has been no continuity.

"We have from 30 years ago been changing the orientation every day and destroying what the last government had done. And everyone of us fighting about it—this guy's not good and blah, blah, blah. We have not cooperated.

"But I think that now we have realized that we all have to work together, be it Peron or another one in the presidency. Try to keep an orientation, good or bad, but to maintain something and to go to one objective without changing and without wasting time.

"So my personal opinion is that there is a bright future. But when we will begin to work and to be serious is the difficult thing to establish. I hope that with this election we can begin going that way."

My visit to Argentina had a stuttering start. Hugo had offered to meet me at the airport and deliver me to the Sheraton Hotel. Admittedly, I never have learned how to make sure I'm not being fleeced by taxi drivers my first time in a foreign country.

But it seemed an imposition to ask Hugo to drive to the airport at 11 o'clock on a Saturday night, especially since he lived on the other side of the city.

Air traffic into Buenos Aires was light. On most days there are only four flights between Sao Paulo and Buenos Aires, though these are cities the size of New York and Chicago and about the same distance apart. The immigration and customs procedures were fast, an express system compared with Brazil's. Everything appeared smooth and efficient as I found a window for changing money and a bus for transport into the city. I cashed a $50 traveler's check for 493 pesos, roughly ten pesos to a dollar, and bought a bus ticket for 25 pesos.

The old, snoot-nosed bus chugged slowly into the city, via dimly lit streets. When eventually the bus stopped, we seemed to be nowhere—no terminal, no hotel, just a spot where the bus pulled off the street and parked.

"Sheraton?" I asked, and the driver pointed to a car across the street. This, I correctly assumed, was a taxi, though it wasn't marked. And since there was only one, I decided to grab it quickly rather than be stranded on a dark corner at midnight.

After what seemed like a ride of some distance, but not surprisingly so for a big city, the driver stopped near what I later discovered was the Sheraton's rear entrance. The taxi meter, barely visible, appeared to show all ones, like 11.11. I figured that 20 pesos would cover the fare and return some change, but the driver expounded at length in Spanish. I had no idea what he was saying, though I did know that in some cities, Rome for instance, there are legal surcharges for a variety of reasons—baggage, trips after 10 p.m.—and maybe he was explaining something of that nature.

Hugo Vivern

I tried English—"I don't understand a word you're saying"—took back the two 10-peso bills and gave him 100. Since this was about $10, it surely would solve the problem, with change.

While I was putting the two 10-peso notes away, the driver started a new flood of Spanish, so I looked up. He was showing me a one-peso note. I apologized profusely. I had no thought of trying to get by for ten cents. I exchanged the one-peso bill for a hundred.

Now everything was squared away, with change. The driver started handing back peso notes—a 50, a 20, and a 5. I was happy, too. I was getting back about $7.50 out of $10, and in most United States cities the trip would have cost more than $2.50.

I was in my hotel room before I fully realized what had happened. Of the four 100-peso bills in my pocket when I got in the taxi, I now had only two. So it had been a hundred, not a one, that I had handed the driver originally. He had made a switch—my

hundred for a one out of his own pocket—while I was putting away those two tens.

Then a close look at the Argentine bills brought more gloom. All except the 50 were marked "nuevo pesos." Because in Brazil I had seen many 10,000-cruzeiro bills stamped with a mark to indicate they had been revalued to ten new cruzeiros, I now had another suspicion. The cashier in the hotel's coffee shop confirmed: The 50-peso note was worth only five-tenths of one new peso, or $.05 instead of $5. I told myself that it's a lot easier to be bilked when a currency is revalued by 100, as in Argentina, than by 1,000, as in Brazil.

Oh well, I had a choice—write off $17.63 for a taxi ride, or $1 for a taxi ride and $16.63 for a lesson in Argentine currency.

I never told Hugo about the taxi ride. I was embarrassed at being clipped. And besides, this was minuscule compared with the million-dollar kidnappings that had been successfully perpetrated in Argentina. I asked Hugo about this activity.

"During the past two years we have had a very large amount of political terrorism, which began with this kind of kidnapping. Now the political terrorism has decreased to a very low scale—but the people who steal things have learned a profitable business. They saw an easy way to get money without any effort. And, most important, without any risk, like in attacking a bank. So this extortion, started by the political terrorists, now is more or less 95 per cent being done by single individuals.

"The last government we had was a military one. It was called a dictatorship by the present government, and it acted in a very strong way to both the terrorists and the thieves—caught a big number of them, and put them in jail. But the present government said the terrorists had been fighting for the liberation of the country, and that there was no reason for them to stay in jail. So they opened the doors of the prison. Now the problem is with a big portion of those that were released.

"From May till now, the government has changed the way it has acted and is trying to eliminate this problem. Every day you can read in the paper that two or three guys were killed by the police. When they found terrorists or common thieves, they began to shoot them, eliminate them.

"Except for kidnappings and extortion, Buenos Aires really is a city without crimes. You can go to dinner late at night with your family, your wife and children, without any problem. You can walk the streets any time, 3 o'clock, 5 o'clock in the morning, with no problem.

"Some aspects of the political situation are really hard to understand for us, and even harder for foreign people. When the old military government called elections, Peron was not allowed to be a candidate, so he supported another one by the name of Campora. No one of the middle and upper classes thought this guy was going to succeed, but he got more or less 51 per cent of the total vote. So he became president and—with the vice president—they made a political alliance between the Peronistas and other parties.

"They began to work together, but couldn't control the more radical members of the joint party, which began to plot against them. I think that this was the reason both the president and vice president resigned. They called elections in order for Peron to be nominated, which wasn't possible during the military government because it was completely against Peron.

"When Campora resigned, the people talked about a coalition of Peron and the president of the other main party in Argentina. This coalition would represent about 80 per cent of the population. But with this kind of joint ticket, the Peronistas have some internal fights and this will not be.

"Now there is the ticket of Peron and his wife. This kind of ticket has caused no fight among the Peronistas, because she does what Peron wants her to do, instead of having another orientation.

"I am not a political specialist, but my idea is that there is a period of time Peron needs to be president to form the base of his party. I think we all need two years of Peron as president. If something happened to him in six months, I don't know what could happen here." [The Perons won the election. President Peron died in office and his wife, Isabel Peron, succeeded him as President of Argentina.]

Turning to the chemical business—complex, but not so much as Argentine politics—Hugo voiced disappointment that Dow had shelved plans for a large production complex, the Bahia Blanca project, in southern Argentina.

"As you know, Dow has been working five or six years ago to put in local plants for VORANOL products and other products. The project at Bahia Blanca was very important for both Dow and the country, more so for the country, I think. For the development of the country, it would be encouraging to have local production.

"When you have to depend on imported raw materials, you have to suffer from the international conditions. For instance, two or three years ago there was an important shortage of TDI [toluene diisocyanate, the companion product of polyols used in producing urethane products]. This caused a real impact in the industry here. There wasn't the growth that everyone had hoped for.

"I think that in Argentina the market for flexible foam, especially for the bedding industry and upholstery, really has grown very quickly. And Dow has about 40 per cent of the total market.

"It's really very interesting, the things that must be considered by the suppliers of this kind of industry. The customers begin making foam in a garage, and then they begin to grow, and it is a special market where the credit risk is really very high. We had, for example, a real problem three years ago. The biggest foamer here went bankrupt, which put all the suppliers in a very difficult situation. But now the situation has changed, and everyone has learned how the business has to be managed.

"The situation is quite improved as compared with five years ago. The technical aspects and the quality of the products made by the customers have changed, so now the only thing that we need is to have polyols, and everyone will be happy.

"Last year the market was spread among Dow, Carbide, and Bayer—and several others who do not operate on a continuing basis here but who offer material when they have it. Dow's share of the market is among the stronger customers from the financial, production, and technical points of view. We import the polyols in bulk, and we have our own terminal in La Plata, which is a city and a port about 30 miles from B.A. We sell to the major customers in bulk and to the smaller ones in drums, and about 90 per cent of our sales are in bulk.

"I wasn't an employee when the Bahia Blanca project was born, but I've heard there were a lot of problems with the small, local producers of the materials that Dow would have produced. It is one of the characteristics of our market. Argentinians do not want another company to produce better and more than their own. So there were problems, for instance, with the local companies that have polyethylene plants here, and with all the producers of the raw materials that Dow would produce here.

"This was at the beginning, I understand, but afterward everyone understood it would be convenient for all of us. But when the project was growing in a really good direction, the political and the economic position of the government changed. It became more nationalist. The government

tried to support projects of Argentine companies. The idea is that the petrochemical industry has to be controlled locally by the government or an Argentine company.

"So a plant is going to be built in Bahia Blanca to produce ethylene and propylene—similar to the project Dow had. But it will be managed by the government in a joint venture with local companies and use technology bought from another international company. Dow has projects for plants that could use these raw materials, the ethylene and propylene, which are not available now. When I started with Dow in 1970 I joined a company that had a really bright future in Argentina with the Bahia Blanca project, but now we are just waiting to see how things develop.

"Since last May I have been working as a salesman of the VORANOL products. There are little companies working in the interior, and one of the big customers is in Tucuman in the north, about 1,100 miles from here, but my work is concentrated in B.A.

"The foamers make mattresses but also sell blocks of foam for use in upholstery and autos, and they also sell to other people who make mattresses. All the production is sold in Argentina, though I think some mattresses are smuggled across the border to Paraguay—but by the buyers, not the sellers."

Hugo traveled in both the United States and Europe during 1970, before joining Dow. "In April of 1970, I went with my wife Susann to New York and Boston, and we stayed at the home of a friend of my father. So I had the opportunity to know the American way of living, the kinds of things they are doing. While I was there I got an international exchange scholarship to work in Portugal. In Portugal I worked two months in a cement company, then I traveled in Europe before we returned here in September. One month later I started working for Dow."

While Hugo has seen a good part of the world, it's in Argentina that he sees his future. And for the long run, he feels it's a future that looks good.

"I think Argentina has the base and the people to go ahead. For instance, we have a very good spread of classes in Argentina. I can say that 70 per cent of our population is middle class. When I'm talking about low-middle, I'm talking about workers who have their own homes. The lower class are the ones who don't have work, don't have a home. The lowest worker here earns perhaps $100 a month, which is not good but is more than in some Latin American countries.

"And the characteristics of this kind of government we are going to have, is to give plenty of support to the lower classes. This doesn't mean the other ones will suffer; but they are concentrating on trying to teach the lower classes, trying to make them help themselves and to think of their development.

"However, one of the difficult things to do in our country is to plan for the future. My idea is to develop with the company, and to develop myself together with the country. Some day I'd like to manage the business in Argentina with a lot of Dow plants surrounding me."

113

22 | Market Oriented

"We always are deleting or adding new products. I can think of only one product we have now that we had ten years ago..."

From the standpoint of style, two persons put more of their personal imprint on the Dow manufacturing organization—especially on the Gulf Coast—than any other individuals. One was the late Dr. A. P. (Dutch) Beutel, founder of the Texas and Louisiana Divisions.

The other is J.M. (Levi) Leathers, a native of Guy's Store, Texas, who started as a chemist in the Texas Division and worked there 27 years before moving to the company's headquarters in Midland. He is now a member of the Dow board of directors as well as executive vice president and director of operations for Dow U.S.A.

Beutel and Dr. Herbert H. Dow, the company's founder, were known for their strong interest in how their plants operated, and the people running the plants. Leathers is best known for the extent of his interest in the details of production processes.

The style of Texas Division production managers is characterized by informality, a low tolerance for "sophisticated management techniques," a passion for working long hours and going after process improvements, a quiet emphasis on loyalty to the organization. Equally characteristic is a soft drawl, with a rounding off of word edges in a distinctive sort of way sometimes described as "South Texas."

Leathers was general manager of the Texas Division before moving to the company headquarters. Now he not only directs U.S. manufacturing divisions but also has a clear influence on Dow production everywhere. And people who started with Dow in Texas in the 1940s can be found in the top layer of manufacturing management worldwide—in Europe, Canada, Latin America, and the Pacific. Like the 53-year-old Leathers, they were born in the 1920s, grew up in the depression of the 1930s, and came

into the industry just when petroleum-based chemicals and plastics were booming to the fore as the big, growing part of the business.

Whatever other likenesses he may or may not have to this style of Dow manager, Bob McClure has the soft way of talking. Bob is the section superintendent in charge of a two-unit complex that does all the manufacturing of Dow polyols for urethane products. He's 48, has been with Dow 26 years, and was involved in the company's first production of polyols for urethane applications.

"The major thing different about the polyol business is that the market is different. What counts for VORANOL products is how our product performs for the customer in the products that he manufactures, in the end uses.

"In a commodity-type plant, say for propylene oxide or glycols, we sell strictly on specifications. Of course we have specifications for VORANOL products, but the final say is good performance and good properties in our customers' products.

"A commodity-type plant has fewer products and larger volume. We make some 40 to 50 different products. Our type of plant is more market-oriented. The research backing us up is more oriented to product research—to developing a product, rather than a process for making polyols.

"The process for VORANOL products is not complicated if, for instance, I compare it with the process for making glycerine or glycols. But the market is more complicated than for glycol or glycerine.

"At Glycol A, when I was superintendent there, we didn't have occasion to know all the field salesmen. In this plant, the people who report to me know the field salesmen on a first-name basis. I'm closer to the marketing people than to the field salesmen. Wiley

Barton and Gene Newton know the marketing people, but they also deal with the field salesmen on a day-to-day basis."

Wiley is the superintendent in charge of the No. 1 unit manufacturing polyols, all for flexible foam. Gene is an assistant superintendent, responsible for the No. 2 unit, which produces all of Dow's polyols for rigid urethanes, and some for flexibles.

"We always are deleting or adding new products. I can think of only one product we have now that we had ten years ago, and that is CP-3000. The rest of the products have changed or varied since 1960."

Bob had just returned to his office from a meeting of the urethane chemicals business team. This is a management group made up of representatives from development, research, production, marketing, and the business management function.

"We discuss the total business and the problems. We are very informal. We understand one another's problems much better than you would in a more formal setup.

"Some plants and product groups don't get the value out of a business team that we do, because of the changing market we are in. As a matter of fact, before the company started the business teams, we had a management team group—set up by Ted Doan back in 1960 or 1961. Ted was the first chairman of our group."

"Ted" is Herbert D. Doan, organizer and first manager of the company's original Chemicals Department. He became executive vice president of Dow in 1960 and was president from 1962 to 1971.

"Since we moved the production to this block in 1960, we've grown 15 to 20 per cent a year—and we're projecting the same rate for the next several years, barring unforeseen recessions or that sort of thing. The world market has been an advantage to us. When we were long on production capacity, we had export markets we could ship to. At the same time, it has been an advantage to the areas outside the U.S. because it gives them time to build their markets before they have to invest capital. If we have excess capacity and they're short on capacity, they may not build a plant right away—until the market has grown to the extent needed.

"Of course this is not always the case, because right now our domestic market is booming. We can be short here, too. But there's a broader base when you can grow worldwide than when you have a limited market.

"When we first started producing the VORANOL products, prices were very high compared with now. But our costs were high

too. As the plant has grown, our costs for converting the raw materials to polyols had a dramatic drop.

"We've kept our profitability up pretty good even though we've lowered prices by 25 to 30 per cent. But everyone is affected by the higher prices for hydrocarbons, and this plant more than most because a larger portion of our costs goes for raw materials.

J. M. Leathers

Earle B. Barnes

Our prices went up last year, and there undoubtedly will be more increases."

Although he wanted to start in research, Bob has been in production ever since he joined Dow.

"Earle Barnes [now president of Dow U.S.A.] is the fellow who interviewed me and hired me, so to speak. I applied for a job in research, but my brother Holmes was work-

ing in research and Earle said he didn't want relatives in the same department. So he set up an interview with Jim Means at Glycol 1. Barnes had worked in glycol also. He was an assistant superintendent under Walter Roush when they started up the glycol plant. When Roush took over organic production, Barnes set up the organic lab. That was the beginning of organic research in the Texas Division. Then Means took over at Glycol 1."

Holmes McClure is now the Texas Division's director of research and development. If Bob hadn't been diverted to production, he probably would now be working for his brother. And it was his brother who urged Bob to come down from Oklahoma for a summer job after he was discharged from the Navy in 1946.

"Most of my naval career was going to school. Good ol' Uncle Sam paid the bill. Finally, when the war was over, I wound up as an electrician on a ship escorting troops back from the South Pacific. After working that summer for Dow, I went back to the University of Oklahoma and got my degree

Dr. A. P. Beutel

in chemical engineering.

"My home town was Lindsay, Oklahoma, a thriving metropolis of 1,200 when I was a boy. I don't know how big it is now, probably 2,000 or 3,000. They struck some oil around there and that brought in some business. It was a pretty poor community during the depression."

For three or four years in the 1960s, Bob was out of the polyol business, but not far away. He was assigned to a team to build the Louisiana direct-oxidation plant for E.O. [ethylene oxide]. This was the plant that began freeing older facilities to give Dow the world's largest capacity in propylene oxide, a basic for the VORANOL products.

For Bob, the job of a production man is "getting the production out at low cost, with good quality, safely, without affecting the ecology, and maintaining the morale of the troops. This is basically the job of whatever you want to call the person who is in charge of a plant or plant group. Production, cost, quality, safety, morale, ecology—all equal, equal emphasis for all.

"We don't really look for a project maker. We look for someone who can do a number of things—not what you would call a specialist. Maybe the word we'd use would be general practitioner. I look for a person who is aggressive in taking the initiative, being a self-starter. I like to delegate as much as I can. When you get down to it, I guess everybody is looking for the same person—one who can do the job, get the job done."

Bob met his wife, Betty, a Canadian nurse, after she moved from Denver, Colorado, to Brazosport to work for Dow in industrial medicine. They have two daughters: Pam, 14, and Meg, 12.

"Betty still is a citizen of Canada. I haven't converted her over to be a United States citizen yet, and I think that is going to be hard. Her dad is German, and he didn't become a Canadian citizen until he was 80—though he moved to Canada when he was 17 or 18."

While Bob has trained many people who now work in Dow plants outside the United States, and others who've had foreign assignments and returned to the United States, all his travel abroad was in the Navy. And he's happy it's been that way.

"I like it here. I'd just as soon be here as trouncing around the world."

The Texas Division is a very comfortable place for capable production managers.

23 | On Sycamore Street

"And we survived the summer of 1972."

Patsy Adam is an attractive production clerk in the Texas Division polyol plant. Stylishly dressed, a touch of sophistication in her makeup and a natural smile for greeting visitors, Patsy would be as much at home in an executive office as she is in a production operation.

Her husband, John David Adam, works in another plant, polyethylene, where he has been an operator for 17 years.

"And we survived the summer of 1972," Patsy said.

As we talked in the Adam home on Lake Jackson's Sycamore Street, it was half a minute before I realized what she was referring to. It was the 84-day strike by unionized employees in 1972, during which the Texas Division maintained production and other operations. John David, a union member, was out on strike; Patsy, a salaried employee, remained at work.

"You have mixed emotions. I've worked for Dow a long time, and I have my loyalty to Dow, and I have my loyalty to John David. Boy, that puts you right in the middle. It gets kind of hard.

"I was raised here, and it was a good place for children. We had a good time, and we didn't get in trouble. I'd like for my girls to enjoy growing up here as much as I did. And we hate to see the area torn apart by bitter feelings. But even I got furious because the women, the ladies on the picket line, said things like, 'What's *your* husband doing *right now?*' Well, I wanted to tell them what he was doing right now, but there was no way since we couldn't say anything.

"But we weren't alone. There were 300 women [salaried employees who continued working] whose husbands were on strike."

Drawing on personal experience, the New York newspaper strike in 1958, I ventured that a strike must be a lot easier when the wife has a salary that continues. But it was obvious the Adams viewed that as an observation of limited merit; a strike that puts husband and wife in different positions "is quite a strain."

The Adams live in a white-shuttered brick home, just six blocks from the four-lane highway separating Lake Jackson from the Dow site. Developed over the past five to ten years, Sycamore is a street heavy with trees, and nearby some were giving way to new homes going in on side streets a block or two away.

In the driveways on every block were boats and pickup trucks with camping units. The homes are brick, in a variety of colors for both brick and trim. Most are two-story homes. The Adams have a ranch-style home with a big white door on their double garage.

John came to Brazosport from Marlin, Texas, because he had a sister working for Dow who told him it was "a good place to work." She had been interviewed and hired by Dow in her senior year at what was then known as Texas State College for Women, in Denton. She now lives in Houston, where her husband works for Dow Engineering and Construction Services.

John David and Patsy Adam

119

Though she was born in the lower Rio Grande Valley, Patsy has lived in Brazosport since 1947.

"My stepfather worked here during the war, then moved back to the Valley. He bought and sold cattle there, but working here was a more sure income. He was an operator in the lime kiln and retired about 12 years ago.

"There now is a plant where we used to live and play when we were first here, during the war. Dow had put up some one-room housing, and there were trailers on both sides of where Technical Service and Development is now, and also where the Beutel Building is now.

"We lived there for a year. Our entertainment was to look out and see trains go across a railroad trestle. And we used to go to movies in B-101 Building, which wasn't quite like it is now."

Patsy's brother, Edward Gillespie, also once worked for Dow as an instrument and electrical supervisor. He is now a contractor in the same field, and his wife Jackie is a Dow secretary in chlor-alkali production.

As a production clerk, Patsy has the usual work of a secretary, correspondence and filing, but she's also involved in calculating daily production rates and sending a

product analysis with every shipment of polyols.

"The customers can't make their formulations without knowing the exact composition of our product. We have something like 48 or 50 different product numbers. The best part of the job is seeing how the orders increase for the good ones.

"For the production rates, we have a new program for the computer called 'manufacturing data base.' Mr. Leathers wants all the plants in the Texas Division to know, on a daily basis, how much raw material and how many BTU's of energy were needed per pound of product manufactured."

The Adams have two children, Michele, 7, and Laurie, 5, so Patsy's Dow career has

been interrupted a couple of times. She started in the payroll department, and has worked in accounting, but her last three jobs have been in production plants.

"I'll take the plants two to one. In all three of the plants, there was a relaxed atmosphere, and you know more about what's going on.

"Of course, you get mad at some of the things they do—and some of the things they don't do. But personally, they always have been very good to me."

The Adams' home was new when they moved in seven years ago, just four days before Michele was born. Now Michele was going into second grade, and Laurie was starting kindergarten.

Patsy leaves for work at 7:15 in the morning. A housekeeper comes in to get the children off to school, do the housework, and pick up the children after school if it's raining. Patsy is home a few minutes after 4 o'clock. The part that she doesn't like, of course, is that John works shift. That makes for days when he's gone before she is home, and communicating becomes a matter of "writing notes to each other."

John works in a plant where the Texas Division is experimenting with the "whole job" concept. The concept is based on the view that "most Dow jobs can be improved, job content is related to job satisfaction, whole jobs are a means for individual and Dow growth, motivation comes with personal freedom to plan a job, whole jobs can increase output and productivity, Dow employees seek and need meaningful work."

John is skeptical. "They started out with how happy we were going to be. They were going to make us happy. So far, I don't think they've really made a lot of people happy—changing so many jobs, taking parts of a job away and giving it to another guy.

"I guess people just don't really like change, especially when it's forced on them. If you'd asked for it, maybe you'd like it. They [the company] can't do everything they want because of the union contract, and they didn't think they'd work it out anytime soon. It's a long-term project, probably two or three years."

"I might like it, but I told them I already have a job and a half," Patsy remarked with a laugh.

Both John and Patsy enjoy living in Lake Jackson. John also likes fishing in the Gulf, and this was a day when he'd had a good catch.

"I fish quite often, mainly surf fishing is what I like. If the water was perfect all the time, I'd probably stay out there in the mornings when Patsy is gone and I'm home. It looks like the river is getting better and this will be a good year. You can tell by looking at the water."

As for the improvement in the quality of the river, Patsy commented: "You don't have any choice if you want to run the plants. And I think it is only right—for the children's sake, and for their children."

John spoke of the annual "Fishing Fiesta" in Freeport, which runs four or five days over the weekend closest to July 4. There are 50 to 60 categories in the fishing contest, and "the off-shore fishing in Freeport always has been fantastic."

Patsy noted the Fiesta also includes entertainment. "They have a street dance, a shrimp-eating contest, and things like this. Last year they had two bands for the street dance. If you didn't like one type of music, you could go over and dance to the other."

Back at her desk the next morning, in white slacks and shoes and black blouse, in the small office building close to the two production plants, Patsy said the last couple of days had been "the least busiest" since she started working in the polyol plant. The previous summer Patsy had extra work because of the strike, but she didn't mind that. What she didn't like was that John David was on one side of a picket line, and she was on the other.

24 | From the Bottom Up

"If the material is so darn good, why don't we use it ourself?"…
"I said to myself, 'I'd hate to spend my life scattering shell.'. So I went back to college."

Elvis G. (Gene) Jones, 38, a senior research chemist, and Harold G. (Gene) Newton, 35, an assistant superintendent in production, have much in common. Both started with the Texas Division as laborers, moved up in the organization, and worked in laboratories while earning college degrees. Gene Jones and his wife went to school together from the first grade through the 12th in Sweetwater, Texas; Gene Newton and his wife grew up just across the fence from each other near Comanche, Oklahoma.

Several years ago Gene Newton and Bob Heard, the general foreman in production of VORANOL products, received a patent for a new polyurethane material. Now Gene Jones is working on commercial development of the technology needed to put that material to use and he believes it "will open up a whole new field in plastics.

"This is taking all the knowledge and experience I have gained in urethane chemistry and applying it to a completely new field. This technology enables us to do things with polyurethanes we never conceived of doing with any plastic. The technology may be unique to urethanes, but there is a chance it will apply to other thermoset resins—and we hope to get into those eventually. For urethanes, the project has the highest probability of success of any I've ever worked on.

"There always have been areas where plastics simply could not do the job. Or if they could do the job, it was impossible to mold them in the shapes needed. With this material we have the capability to mold massive parts, very thick sections that historically just could not be produced in plastic.

"We are doing a tremendous amount of our own engineering for machinery to process this material. There is no equipment available commercially that would give us a total processing package. Because of the mechanical dealings I've had in the past with urethanes, the project was turned over to us, Gerald Wittenbach and me, to develop processing machinery and to investigate all phases of the formulation. We have almost total project responsibility.

"I have no idea what Gene Newton was trying to do when he formulated some materials and found that they instant-set into this plastic. It was a laboratory curiosity for two or three years. It was taken out to the marketplace, but it fell completely flat. People simply did not know how to process it.

"However, people began to realize that the technology Gene had discovered could be employed over the whole broad range of urethanes. It did not require these specific ingredients to do this magic trick that we do. Applied to all urethane technology, this made the thing so broad, so huge, that we said there has to be a tremendous business potential here.

"People come in and we show them in a beaker how you can stir this stuff up and it changes like that [with a snap of the fingers] to this rigid plastic, and they begin to pour forth ideas for applications of the material. It is unbelievable the way people have accepted it within the Texas Division. And we feel the acceptance rate will be as great or greater outside of Dow.

"One thing I really get on my soapbox about is the way we are handling this project. And this is Earle Barnes' idea, as well as ours.

"We are trying to lay a broad foundation, learn all we can about this material while we develop it into a market entity. As Earle phrases it, if the material is so darn good, why don't we use it ourself? And this is what we are doing. We are solving problems for some of the plants—giving them plastic parts that replace metal or ceramic or wood which has not been serviceable—and, at the same time, we are learning how to mold the material. When we do take it outside, we will be able to tell customers: 'You can't mold it that way, you have to do it this way.' "

"We are waiting right now for a mold to manufacture 1,300 lids for some conveyors in the Dow magnesium cells. The material also has shown great promise for applications in the electrical field. We have been very careful about end-use testing. If we don't see a 50 per cent chance of success, we're not messing with it—because there are too many areas where we've got a 90 to 95 per cent chance of success.

"Polyurethanes as a family of materials have unlimited potential. Right now, I don't think we have touched the hem of the garment as far as what we can do with these materials. My belief is that, in seven to ten years, the rigid urethanes will catch up with the flexibles as a sales item. With the developing potentials such as we are working on here, the flexible market had better watch out."

Before this project, Gene worked on getting Dow into the business of producing THURANE brand plastic foam. The only end-use urethane product manufactured by Dow, THURANE foam is a rigid material produced in billets and boards at Dow's Hanging Rock Plant near Ironton, Ohio.

"For 10 or 11 years I worked through the laboratory conception, the development work on a semi-plant scale, through to the actual production of the THURANE foam. Because of the way Bill Davis runs this department, I was able to go with that one product from my idea in the laboratory to the production plant at Hanging Rock.

"If you can do that, you've got to stay excited. You are very proud of being associated with the project and product, and it becomes your child. If we could get this concept involved in all of research, I think our capabilities would be far beyond what they are right now.

"When one group works on the basic research, and another group takes over in the pilot plant, and another group in the production facility, each is divorced from the basics and semi-basics in the various facets of the whole development program. I think people stay more interested if you keep the whole thing within one group."

Gene moved to Brazosport from San Antonio, Texas, in 1956—hoping to land a job in a Dow laboratory. But he started as a laborer in a utility gang. From a family of seven children, he already had a brother working for Dow; and his wife, Deon, who was one of 12 children, had two brothers with Dow.

"They came down here simply because the living in Sweetwater was kind of scarce at the time."

Sweetwater, incidentally, isn't just around the corner from Brazosport; it's 450 miles northwest. Gene proudly notes that in this town of 12,000 he went to the same high school that had been attended by Clyde Boyd, now the president of Dow Canada.

After six months in the utility gang, Gene was given his chance as a laboratory assistant. He moved up rapidly, becoming a salaried technician in 1959. Four years later he began working earnestly for his college degree, having started taking a few courses in 1957.

"With four children, working and going to night school, that got pretty interesting."

Gene first attended nearby Alvin Junior College, then received his bachelor's degree in chemistry from the University of Houston in 1970.

The other Gene—Gene Newton—didn't have a job when he moved to Brazosport from Oklahoma in 1958. But he had an aunt in Jones Creek. He went to work driving a milk truck, then started at Dow just before a layoff in the 1958 recession and wound up back in Oklahoma. He returned to Brazosport in 1960, eventually winning a Dow loan-scholarship that helped him earn his degree in chemical engineering from the University of Houston in 1972.

"I started at Dow in the antifreeze plant. Everything was going smooth except that the 1958 layoff caught me. I'd had my first child born down here, so I had this little baby, and I needed a job. I went downtown and started asking at the stores. It was near Christmas time, and sure enough, the third store I went in, the guy asked if I could sell dry goods.

"I said I could sell anything. So I went to work, and I worked through the summer of 1959. When the summer rush was over, the job was gone. But the guy said: 'Would you like to transfer back to Oklahoma?' So lo and behold, they transferred me to Duncan, nine miles from where I was raised at Comanche.

"Later, I went to work for a company that cements oil wells, and they wanted to transfer me to Mississippi. I turned that down and, instead, bought a truck and started hauling bales of hay. I was hauling hay in the daytime and plowing at night.

"Meanwhile, at the antifreeze plant, they were going over the records and Blaine Esmond, who is now the supervisor of the quality control laboratory for VORANOL products, said, 'I wonder what ol' Gene is doing?' Blaine had the personnel department call me and ask if I'd like to come back to work.

"I said, 'You bet!' My wife and I saddled up that night and moved right on back. I went to work where I was before, canning antifreeze. When the antifreeze season was

over, I went into the yard department and scattered shells all over the place. [Oyster shells are used like gravel for a ground surface in the Texas plants.]

"I said to myself, 'I'd hate to spend my life scattering shell.' I'd had a little college just after high school, so I went back to college at Alvin Junior College."

From the yard department Gene moved to the laboratory for VORANOL products. In the laboratory, Gene was promoted to salaried technician. He also got his "teeth into this foaming and operating. And I asked Bob McClure, the superintendent, if I could move into operations.

"After a few months they had an opening in the glycol plant for a shift foreman. Romey Davis was the manager, and he asked if I wanted that job. I knocked it around for a long time because it was shift work, and I was on straight days. But the money was better, so I decided to become a shift foreman.

"This was a big change. It was one of the first times they ever made a young man a shift foreman. They always had picked older guys who'd been operating for 20 years. So it was a real adaptation—not just for me but for all the older fellows who had been operating so long. I was just new enough to lead 'em. They all were real eager to help. Once you get their confidence, you can't beat the fellows with 20 to 30 years' experience.

"The tendency now is to have young shift foremen, but then it was new. I guess Romey Davis was one of the first to do that, bring in new people that had a little more education, that had a lot of eagerness. You know, that's what you need in shift foremen. You need that fire-knocking, gung-ho commando type who will lead people to do a good job."

Eventually, after working in plants

Gene Newton and Gene Jones

producing ethylene dichloride and ethylene oxide, including the start-up of the direct-oxidation plant in Louisiana, Gene returned to the polyol plant as a shift foreman.

"And then somebody suggested I ought to go ahead and apply for this Dow scholarship and finish my education. I lacked only one semester, so I told Bob McClure, 'I believe I'm going to go ahead and make it on my own.' Bob said, 'Why not try for the thing and apply for the time off—and really enjoy yourself and study better, too?' I got the

scholarship and that semester, from January to May in 1972, I was off work and went ahead and wrapped it up. Sure enough, I did enjoy it. Best thing that ever happened to me, really.

"You wouldn't believe how much trouble it is working shifts and meeting regular school hours. The last year or two I went to school in the daytime, and I worked nearly straight graveyards. I hated to ask a fellow to trade his days off because that's the best part of shift work. So, most of the time, I

swapped for graveyards when I was on days. Most of the fellows liked that. However, if it hadn't been for these shift foremen really making sacrifices and trading with me and that sort of thing, I just couldn't have made it.

"It was pretty tough for my wife, too. She's kind of a homebody type, and when I'd be gone she'd have to make a lot of decisions that other women wouldn't be facing alone. It's just simple things, like kids getting hurt. The boys are growing up now—Steve is 15,

Phil 13, and Bryan 11. The sacrifice has been hers and the children's too, but I think it has been worth it for all of us.

"The time I had free—well, I realized I was cutting them short on my time, and I tried to spend that time with them. I still do. What I'm really saying is that I didn't take up a bunch of hobbies and civic work, that sort of thing, because there wasn't enough time. I don't know what excuse I'm using for not doing more in civic work now. We're very active in the church, the Baptist. Between the church and my work, that's about it."

It was while he was in the lab that Gene and Bob Heard came up with the material on which Gene Jones is now working.

"We found we could foam about anything in the way of polyol starting materials. We were just puttering around the lab. It's called polyurethane plastic, an elastomer, but Dow isn't putting out much information while it's in development."

Except for limited production in Europe, Gene's plant produces all the polyols sold by Dow for rigid urethanes. That means he stays somewhat familiar with orders from various parts of the world.

"Like here, this is a new one on me, an order for this product from Australia. And here's another order that says Brazil, for a while at least, will take all of this product we can supply. We make this one by a high-pressure process, and we have the only high-pressure process in the world.

"I like the business end of this job. I didn't think I would, because I just couldn't see myself sitting in an office all day. But when you get involved in a business, it's fun. My days go zoom, just like that.

"So I'd like to go ahead and work up in the business end. And if I'm ever talented enough to go higher in management, that would be great—to oversee several produc-tion plants instead of just one. I don't have any aspirations of changing directions.

"Normally the business is intriguing, even though we have a lot of pressure. It seems like production people spend 90 per cent of their time doing things other than running the plant. We have all kinds of crises, like the energy crisis [and this was six months before the Arabs cut off the flow of oil to the United States].

"I'm working on planning up through 1975 on what we're going to have to spend to cut down our energy usage. It's the same thing as hit us with pollution: What are you going to have to do to completely recycle your wastes? These are big problems, you know.

"If there weren't any problems, maybe they wouldn't have anybody out here. I'm happy where I am, I feel real lucky I'm an assistant superintendent after being out of school only one year.

"It almost looks like I haven't wasted my time working at those other jobs. You know, you'd think 'Here I am 34 years old and just getting my degree'—but it seems the people at Dow think experience is as valuable as the education.

"I don't see how anybody could have learned more than we have the past year. The products you have this year won't be the products selling next year, because somebody has come up with a new concept."

And next year that new concept may be the one Gene Newton discovered, the one Gene Jones is now developing in research.

25 | Then, and Now

"The black man has made tremendous progress...When I got out of high school, I don't think they would even take your application at Dow."

Willie Caldwell is 53 years old, and his skin is very black. And where there once were three teeth in the front of his upper jaw, there is now one gold tooth.

Willie—and that's his name, not William—is a labor foreman for the Cardinal Construction Company of Freeport. Cardinal has 300 people doing maintenance and miscellaneous work in Plant B of the Dow Texas Division, and also has a construction project at Plant A. Willie has 45 to 50 people—white, brown, and black—working for him.

Stockily built, Willie looks ready for rugged work in his blue hard hat and heavy shoes. You have little doubt that he has the strength of a bull. Willie is a lifelong resident of nearby Brazoria, where his father drove a bus and did utility and maintenance work for the school system. He recalls:

"There wasn't a building here in January, 1942, when I came in this plant [Plant B, which includes the production and research facilities for VORANOL products]. There wasn't a railroad or a highway."

Willie's first Dow-connected job was in building the Plant B railroad system. Later, he did maintenance on the railroad. In 1946 he became foreman of a railroad work gang. At that time, all the people working in the railroad gangs were black.

Willie worked many years for the Tellepsen Construction Company, a unionized contractor, whence came the management roots for the Cardinal company, an open-shop contractor. He also did part-time work as an electrician in residential construction. Much of this work was in Alvin, Texas, and the name of the man he worked for was Eddie—hence the name, Eddie Alvin, for one of Willie's sons.

Willie once applied for an electrician's job in Houston, but never heard from the company where he applied. If Willie felt the

Willie Caldwell Jr. and Willie Caldwell

reason was because he was black, he doesn't say so.

"Maybe I should have followed up on the application, but I never really worried about it. I imagine I'd have to go through a trainee program to be an electrician. I wouldn't quit a good job like I have now to take an electrician's job."

But asked straight out if he felt being black had been a handicap in employment, Willie said: "I do feel that if I were of a different race I would have had a better job. People less qualified had jobs I couldn't get.

"That's in the past. It doesn't seem like it really existed. It didn't really affect me. My dad had a good job all of his life. I've always worked full time, and I've liked it here in the plant. I've done real well, I can't complain."

Willie built his own home in Brazoria, a four-bedroom house 60 feet by 30, with a double garage and a 10-foot breezeway between the house and garage. One of eight children, he also fathered eight, and the seven now living are ages 22 to 32. In addition to Eddie Alvin, who works for Dow, they include Willie Jr., the oldest, who also works for Dow; and two graduates of Prairie View A&M College—Ruthie May, a dietitian, and Audrey Fay, a nurse, both living in San Antonio, Texas.

"I love it here. One reason is that it stays green most of the year. During World War II, I was in the Army and I got to see most of the world—France, Germany, the South Pacific—but I still love living here."

Willie was a supply sergeant in the Philippines when the war ended, but it was the following year before he returned to the United States. In between, he took advantage of the opportunity to add to his high school education. "We couldn't get transportation home, and I didn't want to just walk around. So I went to the Philippines Institute for six months."

The office where we talked also was occupied by two other men, both white. After Willie left, one volunteered: "Willie's a good man. He's very thorough." And the other added, "He's the best we've had out here. If everybody was like him, we wouldn't have any problems. And I know, because I had his job before him."

Since there usually are differences in opinion between generations, I thought it would be interesting to talk with Willie Jr. He is a maintenance operator in magnesium production, where many Texas Division employees have started and whence many have moved on to other—and less physically taxing—jobs in the division. Willie Jr. is 5 feet 8, 180 pounds, and at 32 he still looks fit enough to play football with his youngest brother, Ralph, who is attending the University of Tennessee at Martin on an athletic scholarship.

"My work with the mag cells is not hard, it's just the heat. The work's not much of a problem but—if I wanted to do shift work—I think I could get a lot easier job."

Willie Jr. joined Dow in 1970 at a time new employees were being added because of the impending start-up of a new plant to produce both magnesium and chlorine—the plant where he now works. He started in utility work at the epoxy resin plant.

"When I was fresh out of high school in 1958, I joined the Army because I wanted to travel. I saw a lot of Europe and spent most of the time in France, near Verdun. I was a transportation corporal. Later I went to college one year, at Prairie View, and I enjoyed that. But before starting with Dow, I mostly worked as a laborer for contractors. I applied with Dow on three different occasions from about 1965 to 1970.

"The black man has made tremendous progress in the last eight or nine years. When I got out of high school, I don't think they would even take your application at Dow.

"The trades jobs in the construction industry have opened up only in the last five or six years. Now, you can get that kind of a job if you're qualified.

"You can buy a house anywhere you want in this area—and not worry about anybody giving you any problem. There's no problem in the schools. We've always had school buses, even before the schools were integrated, so busing is just a way of life here.

"More and more kids are going off to college. The financing is easier. That has a lot to do with it.

"Anybody who wants a job can find it. Twenty years ago my dad was a foreman, but only over black people. He can be a foreman over anyone now."

In the Army, Willie Jr. soon was traveling, as he had hoped, and he says Europe "was O.K. There's an opportunity for good living there. But the opportunity here is as great as anyplace else, and I was happy to come back home."

In 1966, the year after he left the Army, Willie Jr. married his wife, Shirley. They have one daughter, Therese, 6, and now that she is in school, Shirley works as an aide to a kindergarten teacher. The fact that his wife works days is one reason Willie wouldn't like shift work. For style of living, Willie Jr. has followed his father, living the past six years in a house that has been in the family for some time and which was rebuilt after an uncle moved out.

In essence, there's not much difference between the views of Willie Jr. and his father. What Willie Sr. would rather forget, his son remembers clearly—but mainly as something that no longer exists.

26 | Help From the Barber

"I've been hinting I'd like to spend a few years in Europe, working in the labs over there...I could certainly stand to live without mosquitoes for a while."

He wore his hair longer, until he sensed some reluctance by Dow's urethane customers to communicate as openly and fully as he'd like. That was when Phil Cook, 26, a development engineer—and a recruit from the active campus generation of the late 1960s—asked the barber to cut his hair shorter. The communications barrier disappeared. And Phil found his shorter hair "comfortable and easier to keep, so I'm happy that way, too."

Cook has a degree in mechanical engineering. Now three years out of the University of Texas, he learned his chemistry after joining the company, something of a rarity for a development engineer at Dow. But then, until he visited Brazosport for a job interview, he'd never heard of urethanes.

"While interviewing in school, I didn't know whether I wanted a production job, a sales job, or something else. Development was described to me as a type of job where you see all functions. You work in technical service for a product, plus you do development work. You work closely with production and their problems, very closely with research, and with the salesmen you have customer and field contact.

"This really excited me, the idea of being able to do this, intermix disciplines. I have been most satisfied with the job concept. And impressed with the freedom that we have in how we run our business, so to speak. I still haven't decided what I'd like to steer myself into in the future. But this is an ideal place to start from."

Despite his youth, Phil has found "surprisingly little problem" working with customers more experienced in the business. "I find that once you sit down and start talking, start communicating—and you demonstrate to each other that you know what you're talking about, that you're talking the

same language—age seems to fade completely away.

"Often I have felt an awe of some gentlemen I've worked with. I've been able to meet a lot of the people, and to benefit from their knowledge and experience. There really is no substitute for time in an area, but I really have felt no limitation from age.

"In development, we stay in pretty close communication with the production department and sales, primarily. With research,

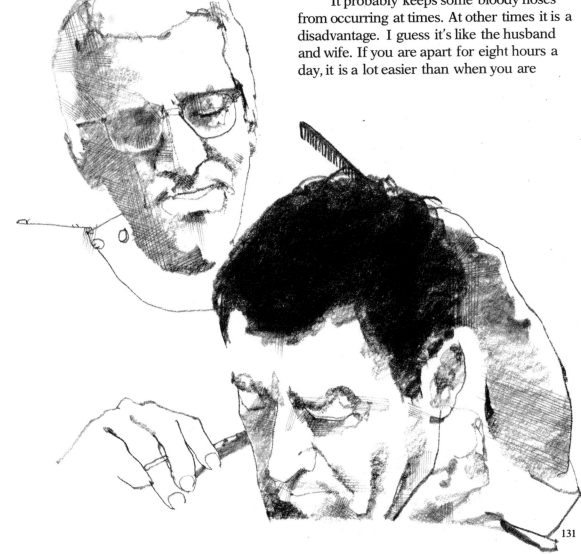

communication is more formalized, and I go down to chat with them from time to time. With production and sales it is a day-to-day interface."

Research, development, and production on urethanes all are in the Texas Division. But marketing, the function for sales planning and management, is in Midland. And the Dow U.S.A. sales force works from 25 sales offices dispersed throughout the country. The location of marketing at a distance from the other functions poses an obvious question.

"It probably keeps some bloody noses from occurring at times. At other times it is a disadvantage. I guess it's like the husband and wife. If you are apart for eight hours a day, it is a lot easier than when you are together for 24 hours a day. I think separation does have some advantages, though it makes for large phone bills."

Phil married his hometown sweetheart from Paris, Texas, and he and Paula have one child, Carrie, 3. They were married just before Phil's senior year in college.

"My idea when I graduated was to go outside Texas to broaden my experience of living and see new areas of the country. Of course, I've been hinting I'd like to spend a few years in Europe, working in the labs over there. I do like small towns. I do like Texas. But I could certainly stand to live without mosquitoes for a while. So long as there is a golf course that I can hit about three or four months a year, I will be happy."

Phil's field is rigid urethanes. Typical of the applications he works on are those in industrial and appliance insulation, "energy conservation as a whole;" to insulate pipelines carrying oil and liquefied natural gas; for furniture, as a wood replacement; and in the automotive industry for safety, for damage prevention through energy absorption in parts such as bumpers, and for sound deadening.

"Generally, urethanes are used for insulation when there are extreme service requirements, where you need maximum insulation with minimum thickness. Also, the foam possesses pretty good physical strength. In any situation combining the two needs—extreme service and physical strength—rigid urethane foam has a good advantage.

"The material can be changed slightly in formulation to simulate wood. It's used quite a bit in the furniture industry—for decorative panels, drawer fronts, mirror frames, bed frames. It's particularly good for pieces of furniture that used to be made out of wood and would require a lot of labor input or craftsmanship. The material can be cast in a mold to pick up all the detail, yet have the same weight, physical strength, sound, and feel as wood. The high-quality furniture market is a good one for rigid urethanes.

"RS-350 is pretty much a general-use product. To Dow it is kind of special in that we are the only company, in the United States at least, making a pure-sucrose polyol. This requires a specialized technique using a high-pressure reactor to make the RS-350. The resultant polyol is strictly from sugar and propylene oxide, in contrast to making a polyol by starting with a blend of sucrose and glycerine, or sucrose and water, or sucrose and some other animal.

"The difficulty is in taking a solid like sugar and stirring it in with the oxide and reacting it. It takes a long time to get the reaction going, and once it goes it's a pretty powerful reaction. It takes special equipment to handle.

"We also have blended RS-350 to meet customer needs for processability and for end properties—to make the end product more like wood, less brittle, more resilient. 'Resilient' is kind of a bad word to use for urethanes because it makes you think of flexible. But 'resilient' in terms of wood is flexural strength, the capability to bend without breaking.

"The sucrose products have been kind of Dow's launch point into rigid urethanes. Ever since its beginning, the rigid industry has had tremendous potential, and it has taken about 10 to 15 years to really get going. I think it is just in its infancy, that we'll see good growth through the rest of the 1970s, and even more dramatic growth in the early 1980s.

"It's really a development market. And it's mainly a matter of taking the raw material, the concept of foaming, and plugging it in and making it go."

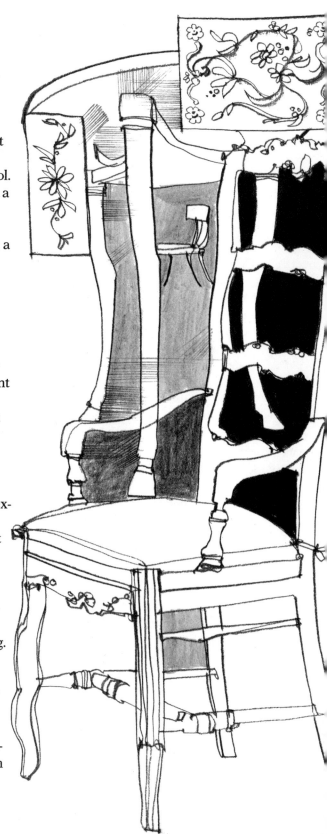

27 | New Plant, New Product

"I noticed my foot was pointing in the wrong direction. So I stopped, fell off my bike, and started moaning."

Bill Olmsted is 25, a year younger than Phil Cook. And his hair is longer. And he races motorcycles. Bill is the process design engineer for construction of a plant that will expand Dow's urethane chemicals business to include toluene diisocyanate.

Bill's father works for Dow in Michigan, and so did Bill during three summers while he was attending the University of Michigan. It may sound as though Bill was eager to join Dow from the time he became interested in chemistry, even before he was a teenager. But that's not the way it was.

"The last summer in Michigan I almost decided I wasn't going to consider Dow for a job interview. I worked for Dow in Midland between semesters—the first summer as a helper in steam trap and valve repair, then in a quality control laboratory, and the third summer in a research lab. From that experience I didn't want to work for Dow at all.

"The jobs weren't very interesting to me. The first year, it wasn't bad because I went into the plant and could see firsthand a lot of the different plants. But then I got stuck in a quality control lab doing the same tests day after day. I guess I get bored too easily. Standing there doing the same thing, I didn't like it at all.

"As a senior in college, I did interview with other companies like Dow, and with refineries and smaller, one-product companies. The more I talked with companies, the more I could see that it was the bigger companies that interested me most.

"My interview with Dow was in the middle of the protests calling Dow 'the warmonger making napalm.' There were a lot of demonstrations while I was at Michigan, on just about anything, though the violent demonstrations—like the bombing of the ROTC unit—occurred after I left. When they started demonstrating against Dow, I

guess that's when I made up my mind to go in for an interview.

"I still went with a negative attitude. During the last semester at school I decided I'd had enough cold weather. I said that no way would I work at Midland; I wanted to go to the south or southwest. A week or so later I came down to the Texas Division for an interview. I visited a couple other companies, but then I stopped because I knew I was going to Dow."

Bill is single and "trying to stay that way as long as I can." His father is director of retiree and industrial recreation activities in Midland for both Dow and the Midland Community Center. Before joining Dow in 1956, Bill's dad was a high school football coach.

"My dad didn't try to influence me; he didn't push me into the chemical business or anything like that. He probably would have been happy whatever I went into, so long as I wasn't a beach bum or something like that."

While we talked in Bill's office in the A. P. Beutel Building, headquarters of the Texas Division, his left ankle was propped off the floor, in a cast. I asked what had happened.

"I race motorcycles. It was one of the races a week ago Sunday. I just got a new bike, and the pegs are a little lower to the ground. I was going down through a rut, a deep rut, and the ground just caught my foot and twisted it.

"It felt like a bad sprain. I looked down, and I noticed my foot was pointing in the wrong direction. So I stopped, fell off my bike, and started moaning. I'd broken a small bone in the back of the ankle and stretched the ligaments. That's the sore part.

"Motorcycle racing is a real big sport down here on the Gulf Coast. I have a

Czechoslovakian bike made just for motocross, for racing on a closed course that's got ditches and jumps.

"Most of the riders I know are from Houston and Galveston. When you talk about motorcycle racing, most people think of a long-haired hippie, smoking pot, wearing a black motorcycle jacket. But most of the riders I've met are real nice. They just don't look like the black-leather-jacket type; just

the opposite, real friendly and helpful.

"I think racing is actually less dangerous than riding a motorcycle on the road. The most dangerous part is falling and having someone behind you run over you. If you have a lot of bikes going the same place at the same time, of course, the odds increase it is going to happen."

Bill's current project represents a major Dow step deeper into urethane chemicals.

When the plant goes into production in 1975, Dow will be manufacturing both of the major raw materials for urethane products—the polyols and the TDI. Besides adding to the company's sales volume, this will remove an advantage some competitors have used skillfully in the past, when they could offer both materials to a prospective customer while Dow had only the polyols.

The TDI plant is the fourth project Bill has been assigned to as a process engineer—and the three previous jobs all were cancelled before construction. So, on this one, Bill is especially anxious for the day when construction begins and then to follow through to the plant's start-up.

Before his string of three cancelled projects, Bill worked on the engineering for the propylene oxide plant at Stade, Germany, and also in troubleshooting at the new

magnesium-chlorine plant in Brazosport.

"On the Stade project, I did reboiler sizing, line sizing, tower design. This was real good. It wasn't a training program; they just throw you in there, and you learn by doing. That helped a lot.

"On my current project, there's a production representative and two instrument specialists whose experience is a lot better than anything I could say. I'll make changes they recommend, because of their experience. It's a pretty complex project, because the equipment includes just about any you can think of. Some will be made in real exotic alloys for protection against corrosion and erosion."

Eventually Bill would like to get into managerial work, as a project manager—"not up in an office, detached, but where you keep your fingers in things." The previous year he'd been in Holland for Dow, leading to the conclusion he'd be happy to spend a "few years in Europe, Latin America, or some other foreign country.

"This was the first time I'd been to Europe. I really enjoyed it over there."

Another member of the TDI capital-project team, John Savaso, the project engineer, graduated from college 20 years ahead of Bill. He's worked on Dow projects in half a dozen other countries—Holland, Mexico, Colombia, Brazil, Argentina, and Ecuador.

"From 1961 to 1963, I was the project engineer for the ethylenediamine plant we built at Terneuzen. The engineering was done in Milan, Italy, so I spent four or five months there before going to Holland. At Terneuzen, we started with a sugar beet patch.

"My family was with me the time we

Bill Olmsted

were in Holland. While we were there, Holland had its coldest month in 100 years. We spent part of that winter on vacation, thank goodness, in Austria."

For the projects in Latin America, John was a consultant on manufacturing and engineering. These projects included the terminals in La Plata, Argentina, and Guaruja, Brazil, where Dow now ships VORANOL products and propylene oxide.

John, 44, joined Dow in 1951, two years after he graduated from Louisiana State University with a degree in mechanical engineering. Before joining Dow, he worked on construction of a transcontinental pipeline and suspension bridges over the Colorado and Brazos Rivers.

"This project is a lot like a pot-and-pan chemical process. It's complicated, and there are quite a few units of operation, so there will be more steps in this one than I'm accustomed to. It's nothing like an ethylene plant or a chlorine plant.

"The recycle streams are very large compared with the product coming out at the end. From the pollution standpoint, this plant could be a troublemaker—so we are planning to make it essentially a closed system.

"I don't believe the anti-pollution measures are going to cost us a lot of premium money, but neither do I think we will save enough through recycling to make the investment justifiable on economics alone. I'm saying that just from the feel. We haven't done economic studies on this question because we're going to make it an essentially closed system anyway."

John and his wife Adele have three children, and the oldest, Charles, 19, is following his father in studying engineering. He's enrolled in building and construction engineering at Texas A&M.

28 | Mouth of the Brazos

"We've come a long way from where we started. Dow just keeps wanting drums, and we just keep making 'em."

The Tobey Hardware store was doing business in Freeport before the birth of its present owner, Edward E. Tobey. Ed was born in the family's second-floor quarters above the store's original location on East Park Street in Freeport.

Ed's father, Edward C. Tobey, who died in 1965, came to Freeport in 1917, a few years after the town was founded. He had read a leaflet praising the merits of the area in agriculture, fish and game, and the potential of the port. Edward E. was born two years after the business opened, and started working in the store when he was eight.

During World War II, Ed was a pilot in the first outfit organized to fly B-29 bombers, and he went around the world before he was discharged. He flew 800 to 900 hours of combat time ("They counted combat time from the time you took off on a mission till you got back") and participated in what he thinks was the longest mission flown by B-29s. His plane took off from near Calcutta, India, bombed Singapore, and returned 20 hours and 20 minutes later—after a round trip of 2,000 nautical miles that left only 400 gallons of fuel remaining from the 8,100 he had at takeoff.

Ed owns two small planes, though he doesn't fly much anymore. "I try to get in about an hour a week to keep the planes in condition and to keep my hand at it. Last year I flew about 60 hours and took trips with some friends to Monterrey, Mexico, and New Orleans.

"A lot of people have left here, a lot have come back. There used to be an old saying, 'If you ever drink the water from the mouth of the Brazos, you never leave.' People go where they can make a living, but I think this is the best place in the world to live."

The community of Velasco, now part of Freeport, and often referred to as North Freeport, was started 21 years before Free- port. There was an earlier Velasco estab- lished at the river's mouth in the 1820s, and across from it was—and still is—Quintana. The original Velasco was wiped out in a great hurricane in 1875. The town was re-estab- lished upstream in the 1890s. The town of Freeport was developed to house employees of the Freeport Sulphur Company, much as Lake Jackson was started three decades later for the growing work force at Dow.

"The storm of 1900 took everything out," Ed says. But he has a promotional leaflet that survived, because it was safely in the vault of a hotel. That leaflet tells of the Brazos harbor's great potential for trading in wheat, cotton, cattle, corn, iron, coal, timber, and sugar. Nothing is said about salt or petroleum—petrochemicals hadn't even been invented—and there is no mention of sulphur.

The tarpon were noted. "Hooking tarpon here is as simple and easy as catching catfish

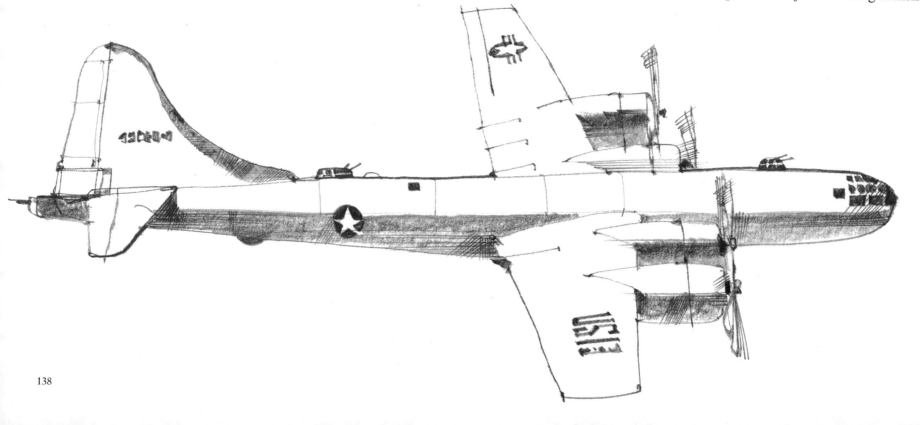

in a mill pond," the leaflet says. Also: "Stephen F. Austin and his associates made their settlement in Texas on rich lands near the mouth of the Brazos and established their trading point at Velasco. There is no doubt that the principal city and port of Texas would today be found in the Brazos' mouth but for the poverty of the people in its early settlement and their consequent inability to remove the bar at the mouth of the river."

The water was then only four and a half feet atop the bar in the Gulf at the mouth of the Brazos. But work on the harbor began in 1889, to enable vessels drawing 18 feet to enter the harbor.

"On July 9, 1891," the leaflet reports, "the Brig Atlantic from New York, drawing 15 feet of water with a cargo of granite, without the aid of a tug, sailed over the bar through the jetties and directly to the wharves at Velasco."

The area's recreation potential was noted very early, with Surfside touted as "the Manhattan beach" of Velasco. Ed Tobey recalls a trolley car, maybe horsedrawn in the 1920s, that ran between the hotels in Velasco and Surfside, and a car ferry for crossing the Brazos between Freeport and Velasco. Land was sold in combinations of 25-foot lots in Velasco and five-acre plots outside of town. Buyers were from many parts of the United States, a fact that later caused problems in getting clear titles to parcels of land.

Freeport Sulphur was a steady employer for many years, so that the depression in the early 1930s didn't hit the area as hard as many other parts of the United States. Ed remembers that it was 1938—when Freeport Sulphur was phasing out and shortly before Dow came to town—that the community had its worst business year.

"We very definitely were happy to see Dow take an interest in the area. There was a big boom going by 1941 when I left for the service. I had started working for the Austin Company in building Dow's Plant A."

The Dow production was important for the American war effort. Although he was away from Brazosport during most of the war, Ed remembers gun emplacements around the mouth of the Brazos, and Navy blimps patrolling the shore.

Tobey Hardware expanded into another location on Gulf Boulevard in North Freeport in 1965 "because we needed a place to expand and there was no way to do it at our original location. This street didn't exist when I left for the service. The building we're in now was built in 1959, about five years before we took it over."

The Tobey business continues to grow, supplying the operators of the shrimp boats, construction contractors, the Dow plants, and other companies supplying services to Dow.

"The bulk of our volume with Dow is in stainless steel bolts, but they also buy fasteners, sprayers, and a variety of miscellaneous items they may need from day to day. We see a lot of individual people in here, but less than ten per cent of our sales volume is in retail sales."

John A. Simmons was honored as "Texas Lumberman of the Year" in 1973, selected by his fellow lumber dealers for "outstanding service to his industry, customers, and community." This was the same year he expanded his business out of Freeport's old Missouri Pacific railroad passenger depot into a new building next door.

After some 40 years of passenger service, the 60-year-old depot also had served John well, keeping the business high and dry through a couple of hurricanes—though he lost the roof of a warehouse during Hurri-

cane Carla in 1961. One reason the depot was a good spot for John's business is that it was built a couple of feet higher above sea level than most stores in Freeport and Lake Jackson. John just wishes his home in Jones Creek were as high as the old depot. Carla put two feet of water in his house.

The name of the business is Simmons Building Supply, and it was shortly before Carla's visit, in 1961, that John became sole owner and moved into the old depot for easier unloading of lumber from rail cars. John had come to Freeport in 1941 to work for a highway contractor, then he joined Dow in construction and engineering in 1942.

"I remember being in Dow engineering when we were working in maintenance and on process improvement at the styrene plant, when it was owned by the government and C. B. Branch was superintendent. Dow took over the plant after the war." And Branch, in 1971, became the president of Dow.

"In 1947, Bill Schambra was president of the school board. The school district was starting a construction program, which was badly needed after the growth of the area during the war, and Bill asked me to head up the construction program. I figured some day I would go back to Dow, but instead I became the partner and manager of a lumber yard in 1951. The business started with four employees in 1941; now we have 20."

There's one thing about John's business different from that of many building suppliers—its participation in the Dow vendor supply program, an innovation by the company for routine purchasing. John's company gets orders from Dow by teletype, delivers the material to the end-use point in the plant, and a Dow computer does the rest—sending him a check without the necessity for any billing. You can imagine how happy he is to be free of all the paperwork, and the cost savings benefit both companies. Because they deliver to so many different places, John's drivers know the plant "probably better than most Dow people."

The Simmons store is also tied in with the Dow shortwave radio network so that if a storm knocks out the phones, the plant can still keep in touch. And during a hurricane, Simmons keeps a man on duty within reach of Dow. "After a hurricane, the lumberyard is the first place people want to get to."

Among John's customers are the ocean freighters that call at Brazosport. They buy lumber and plywood for bracing and palletizing, and polyethylene film for covering cargo inside the holds.

"There was no harbor, as such, when I came to Freeport. But I remember a prediction by Dr. Willard Dow, who was the company's president at that time. He predicted the time would come when Plants A and B would be joined together with a string of power plants in between. And I can see that coming right now."

Tobey and Simmons are only two of the businessmen who have been in Brazosport throughout the period of Dow's growth. Darrell V. Collins, chairman of the board at the First Freeport National Bank, was working in Angleton, Texas, as an office manager for the Community Public Service Company, when he had a chance to join the bank.

Collins has seen both the area and the bank grow steadily, "with a couple of leveling-out spots." He became president of the bank in 1961 and board chairman in 1965, gave up the presidency in 1972 and now, at the age of 65, is continuing as chairman "on a year-to-year basis."

The bank itself is 60 years old, five years younger than the Brazosport Bank of Texas, which started as the Velasco State Bank. The

gray brick building where First Freeport was first located still stands on Park Street, near both Simmons Building Supply and the original location of Tobey Hardware.

"You'll notice the windows were built high off the ground to make it difficult for robbers or hijackers." The bank now owns one of the largest and most impressive structures in all of Brazosport. It has $30 million in deposits, and it is one of five banks to which Dow transfers payroll money from Houston every week.

Waiting outside Collins' office was Wayne Richardson, president of the Styrothane company, a business started by his father in 1963. His father, C. R. Richardson, came to Freeport in 1942 from Cisco, Texas, where he was "pumping gas." He worked for Dow 20 years, starting as an insulation helper and becoming one of the Texas Division's first experts in protective coatings.

"Then he decided to jump to the other side of the fence, take a chance, and go into business on his own."

Now Dow is a customer of the Styrothane company, and Wayne Richardson heads an organization that has 80 employees when the work is heavy. At the moment his company was doing "more work than we've ever done." Also among his customers are the shrimp boats.

"The shrimp boats can stay out in the Gulf only as long as their ice holds out. There are very few boats that are not insulated with urethane foam."

At the Gulf Supply Company, Harry Thorne is back in Brazosport as district manager after a previous stay from 1960 to 1963 as store manager. In between, he's worked for Gulf Supply in Baton Rouge, Beaumont, and Houston. From 1960 till 1973, the number of items stocked by Gulf Supply increased from 2,700 to 4,800, and its work

force grew from 20 to 46.

As Harry remembers it, Dow originated its vendor supply system with Gulf in 1960. From that point it spread, not only to John Simmons' company but also to other Dow suppliers—and to hundreds of other companies, including both customers and competitors of both Dow and Gulf Supply. Drivers for Gulf Supply also know the Dow complex well since they handle deliveries for Gulf and also for five other suppliers.

"Our problem right now is shortages of supply. Pipe is on allocation, but we expect to get our share. We are not in the lumber business, but I understand things like plywood are short—things you'd never expect this country to run short of."

Wayne Richardson's father and John Simmons are examples of men who switched from working for someone to going out on their own; Bill Tutor went the other way. He was a self-employed electrical contractor in Houston. Now he does maintenance and electrical work at the Rheem Manufacturing Company's plant for manufacturing steel drums in Freeport.

Bill was "a farm boy" from Central Texas, from a family of 15 children, when he moved to Houston. He'd never seen a big city when he married his wife in the town of Troy.

In 1960, his three children grown and married, Bill decided it was time to get out of the construction business. He started work at the Rheem plant before the first machine was installed.

"I was the lead man for a number of years, but when the plant was expanded they sent in new supervision from Houston. So I got to go back to the electrical work that I love. Really, I've loved every minute I've been here. It's a pleasure to work here. If you want to move up, somebody's got to die.

Everybody's happy and won't leave."

The Rheem plant supplies drums to Dow, a big variety of drums, including those that carry VORANOL products to many parts of the world. It also produces a few drums for another chemical plant in Corpus Christi. The plant's drum-production equipment is among the most modern in the industry, and its production rates are among the fastest. Since the start-up, the plant has been expanded and production has more than doubled—even though Dow continually looks for opportunities to ship products in bulk rather than in drums and bags.

Bill lives in Lake Barbara, which lists its population as 605. "Most of the people are country people like me, or at least they seem to be. They are real friendly. I love to fish, and so does my wife. As long as there is any bait left, she won't let me come home. That's what makes it so nice. We have everything in common pretty well."

If manufacturing drums sounds monotonous, perhaps it's how one looks at it. Basically, the drums are made with mechanized equipment, and Bill's job is keeping the equipment running—and that equipment is more complex than when the plant was opened.

"We've come a long way from where we started. Dow just keeps wanting drums, and we just keep making 'em. Some times we have to work 10 or 11 hours. But everybody likes it that way, working days. And there really isn't enough work for two shifts, anyway."

Except for the depleted sulphur resources, just about everything in Brazosport has "come a long way from where we started." But the businesses are a bit different from those envisioned for the mouth of the Brazos by the Velasco promoters of the 1890s.

29 | Mired in Mud

"You worked around the clock... because it might be two weeks before you saw another ship. Since then... Dow's exports have grown at least four or five times."

Brazosport and Galveston are about equally distant from Houston, 50 to 60 miles, and they are 40 miles apart on the coast of the Gulf of Mexico. To drive from Brazosport to Galveston, you cross the Surfside bridge over the Intracoastal Waterway and go 18 miles along the shore until crossing over to Galveston Island by a toll bridge at San Luis Pass.

At Surfside and on the island you drive past resort cottages built on stilts to keep from being flooded when rain and the Gulf waves are swept across the beaches by high winds. Going back to the mainland from Galveston, it's another 40 miles to LaPorte, and if you keep moving down the main street of LaPorte, beyond the city limits, the road ends at the water's edge. You are then near Morgans Point, which overlooks San Jacinto Bay and Barbers Cut, where the Houston Ship Channel empties into Galveston Bay.

It's sort of desolate toward the end of the road, though it's a scant dozen miles or so from the Manned Spacecraft Center at Clear Lake, a Houston suburb. But when it's storming, with the wind shaking the creaking old fishing docks that jut feebly into San Jacinto Bay, it reminded me of that old Edward G. Robinson movie, "Key Largo," set in the Florida Keys.

When I looked around at Morgans Point, there was the *Munchen (Munich)*, the big barge carrier that's identical to the *Bilderdyk*. The *Munchen* is owned by Hapag-Lloyd, a German shipping company. Together with Holland-America's *Bilderdyk*, it operates under the name Combi Lines, each ship crossing the North Atlantic between the Gulf and north European ports about ten times a year.

This was on a Saturday, and I had left Brazosport to satisfy my curiosity on two

points—to take a look at this twin of the *Bilderdyk*, which I would board three weeks later for the trip to Europe, and to see my first baseball game in Houston's Astrodome. As in Savannah, Georgia, and Sheerness, England, ports I later visited aboard the *Bilderdyk*, these ships don't dock in conventional port facilities. Instead they tie up at specially-built dolphins downriver from the cities.

It wouldn't have made the same impression in a port with other ships, but the *Munchen* in Barbers Cut loomed up like a big hotel in the middle of a desert. I turned onto a side road toward a small building at

the end of a concrete pier leading to the ship. Twenty cars were parked near the building, and there were men in several of the cars. I assumed they were longshoremen waiting for the rain to stop.

But out on the pier, I noticed that the ship's big crane was at work moving barges. And aboard the ship, Captain Hillard Smid—over a stein of German beer in his office—assured me the barge movements aren't delayed by rain.

What Captain Smid lamented was that in United States ports the longshoremen's contract with the shipping company requires the hiring of two gangs of 16 men each, plus

Back in Brazosport the following week I watched the loading of drums and magnesium metal into barges that would go aboard the *Bilderdyk*, and more magnesium into another barge that would carry it to New Orleans for loading aboard a ship going to Volkswagen in Germany. At the docks I also learned a good bit more about the shipping business.

In Brazosport there are two local unions of the International Longshoremen's Association, one with a black membership and the other white. The white local, number 1723, was started in 1950; the black local, number 1818, in 1954. There's another white local, 1817, for clerks and timekeepers. One business agent, a white man, represents all the locals in dealings with the stevedore companies.

I was surprised to find this form of segregation still existing in the United States, and it appears the reason is that the longshoremen like it that way, though no one expressed a preference. I talked with both blacks and whites, including the man who started the black local.

The two locals split the work exactly evenly so that, their local having fewer members, the individual members of the black local generally get more work per person than the whites. This is difficult to determine precisely because many of the same men also work ships in Houston, Galveston, and Bay City.

If a black gang loads the aft of a ship, and a white gang the fore section, this is then reversed on the next ship. Apparently this arrangement exists at other Texas ports. I remembered that at Morgans Point the longshoremen on the ship were white, and those in the cars were black. They switch every four hours, I later learned.

On the docks, I had a chance to talk

foremen and a timekeeper, for working the *Munchen* and the *Bilderdyk*. Actually, about the only people needed are one man to drive the crane and a couple to hook cables onto the barges and to secure the barges aboard ship. So there is plenty of time for all the others to fish, if the weather is nice, or listen to their radios. The following month, I saw the same work done with only five men in Rotterdam, and four in Bremerhaven, Germany.

Still, when I returned to my car, I thought it was a blessing for me that there were so many people around with nothing to do. The car was mired in the mud, and sank deeper when I tried to move. The longshoremen, experienced enough to park on the pavement or firmer ground, were a friendly bunch. There was no way they could help me without getting muddy, but they volunteered.

Eight men, and I've got to think longshoremen must be among the world's strongest, grasped the bumper and fenders of the Plymouth sedan. Another got behind the wheel. They pushed, and they tried to pick it up, but to no avail. The car was too deep in the mud. Eventually I was rescued by a tow truck from LaPorte—and in time to reach the Astrodome, cold and wet, for the first pitch against the San Francisco Giants.

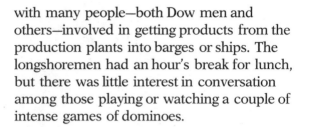

with many people—both Dow men and others—involved in getting products from the production plants into barges or ships. The longshoremen had an hour's break for lunch, but there was little interest in conversation among those playing or watching a couple of intense games of dominoes.

Al Kulcak is a 27-year employee of Dow. He's a materials-handling technician. Al picks up cargo-loading orders at the main office of the Dow transport and warehousing operations. He goes to the production plant to check on product availability, and if everything is in order, he stencils the drums with the order number and shipping destination—maybe Bangkok, quite often Hong Kong. In the case of the polyol shipment I proposed to follow to Europe, it was Dow's Botlek terminal in Rotterdam.

For moving the products Al uses a trailer that can hold 60 drums, and is equipped with a telescopic boom for lifting up to 6,000 pounds from a truck. As on the big cargo carriers themselves, and in the loading at the

dock, the actual tasks of carrying and lifting are mechanized. But there still must be conscientious work to get the drums and bags in the right places, properly handled and protected from damage.

Al commutes 60 miles from near Rosenberg, a community closer to Houston than it is to Brazosport.

"Both my wife and I were born and raised near Rosenberg. My father is a farmer, and so is my wife's father, mainly cotton and grain. I still farm a little. My brother and I each have about 100 acres.

"You can't get that farming out of a person when he gets used to it. My father bought his land in 1933. You fall in love with the land."

Al and his wife, Olga, have five children, one son and four daughters. Mark, 20, is a graduate of Wharton Junior College; Bridget, 18, attends Lamar University, majoring in speech therapy; the other three girls are in high school and junior high.

"Mark is planning to attend the University of Houston and major in government. This summer he's working here at Dow in a materials-handling job. He also likes the farm, and he helps me out when he's home. But if he farms, he will also have to have another job."

Al is among 280 people working in materials handling in the Texas Division. This group recently voted to cancel its union affiliation. I didn't put Al on the spot by asking how he had voted, but he gave no hint of dissatisfaction with what had happened. And certainly Bobby Henderson, the manager of the materials-handling operations, was convinced that the change had been beneficial to both the individuals and the company. He said there has been a definite gain in efficiency and that the jobs are more interesting through elimination of narrow work-jurisdiction lines.

The timekeeper for the longshoremen was Al Wise. Al remembers when the white local was organized to handle shipments of coal coming from Oklahoma to Brazosport by rail for export. He also remembers the first Dow vessels, ships chartered for trips to Port Newark, New Jersey, and barges for Chicago and Cincinnati.

"You worked around the clock, and you had to work all the hours you could because it might be two weeks before you saw another ship. Since then, I'd say, Dow's exports have grown at least four or five times over what we did originally in 1952.

"I work both the Dow and the city docks. I'm a commissioner of the Brazos River Harbor Navigation District, and one of our efforts is to try and stimulate more foreign business, imports of cars and steel—and that would help Dow's business.

"When you have the ships here, Dow could export on the same vessels. Sometimes they have to truck products from here to Houston or Galveston because the quantities are too small for a ship to stop here."

Al lives in Brazoria. He said the longshoremen come from a wide area, not only the communities of Brazosport, but also Bay City, Sweeny, Houston, Old Ocean, and Galveston. Al was born in Iowa, and his father was originally from Oklahoma, as was his mother, a full-blooded Indian. His father moved first to Rosenberg, then to Freeport in 1942. He worked for the Army Corps of Engineers in putting up levees and for contractors who built Dow plants and dug the barge canal going to Plant B.

Henry Harris has been a longshoreman since 1954, when he went to Galveston—where he knew the president of the black longshoremen's local—to get a charter for the black local in Brazosport. Previously, he worked at installing sewer lines in Lake Jackson, and as a janitor for the telephone company in Freeport.

Henry is 55 years old, and when he takes off his blue hard hat you notice his hair is turning white. He says work never has been scarce in Brazosport, "not for somebody that wanted to work." His wife also is a Texan, and he met her in Freeport, where her father had moved to work for the Freeport Sulphur Company.

Before 1954, all the longshoremen's work was done by whites, and Henry has "no idea" why it changed—except that he went to Galveston to get that charter for a black local. "We [the black and white locals] have been working together ever since."

Because longshoremen's work is irregular, Henry also has worked for the sheriff's department as a part-time deputy the last three years. He attended Brazosport College to receive certification as a peace officer.

Blueford (Buddy) Haynes, 51, once drove a Greyhound bus in Florida, but he came to Brazosport with another bus driver who also worked as a shrimper. Buddy stayed, working on a shrimp boat for two months before turning to other work. "The other fellow bought a new boat, but he didn't work it."

Buddy does maintenance work on fork-lift trucks and other equipment owned by seven stevedoring companies that do business in Brazosport. Before the dock was built, he moored all the ships that came into Brazosport Harbor to load rice, flour, livestock, occasional Dow shipments, and other general cargo.

"I sure do like this work better than working in a gang down in the hold. It gets up to 110 degrees down there—and hotter than that when the sun is shining down and there's no breeze."

But this was a pleasant day on the docks in Brazosport, the temperature in the 80s. This is a major export point, but it's not like the piers in Brooklyn, and it's not like Morgans Point either. There was no mud, and everybody was working.

30 | The English Channel

"All the fun and romance are gone...Being a ship captain is not the challenge of previous years... There are no surprises."

It was a Friday morning, and heavy traffic was anticipated in the English Channel. Within view were a tanker, a ferry, a naval vessel, and two freighters—heavy traffic indeed after being on the North Atlantic more than a week, and spending many hours without seeing another ship.

"There's always a big push to get the ships loaded and out to sea before the weekend," explained G. J. A. Amersfoort, the first officer of the *Bilderdyk*, the "chief mate." The dots on the radar screen showed dozens of ships in the area, though most were too far away to be seen with the naked eye.

The weather had been excellent in crossing the ocean, the sky clear and the sea amazingly calm. "I can remember when the fog has been so heavy we didn't see anything from the time we left Europe until reaching the States," remarked Ben de Haas, the second officer.

Only once before in its 15 months on the North Atlantic had the *Bilderdyk* carried a passenger, and that was on its first trip. The ship has no quarters for passengers, so the previous passenger began the voyage in the captain's small auxiliary cabin on the bridge. After the passenger had thrice become seasick—the bridge losing its clean, wind-swept fragrance—it was decided it would be better if he moved to the "hospital," a three-bed infirmary.

Another officer related that the chief mate had said "Never again." He didn't like having to look for a key to the infirmary when he needed medical supplies. And nobody liked the odor of seasickness on the bridge.

But I never locked the infirmary, and my stomach was never tested by the waves. When I'd awaken in the morning, the ship was so quiet it was like being in a berth on a train slowly entering a station. I had the feel-ing I should reach for the shade of the train window, squeeze the latch, and lift the shade to see what city we were pulling into.

This Friday was a happy day for the boatswain, Gerrit Meijers, a big guy with a little limp. He'd won the pool, 60 guilders, on the time the *Bilderdyk* would pass directly south of Bishop's Rock on Land's End at the southwestern tip of England—the first land to come into view, though it happened at 2:40 in the morning.

The captain, Arie Van Dijk, substituting for the vacationing regular captain of the *Bilderdyk*, also was obviously pleased that the voyage was nearing its end—though he knew that at home he'd have to face the question of whether to wallpaper, as his wife wanted, or paint, as he preferred.

The chief engineer, Willem De Wit, sensed that "his horses," his 26,000-horse-power engines, were anxious to reach their stall. This was the ninth day they had been gulping fuel without pause, 50 gallons per mile, since we left Savannah, Georgia. The chief also was in good humor, though he'd just received news that would cost him 6,000 guilders. His son had passed his engineering exams, which meant the chief would be paying off a promise by buying a new car and giving the family car to his son.

Jaap Scholten, who had been the host at mid-ocean for his own birthday party, his 20th, was anxious to see his family, though the reason that he hung pictures of Che Guevara and Chairman Mao in his room was not ideological but just "to bother father and mother."

A Spanish sailor, Ramon Rouco Santos, knew an airplane ticket awaited him in Rotterdam for going home to the northwest coast of Spain. Though he speaks and writes only Spanish—while most of the officers are fluent in Dutch, English, German, and French, but not Spanish—Rouco Santos had sent the bridge a note that the chief mate easily translated as "I'd like to fly to Vigo, but if a good connection isn't available, make it Santiago de Compostela."

Mrs. Johannes Koks, wife of the third engineer and the only woman on board, had her feminine wear hanging up to dry in the laundry room. The third engineer himself had seldom smiled since we left Savannah, where there had been a post-midnight debate about the general intelligence of engineers. But now even he seemed more relaxed.

Probably the only person who wasn't happy was the 25-year-old third officer, Willem Asselbergs. The previous evening the home office had requested that he stay aboard for another trip. The company was short of third officers.

"You're stupid to do it," the third engineer had told him at dinner.

"What?" Asselbergs asked in surprise at the unsolicited advice.

"You're stupid to accept another trip."

"You sound like all Dutchmen. The Vietnamese are stupid, the Indonesians are stupid, the Australians are stupid, the New Zealanders are stupid."

Ben de Haas, the second officer, asked for another piece of bread. Observing the engineer's impatience for the meal to end, so he and his wife could leave the table, Asselbergs said, "If you want to go, go ahead and go."

I asked for another cup of coffee. We had reached the dining room after 6 o'clock, and it wasn't yet 6:30. The third officer explained that dinners had been calculated to average 18 minutes, which in a sense was part of the argument in Savannah. The protagonists had contended the engineers worked so much overtime they never took time for a leisurely meal or for conversation,

Gerrit Meijers

and that therefore the engineers were "getting dumber and dumber."

"May I have some more coffee too?" Asselbergs asked Victor Wustlich, the Dutch-Indonesian steward.

Changing the subject, I asked the second officer to translate to Mrs. Koks, gorgeously sun-tanned from all the time she had spent reading on the top deck, that the trip had been more enjoyable because "We'd had a beautiful girl aboard." Though she had admitted to speaking only Dutch, she smiled immediately. Ben said, "There's no need to translate when you're paying a compliment."

"When there's only one woman aboard, she's always 'beautiful,'" her husband said.

"If I were you," Asselbergs said to Mrs. Koks, "the first thing I'd do when I got back to your room is slap him in the face."

Meanwhile, Asselbergs had figured he had three options for solving the problem of what he was going to do, now that he'd been asked to take another trip at the very time his fiancee would be on vacation from college:

—He could hit the captain. That would get Asselbergs off the ship, but actually he liked this captain more than most captains.

—He could ask Dow Chemical to request that his fiancee, an art student, come aboard for the next trip so she could paint pictures to illustrate this book.

—The second officer could stay aboard for the three European ports scheduled after Rotterdam, relieving Asselbergs till he reboarded for crossing the Atlantic. "But then the home office would think de Haas likes the ship so much, he would have a hard time getting his next vacation."

I suggested he could marry his fiancee during the day the ship would be in Rotterdam, but a speedup of that sort sparked no enthusiasm.

Until word had arrived from the home office naming the men who would go on vacation, this had been a daily subject of conjecture for the 5:30 p.m. gathering in the small bar of the ship's lounge. If either the second or third officer had to stay on for the next trip, Asselbergs said, it should be de Haas. He could bring his wife, while company rules barred fiancees.

Probably the only time an officer and his fiancee traveled aboard a Holland-America freighter was the one trip when the second engineer was engaged to a deck officer—the first woman ever to serve as a seagoing officer in the Dutch merchant navy.

"That was hard," said Johannes Vroegindewey. "The rules wouldn't allow her to ever visit my cabin. She made one more trip on another ship, and then we decided that was no good."

After her short career at sea, which included television appearances in the ports of Baltimore and New York, Mrs. Vroegindewey retired to an office job with Holland-America. Now she was going to board the *Bilderdyk* for its next trip, but as the wife of the second engineer, not as a deck officer.

For this 3,900-mile voyage across the North Atlantic, the *Bilderdyk* had 28 people on board—the captain, three deck officers, five engineers, one wife, the radio officer, an electrician, and the boatswain, all Dutch; 14 sailors, seven of them Spanish, six Dutch, and one Portuguese; and one American passenger. The oldest was the 53-year-old captain, and the youngest was the bearded, just-turned-20 Scholten.

The 857-foot ship, with a deadweight of

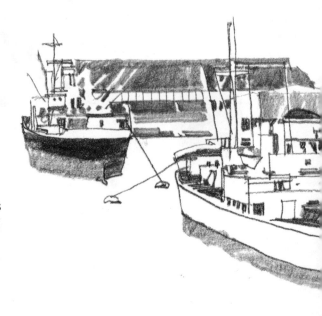

29,712 metric tons, crossed the Atlantic east-bound with a full load of 83 barges, each of which contained up to 370 tons of cargo. The barge cargoes included chemicals, magnesium, liner board, wood pulp, and peanuts. After leaving Rotterdam, the *Bilderdyk* had been to Savannah, Houston (where the barges from Brazosport were taken aboard), New Orleans, Savannah again, and now it would call at Sheerness and Bremerhaven before returning to Rotterdam.

A myriad of technical detail could be written to establish the *Bilderdyk* among the most modern, best-equipped cargo carriers in the world. But I thought the experience and capabilities of the officers even more impressive. Yet, there is a certain degree of incompatibility in those two facts.

"All the fun and romance are gone," the captain commented. "Obviously being a ship captain is not the challenge of previous years, but it's better than working in a factory or at a desk. Things have changed. There

are no surprises. It used to be that you might find you were 50 miles ahead of where you thought you were. Now a half hour [10 miles] is the most, no real surprises."

Bill Asselbergs, still vexed that he wasn't going on vacation when we reached Rotterdam, commented quietly, "With a $20 million ship, there shouldn't be many surprises." Then, a minute later: "Another trip will make 20 weeks aboard ship. This is almost five months. Ridiculous."

That evening the chief mate, the 44-year-old Amersfoort, was going to call Rotterdam to plead Asselberg's case, but the answer

would still be the same. As chief mate on this ship since it was commissioned in 1972, Amersfoort is a man who held the admiration of the younger officers. Extremely competent, mild-mannered, he is the type of person you'd expect to stay calm and make the best possible decision in any sort of an emergency.

Twice he'd been the chief mate on ships when the captain was stricken critically—once a heart attack, another time a stroke. Both captains survived the illnesses. On the first occasion, the ship was diverted to Halifax in Canada; on the other, the captain

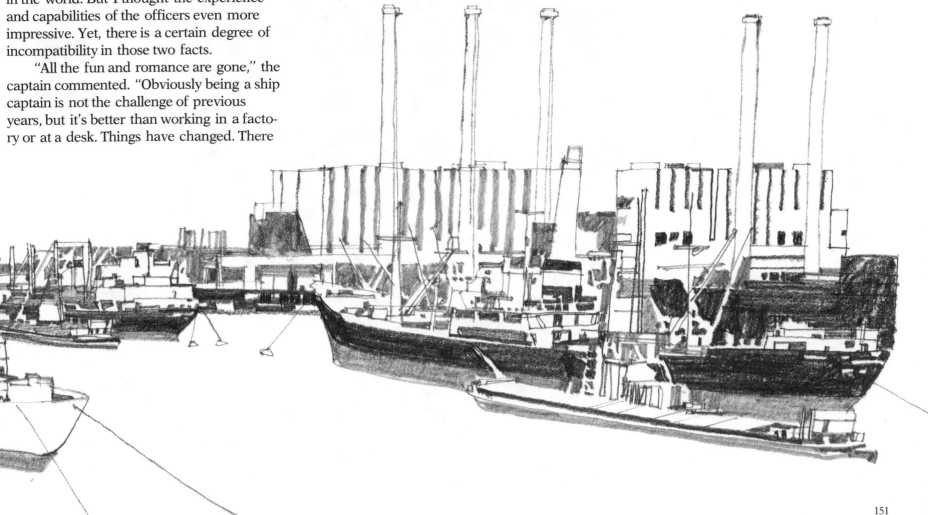

was removed from the ship by helicopter.

When we left Savannah, the officers had an extra bit of work, because the cable on the crane had to be replaced. This work, as well as the handling of the barges in every port, is under the supervision of the deck officers.

The engineers' main job is in the engine room, a mammoth chamber that looks a lot like the inside of a modern, highly-instrumented power plant. The chief engineer, De Wit, agreed to the resemblance, but with one major exception—in mid-ocean there's no place to look for help or spare equipment. The challenge to the engineers is to keep the ship running at maximum efficiency. Preventive maintenance is essential for avoiding expensive loss of time.

The *Bilderdyk* is extremely self-sufficient. Through evaporation, it desalts its own water for drinking and other domestic uses. The ship's desalting capacity is 36 tons of water per day, and normal usage is 12 tons. Perhaps the single item that most impressed on me the self-sufficiency of our city at sea was that the ship carries a coffin. A body can be frozen and stored in the lead-lined coffin if the family wants it returned rather than buried at sea. And the chief mate had once been on a ship that had a fatality. A sailor fell from the mast and broke his neck. The chief also pointed out that among ocean-going vessels there is a system for always being able to learn the location of the closest ship with a doctor, and for obtaining medical instructions by radio.

The ocean voyage actually was the start of my European visit since all the others on board were European, though at least two men had been born in Indonesia and another in Surinam, the Dutch territory in South America. It was a very congenial group, but the repartee about engineers working over-time and the postponement of a vacation had foundations in serious subjects. For seagoing people, time at home is especially precious. And for the Dutch there is a question about extra work, even for premium pay, since the officers said any extra income is taxed at least 50 per cent.

"You may still see people washing the streets in Holland," it was suggested, "but that work is not done by the Dutch any more. South Europeans have been imported for that type of work. And while there's some unemployment, there are more jobs than people. The unemployed are drawing compensation while waiting for an opportunity that matches their skills. A person who in unemployed is not asked to take a position below his level of education."

Jobs on the *Bilderdyk* are among the best-paid in the Dutch merchant navy. And the accommodations aboard ship are excellent. Each officer and each sailor has a cabin of his own. The economics work out quite clearly that it is less costly to have a minimum-size crew, which works overtime when necessary, than to have crews as large as those that formerly manned this size of ship. At the same time there is no doubt that, given their choice, the officers would take more time at home in preference to higher pay.

After we had been at sea for five days, my good friend the radio officer, Rob Van De Berg, thought I might like to telephone to my home in Michigan. Although I knew the ship had extensive radio facilities, I wasn't aware it was possible to call home. But after a good shortwave radio connection with the telephone company's station in New Jersey, the ring in Midland went unanswered—probably because of a Little League baseball game.

Rob tried again the following evening.

But he couldn't reach the New Jersey station because of interference from Europe. The third try was a charm. Reception was good and the timing excellent, for I had the opportunity to give my best wishes from the mid-Atlantic to my daughter Becky just a few hours before her graduation from high school.

The voyage's most surprising event occurred in the English Channel. It was morning, and I was on the bridge with the third officer. There was a tanker off to our left, and then a bit farther ahead a destroyer of Her Majesty's Navy. All of a sudden there were five orange-red flashes from the guns on the destroyer, pointed across the path we were traveling. Five bursts of sound followed shortly after we saw the bright flashes. This was completely unexpected.

"I'll call the captain," said Asselbergs. "He'll know what to do. He sailed during the war."

The captain came to the bridge and looked through his binoculars. The destroyer indeed had the proper flags flying to warn that she was conducting gunnery practice. The captain said the destroyer would have phoned in case of any problem; he also added that, with today's artillery, a ship can easily be within firing range before warning flags are visible.

In the North Sea the captain remarked about the carelessness of sailboats crossing in front of the *Bilderdyk*. "What they must not realize is that, if they lost their wind, there's no way this ship could be stopped quickly enough to avoid a collision."

In our trip through the English Channel, we also saw the *Queen Elizabeth 2* as it crossed in front of us after departing Southampton. There was also a submarine, and on the English coast the nuclear energy complex at Dungeness, and the white cliffs of Dover.

31 | Always in a Hurry

"On a U-boat or a submarine, there's no shelter, no nothing. We stay on top in the open tower. In the bad winter time, it can be raining like hell, very cold."

Sometimes he boards a ship from a wire dangling from a helicopter "like a fish on a hook." Frequently he climbs aboard from a pilot boat at a rendezvous point seven miles up the coast from the Hook of Holland. On this afternoon, however, he came aboard the *Bilderdyk* after riding a train from Rotterdam to Bremerhaven.

Peter Van Eijk is a pilot who guides ships in and out of the New Waterway, which leads to the Nieuwe Maas River, the Rhine River's main outlet to the North Sea. Rotterdam is located astride the Nieuwe Maas, 15 miles inland from the coastal village known as the Hook of Holland.

Van Eijk is among 250 pilots at Rotterdam. Twenty-one years ago, when he entered this business at the age of 24, he was the youngest of 72 pilots. But the increase in the number of pilots is only one indication of the traffic growth at Rotterdam.

"The number of pilots has more than tripled. But in addition, each pilot has increased his personal productivity in number of ships he works." And the ships have continually increased in size.

It was four o'clock on a Tuesday morning when we reached the Hook of Holland, not yet midnight of the previous day in the United States. The sun was just coming up

an hour to operate a ship like this. So the captain asked the Holland-America Line to send a pilot to Bremerhaven. Now we can enter right away when we arrive at the Hook of Holland."

And then another pilot would come aboard for Rotterdam itself.

"We go to France to meet the big tankers. Or by helicopter to the 250,000-ton ships. The helicopter takes us from the Hook of Holland to about 15 miles at sea and drops us on the ship on a wire. The helicopter can't land on the tankers; it is not allowed, too dangerous. So they drop us on a wire, like a fish on a hook."

The day was sunny and comfortably warm. We were within two days of the most-daylight day of the year—which on the North Sea means almost 19 hours, from 3:30 a.m. to 10:30 p.m.—off the coast of Germany. But the weather is not always so nice, and with rough seas the rendezvous between ship and pilot boat can be difficult.

"We have a lot of problems in the winter. When taking a ship out, sometimes we will stay on to the next port. Last winter the captain of one of the big container ships wanted to take me to New York. I finally dropped off in the English Channel, but the captain didn't like to stop because he was in a hurry."

Piloting a submarine is another task that's not so pleasant in rough weather. "On a U-boat or a submarine, there's no shelter, no nothing. We stay on top in the open tower. In the bad winter time, it can be raining like hell, very cold. We put on the commander's parka coat."

Despite weather problems, there's no question that Van Eijk likes his work. Before starting a year's training as an apprentice pilot, he was a deck officer on a general cargo ship, sailing the oceans for seven years.

"But now I get to be home with the wife and family. I see the boys [Peter, 21, and Dick John, 17] growing up day by day. When I was at sea, my trips were usually six to seven months. I left our home when our older son was two weeks, and when I came back he was eight months."

We were arriving at Rotterdam following two weeks in which the port had set world records for oceangoing traffic—854 ships the previous week, and 830 the week before that—records almost certain to be surpassed in ensuing weeks. Riding into Rotterdam on the top deck of the *Bilderdyk* is similar to riding atop a float in a parade on Main Street. Although there weren't many people watching, even a few seemed like a crowd after being at sea for two weeks—and it had been dark when we arrived at both Sheerness and Bremerhaven.

On the left, the port side of the ship, were the villages and the towering, neatly-spaced apartment buildings, trains, and electrical power lines. On the starboard side were the petroleum and petrochemical production and storage facilities of Europoort, then the Dow terminal at Botlek, more oil and petrochemical tanks, and then the dry-cargo docks. Our destination was Waalhaven, almost at the end of the harbor, convenient for sending away the barges destined to go on up the Rhine.

Van Eijk, who has piloted thousands of ships, including the *Hitra* and the *Frosta*, Norwegian tankers that bring chemicals to the Dow terminal from the Gulf Coast, pointed out that this is where many of the barges go—on up the Rhine.

"The Rhine is an open connection between the industrial country and Rotterdam. And that's the natural reason this port is big—80 million people living and producing behind Rotterdam."

over this village and its large train station, where passengers board ferries to England.

Van Eijk had boarded the *Bilderdyk* at Bremerhaven because the captain had decided it would be better not to risk losing time in meeting a pilot boat.

"Captains always are in a hurry nowadays," Van Eijk commented. "That's why I came out to Bremerhaven. If the ship had to stop outside at sea to take a pilot on board, if there was not at that moment a pilot ready to board the ship immediately, this ship would miss its high-water tide—and that would cost 12 hours waiting.

"And I think it costs $500 to $600

32 | The Soviets Want Drums

"Material handling isn't a matter of muscles any more, it's a matter of equipment. We can handle cargoes twice as fast as 10 to 15 years ago, and we can do it with fewer people."

It's possible Holland will build such a reputation as a gateway to Europe—Amsterdam's Schiphol Airport for people and the port of Rotterdam for merchandise—that the charm of the country itself will be mostly ignored. That would be unfortunate.

My previous visit to Holland had been in winter, the season of Hans Brinker and skaters. Now it was summer. The brick homes in the countryside were surrounded by greenery, splashed with flowers, and there was a festival on the main street of Terneuzen, where Dow has a large production complex. From the marching bands of nearby communities to the street-platform style shows, this was a lively event for a community of 20,000—with the big show, the Schelde Jazz Festival, scheduled for the closing day.

The Dutch are more reserved than the southern Europeans, the Italians for instance, but you sense genuine friendliness and never a curtness. And so it was that, in addition to continuing the adventure of following a VORANOL product to its ultimate buyer, I also was invited—and delighted—to make a few side trips in Holland. One was to visit a Dow customer in Uithoorn, near Amsterdam—a large, successful company doing some exploration on expansion into the field of rigid urethanes. The company's office building overlooked one of the canals typically associated with Holland.

Another visit was to Middelburg, returning a Midland visit of five years ago by G. A. de Kok, editor of the outstanding provincial newspaper *Zeeuwse Courant*. Since visiting Midland, de Kok has made three more trips to the United States, an indication of the Dutch interest in the United States and particularly in United States companies doing business in Holland.

I spent the weekend at the home of the *Bilderdyk's* radio officer, Rob Van De Berg,

whose wife, Helen, and children Ingrid, 11, and Erick, 7, were hoping he'd be at home for at least a few weeks. They live in a new home in the small town of Sprang-Capelle, happy to be away from the congestion of a city. The next I heard from Rob he was in Durban, South Africa, en route to Bombay, India.

Rotterdam itself is an interesting city. Everything in the city's center is bright and new, rebuilt after being bombed out during the war. Away from the center are the old but well-kept structures that survived the war.

It's tempting, of course, to write about the interesting sights. And I traveled by train through Holland, Belgium, Luxembourg, France, Switzerland, and to Milan and Venice in Italy so that I would see more than the view from an airplane. But that was not the reason I was in Rotterdam. I was there because it is through Rotterdam that Dow products from the United States flow to all of Europe.

The location of the Dow terminal is an area known as the Botlek, at the tip of a peninsula where the Maas Rivers, old and new, join to form the New Waterway, ten miles inland from the North Sea. This is the site not only of the terminal, but also of a Dow manufacturing operation for styrene-butadiene latex and SARAN film, and for formulating a variety of products for which the raw materials come from the United States—brake fluids, antifreeze fluids, solvents, and DURSBAN insecticide.

Foremost, it is a distribution point with 37 tanks for the storage of liquids and five warehouses for packaged products. A basic part of this operation is a quality assurance laboratory for guarding against contamination as the products move in and out.

The terminal is on the waterfront, close

to the big markets of Central Europe and about halfway between the northern and southern capital cities. It is 1,200 miles from Helsinki, Finland; 1,200 miles from Madrid, Spain; 2,000 miles from Athens, Greece. But Athens is not the most distant point to which Dow ships from Rotterdam. Products also flow from here to Africa and the Middle East.

For the Soviet Union, deliveries are made by truck to ships at anchor in Rotterdam. These shipments always are in drums—because Soviet industry is short on drums, and the Russians want the steel containers as well as what's inside.

The terminal manager is Willem van Noort, 48 years old, a Dow employee since 1964 and associated with Dow interests in Holland since 1948 in his previous job with an agency representing clients in various parts of the world. Dow began using a public terminal in Rotterdam in 1954 and started its own operation at the Botlek in 1957.

"We are quite unhappy we did not take more land here," Bill commented. "We didn't foresee that the Dow growth in Europe would be so fast." This land, incidentally, is all land reclaimed from the sea through massive landfill operations that even today are continuing downstream toward the North Sea.

Products arrive at the terminal in two Norwegian tankers, J. Ludwig Mowinckels' *Hitra* and *Frosta*, each with a capacity of 36,000 tons; by barges from the *Bilderdyk* and the *Munchen;* by freighters from Bay City, Michigan, every three weeks from May till December, when the St. Lawrence Seaway freezes; by small tankers from Bay City; and in the winter by container vessels from Montreal and New York. Occasionally there are shipments from Dow production plants in Spain and the United Kingdom. The

Jan van Male and Wim Sekeris

average number of vessels calling at the terminal is 30 to 35 a month.

The products go out mainly by truck—but also by railroad, and in barges and small coastal vessels.

The operation of a European terminal is more complex than the terminal business in the United States, though the tonnage handled is certainly less than the total exports from Brazosport. In Europe, it involves dealings with companies in different currencies and in different languages.

Shipping to Helsinki, for instance, is not simply a matter of dispatching a truck onto an expressway. The truck first goes to Denmark, passing through Germany. Then it crosses the North Sea to Sweden on a ferry, goes back to a highway through Sweden, then boards another ferry to Finland, And for some destinations, Greece for instance, the truck passes through Eastern European countries where the regulations may be quite different from elsewhere in Europe.

If a shipment is going to a country in the Common Market, all the customs details can be handled at the Botlek. If, however, the product's destination is outside the Common Market—Spain or Romania, for example—a customs agent seals the shipment in the truck or railcar at the Botlek for passage tariff-free through Common Market countries. The tariff then is paid according to the rules of the buyer's country.

Under the direction of Jos Beren, manager of product flow operations, three coordination functions are performed by different Dow people at the Botlek terminal. Product shipping coordinators act as liaison between European sales offices and production plants in balancing orders and product availability. A transport coordinator schedules the carrier—truck, rail, or vessel. A customs coordinator works with a government agent at the Botlek or, for shipments outside the Common Market, arranges customs handling in the buyer's country.

It was the second day after the arrival of the *Bilderdyk* in Rotterdam that the 179 drums of VORANOL RS-350 were unloaded from a barge pushed to the Dow terminal. This operation was supervised by Jan van Male, the supervisor of dry cargo.

"All my professional life has been in shipping, warehousing, and stevedoring. The first seven years were as a deck officer on a ship; then I was the assistant manager for stevedoring at Surabaja in Indonesia until President Sukarno expelled the Dutch. From 1956 to 1959, I was with a stevedoring firm in Amsterdam. Then, till I joined Dow in 1966, I was a marine superintendent loading and unloading cargoes for the U.S. Department of Defense.

"Material handling isn't a matter of muscles any more, it's a matter of equipment. We can handle cargoes twice as fast as 10 to 15 years ago, and we can do it with fewer people."

Jan's counterpart for bulk liquids, Wim

Sekeris, remembers the Dow terminal site when it was farm land. He started to work for Dow in 1958, riding a motorbike. Wim attended neither high school nor college, but he has steadily moved up in the organization. And he remembers when he acquired a second-hand car, then another second-hand car, and finally his first new car—at the time he became an assistant supervisor. I wonder if the gasoline shortage put Wim back on his motorbike.

"The challenge of this job is to maximize utilization of the tanks, not have a tank half-full, but to switch the material to a smaller tank if the larger tank is needed for another product. And the biggest problem of all is when the *Hitra* and the *Frosta* arrive from the Gulf Coast only a few days apart, rather than at the normal three-week interval. We really have a job finding space for everything."

It was Furges Molugnhey, the shipping coordinator for VORANOL products, who pointed me toward Italy as a major market for RS-350, though this is a product for which the European demand had exceeded supply frequently in the last two years. Furges, an Irishman who speaks Dutch fluently, has been a Dow employee the past eight years.

Different businesses have various ways of keeping score on how well they are doing. For Bill van Noort, the key figure is "turnover"—the total tons of product handled through the terminal in a year divided by the terminal's capacity. A public terminal estimates it needs a turnover of four to make a profit; a turnover of ten is regarded as the practical maximum. Bill's figure for 1972 was 8.5, up from 6.3 in 1971. And he just hoped there would be enough product available to come somewhere close to 8.5 in the product-short years of 1973 and 1974.

33 | A Multiple of Nationalities

"We have 17 or 18 different nationalities working in this building. It is rather interesting, when you think about it, because our fathers fought a war."

The headquarters for Dow Europe is Horgen, Switzerland, 15 miles from Zurich and nestled between Lake Zurich and the Alps. For travel in Europe, this is an ideal base of operations. But the attractiveness of the region must have been one reason the company decided to headquarter here.

The individual with the longest urethane experience of any of the Dow people now in Europe is Ron Sorensen. He is at Horgen as the development manager for organic chemicals.

Ron first became acquainted with Dow as a competitor in the magnesium metal business. From 1955 to 1958 he worked for Norsk Hydro, a Norwegian aluminum producer that is second only to Dow in its capacity to produce magnesium.

A native of Norway, Ron returned to his homeland after receiving a chemical engineering degree from Gothenburg University in Sweden. At Norsk Hydro, he came to know a great deal about Dow when he was assigned to study the Dow patents in magnesium.

In 1958, at 27, Ron moved to the United States, where he combined urethane work for a United States chemical company with evening classes at Fairleigh Dickinson University in New Jersey. He received a chemistry degree from Fairleigh Dickinson in 1963 and then joined Dow Europe.

Ron's first assignment was an eight-month training program in Michigan and Texas. Several years later he returned to Midland on an assignment in research, six months with a group working on designed polymers, and six months in organic chemicals. Now he is back in the Technical Service and Development laboratories in Horgen.

"Tom Sparta was Dow's first urethane man in Europe. He made the first sale in 1961. When I came over, Tom handled the sales, and I was the development man.

"Urethane is one of the rare areas where Europe might be ahead of the United States because urethanes were developed and commercialized by Bayer in Germany. The equipment for processing urethanes is generally more sophisticated in Europe than in the U.S. In Europe there are companies specializing solely in the manufacture of equipment for the urethane industry."

Still, Dow Europe's polyol sales have recorded a steady annual growth of 15 to 20 per cent. And one of the biggest reasons for that growth, Ron says, is Dow Europe's completely different—and typically American—approach to the urethane market.

Traditionally, European chemical producers have served their customers by delivering ready-to-use, tailored-to-your-need materials. The chemical companies develop great technical strengths so as to be able to do this. And, equally traditional, they then maintain a close hold on the technical know-how involved in their products. And this was the general situation in urethanes.

"Dow has the typical American approach, very open. We started educating the people. We were able to help the people make foam. This was a completely different attitude."

Today, Ron believes, there should be caution in predictions on the growth rate for urethane products. "Because the whole polyurethane industry is hearing a lot of criticism because of foams that burn.

"And I think it is proper that we should think more about fire retardancy. I do not think we need non-burning foam in all kinds of furniture. I think if we have a certain kind of fire retardancy, and also more fire-retardant fabrics, we can really improve the furniture quite a bit. But everybody has to sit down and say 'this is going to be law.' We can supply the fire-retardant system."

Dow's "very open" approach to the urethane market has been combined, Ron said, with Dow Europe's basic philosophy of attracting individuals of various nationalities to work in their own countries.

"Mr. Merszei [Zoltan Merszei, the Hungarian-born president of Dow Europe] always has tried to put nationals in each country—let Germans deal with Germans, Scandinavians deal with Scandinavians, and so on—and of course he has been very successful. We are truly a European company, an international company.

"Of course, it is a little different here in Horgen. I think we have 17 or 18 different nationalities working in this building. It is rather interesting, when you think about it, because our fathers fought a war. That was not two generations ago—just one generation.

"I have never seen that we have any problems because of nationalistic feeling, and this is very encouraging to me. Because it means that it is not really people, as humans, but it is the systems that have created these big wars. It is not the people because, if it would have been that, we wouldn't have been able to operate."

Ron himself is one of the most multinational Dow people—a native of Norway, student in Sweden and the United States, employment in both the United States and Switzerland, and Holland too, because that is where the Dow development facility was located before it moved to Horgen. Now the oldest of his three daughters, Marion, is back in the United States as a student at Michigan State University.

Another multinational scientist at Horgen, the development individual closest to the rigid urethane business, is 30-year-old Dr. Matthijs van den Engh. A native of Holland, he received his bachelor's degree from the municipal college in his home town

Dr. Matthijs van den Engh

of Dordrecht, went on to a master's degree at the technological university in Delft, and then studied three years in Regina, Canada, at the University of Saskatchewan. While in Canada, he married a girl from the Philippines, also a chemist, who worked in Zurich at the Federal Institute of Technology until recently she became a mother.

Matthijs joined Dow Europe in 1972 after receiving his Ph.D. degree in physical organic chemistry. Of urethanes, he believes that "chemically, this is the most challenging of all the areas" being explored at Horgen.

"Basically what we are doing here is helping to push our polyols by adapting and modifying systems to meet the needs of our customers, to develop formulations for various applications. Because we can really vary the quantities and choices of compounds to make foam formulations, there are a great variety of possibilities.

"That is what makes this area so challenging, figuring out how to get optimal formulations."

And it's difficult to imagine a more delightful place for juggling molecules than the Dow laboratories in Switzerland.

34 | An Italian Company

"Then I say, 'Why continue working for an agent...?' I said that is a good chance for me, a good occasion to start a new life..."

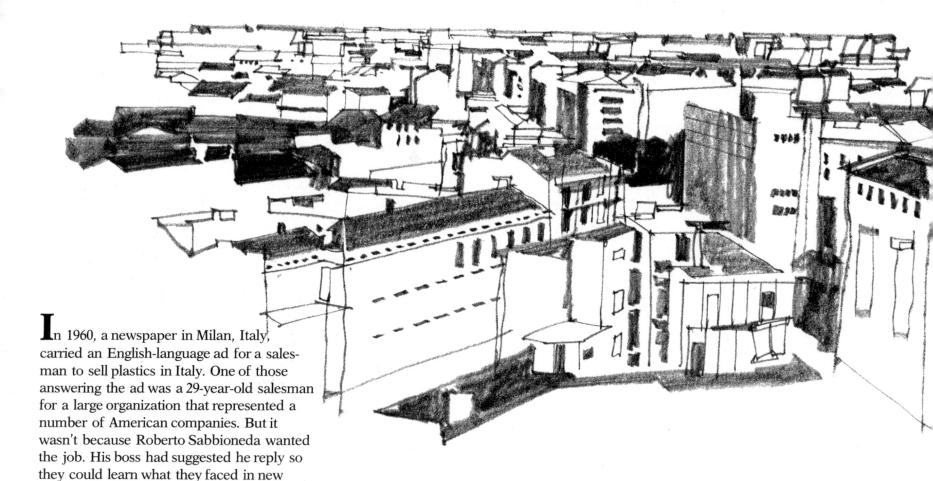

In 1960, a newspaper in Milan, Italy, carried an English-language ad for a salesman to sell plastics in Italy. One of those answering the ad was a 29-year-old salesman for a large organization that represented a number of American companies. But it wasn't because Roberto Sabbioneda wanted the job. His boss had suggested he reply so they could learn what they faced in new competition.

"The ad said just, 'U.S. company ready to start operations in Italy with an Italian plant to produce thermoplastics,' looking for a salesman, and so on. So my intention, really, was to check what American company was coming to Italy and starting thermoplastic operations—because we were selling products such as ABS, methyl methacrylate, and so on that would be affected. We were really interested to know who.

"Then when I understood that the company was The Dow Chemical Company, then of course my interest grew, really, at that point. Then I said, 'Why continue working for an agent who sooner or later will disappear because a lot of American companies and European companies are opening offices here?' I said that is a good

chance for me, a good occasion to start a new life directly with a producer, with a commercial organization."

At the same time Sabbioneda was joining Dow in Milan, Enrico Aliboni was being hired as a trainee in production management. And he participated in the engineering and construction of the polystyrene plant at Livorno.

A month before either Sabbioneda or Aliboni was hired, a week before the opening of the sales office in Milan, Lucilla Mondellini joined Dow as a secretary. At that time there were two Dow companies in Italy—the production company and the sales company.

Two Americans, Bob Reinker in production and Roger Zoccolillo in sales, were launching Dow's venture in Italy. Actually, they were responsible for more than the

business in Italy. Reinker also was in charge of another plastics plant under construction in Greece; Zoccolillo also was responsible for Dow sales in the Middle East. Miss Mondellini, meanwhile, stepped into a big job as secretary—because the business required letters of credit, paperwork for customs, and numerous other items of documentation.

Since 1967, the production and sales units have been combined in one company, and all the people in the company are now Italian. Aliboni transferred from Livorno to Milan to become general manager, Sabbioneda is the general sales manager, and Miss Mondellini is the secretary for both Aliboni and the personnel manager.

"We've grown a little bit since May, 1960," says Sabbioneda. "When we started operations in Italy the sales were around $2 million; this year they will be above $40 million. Last year we had an increase of 29 per cent.

"In 13 years we really have been able to put the Dow name in front of the chemical and various other industries in Italy."

Aliboni, 45—who became the works manager at Livorno in 1963—and Sabbioneda both emphasize that Dow is an Italian manufacturer, an essential element in its sales growth in Italy.

"It is absolutely necessary to have production in Italy," says Aliboni. "I think the success we are experiencing in the products which are produced locally—polystyrene, styrene-butadiene latex, and the formulation of PLICTRAN pesticide—is absolutely due to the fact that we are local producers. We are recognized as part of the Italian industry in those fields, and I think this is really important.

"We are producing 45 per cent of our total sales, and this is a minimum percentage that we should keep in the future. Our growth rate in sales always has been higher than the Dow Chemical average with the exception of this year, when the economic conditions in Italy have not been so good. There is a direct relationship between sales and our production, and becoming a part of the system instead of being the people who always have material abroad."

Aliboni is confident Dow sales in Italy will more than double, perhaps more than triple, by 1980—"a big achievement if we can do it.

"This forecast is on the assumption that we continue to produce at least 45 per cent of our total sales. It is practical for us to bring in raw materials, such as styrene, but it is not practical to import finished products in the volume needed to meet our sales goals."

On the marketing front, Sabbioneda attributes the Dow growth in Italy to three reasons.

—Gaining "our share of the market," which was almost zero in 1960.

—Introduction of new products for new applications.

—Participation in Italy's industrial growth.

"We have been able step by step to take our share from other producers or importers into Italy. Dow is considered an Italian company, and an Italian producer, and this is an advantage over other importers who are not local producers.

"So that we can handle all the material we can import from abroad, we are building a reputation as a local producer. And the service we are giving is that of a local producer, even for products we are importing.

"That is our main concern—to beef up our reputation by having a local warehouse, local storage tanks where we store the VORANOL polyols, where we store propylene glycol, where we store chlorinated solvents. We can really deliver a tank truck of material to customers in 48 hours. That is the kind of service that is given only by local producers."

I can assure anyone that 48 hours is indeed fast service in Italy. During my visit the government-owned railroad announced it would accept no freight shipments of any kind for three days, because the system was so clogged and because it needed the locomotives to pull passenger trains. And a letter sent air mail from Rome arrived at my home two weeks after I had returned.

"Looking at the way customers see us," Sabbioneda continued, "we have been able to convince people that we can deliver many products the same as a local producer. That is one of the main reasons we have tank storage facilities around Genoa. We can

bring material by ship from Terneuzen, and then distribute it here, and that costs certainly a cent less per pound than direct shipment by truck or tank car from Holland or Germany."

For products that sell for 10 cents to 20 cents a pound, a one-cent saving is a major gain.

"In addition to giving faster service, we really are saving money. Direct shipments by truck or railroad tank car from Terneuzen to Italy cost about two cents a pound. That is quite heavy if you consider that moving the same material [from Terneuzen] to the north of France or the center of Europe costs three-quarters or half a cent.

"You can see how we really are penalized by this distance to our markets from the major production points. So we have to find all the ways to save on transportation.

Lucilla Mondellini

"That is why we are bringing chlorinated solvents here in bulk, and drumming the CHLOROTHENE, DOWPER, and methylene chloride solvents in Italy. Otherwise bringing material down in drums would make it costly for us to compete.

"From the United States we are selling ingots and rolls of magnesium for auto wheels. The magnesium is shipped in lots of 20 to 60 tons, which are loaded directly on trucks and delivered to the Fiat plant at Turin.

"DOWFUME fumigant also comes from

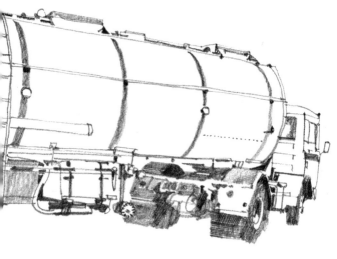

the United States to Genoa and Naples. The other products go to Rotterdam. That is because the volume is not large, and when there is not really a need for fast service we save money by bringing the material on a special train that runs from Rotterdam to Milan."

Turning to the business of urethane chemicals, Sabbioneda is quick to give credit to his American predecessor, Tom Sparta, who moved to Europe as a technical salesman and was the general manager for the Middle East, headquartered in Athens, Greece, before transferring to Milan.

"In flexible foam, we have been able to take a good share of the market, starting back in 1963, due mainly to the Tom Sparta activity in Zurich and later on in Italy.

"When we made the first sales in Italy, nobody believed very much in the Dow products. Bayer was the leading urethane company in Europe and our VORANOL products were completely unknown. We made a lot of trials, and people became convinced we had good products too—in some cases later on, even better products. Today we have our good share, I'd estimate between 15 and 20 per cent.

"You have heard of the Corradini company, a good customer for RS-350 and other polyols. Corradini was a company that started almost with us, ten years ago or something like that. I remember the first call we made there. They were working with one small machine, making these rigid panels and trying to sell in the market.

"So we gave them a lot of help technically, and they've always been grateful for it. They always have been good customers for over 50 per cent of their requirements. And they grew, of course, and today they are a very good name in this type of business. And they certainly are well known not only in Italy, but even in exporting to Africa, the Middle East, and so on.

"Corradini was working in the area of rigid foam where, I am of the opinion, we missed the big opportunity—foam-in-place insulation. As you probably know, here in Italy there is a big refrigerator industry. Five to six years ago they were in a complete boom, and they were looking for people able to go to their plants and teach them how to use the proper foam and the proper product. The refrigerator industry is picking up again. The trend is still good, and they have good forecasts to export a lot of refrigerators from Italy.

"And I must say we, Dow, have missed here in Italy a good business of $2 or $3 million—well, maybe because we do not have a good product for this application. We have been polystyrene suppliers to all those companies so we were very well accepted, and we had possibilities that other companies did not have.

"As for urethane chemicals for making synthetic wood, there has been a lot of talk about this, but I haven't been close to that part of the business. The furniture industry is one of the big ones in Italy. We have a lot of good designers, and they are trying to use as much synthetic material as possible—ABS plastic, glass-reinforced polyester, polycarbonate, polystyrene, any type of synthetic material.

"The price of wood is going up very fast. One reason is that we are a net importer of wood in Italy, we rely on an external supply. Also, the cost of manpower is going up very fast, and in the past all of this furniture really was hand made, I would say. Today that is impossible—except that in family-style businesses you can still find some people making furniture by hand.

"Manpower is getting more and more expensive, and even short. There are a lot of people looking at these new materials as substitutes for wood in furniture applications, and this can be any type of material, depending on how people can see the best future for the end use."

Sabbioneda's career has been in sales, and Aliboni's in production, plus some professorial assignments at the university in Pisa. But each is certain that one part of the business won't grow without the other, and that the sale of imported products will be handicapped if Dow lags in building its position as an Italian company, an Italian manufacturer.

35 | A Pink Fourth of July

"These are Italian communists. Many families are communist with two cars and two TV sets, more communist in ideology than in economics."

On the Fourth of July I visited a group of communists on a farm in Italy. And it was quite enjoyable. We'd gone to the farm to buy a watermelon, and they uncorked some of their best wine, one of the last four bottles left from the cask of a vintage year.

This was in the cheese and wine country near Correggio, a hundred miles from Milan toward Bologna. Since we didn't talk politics, how do I know the people were communists? Because they said so—after I insisted that Aldo Polacchini ask, even though he contended it was a foolish question because in this region "all the people on the farms are communist."

It wasn't quite like those Fourths of July when I was a boy shooting firecrackers, but it was an unusual day. We visited the farm, and a winery and a cheese maker, and had lunch in Campagnola, birthplace of Franco Pecorari, manager of the Corradini company.

Aldo, the 31-year-old salesman in charge of VORANOL products in Dow's Milan office, was just a bit glum. This would be one of his last calls on Corradini, a company whose polyol purchases from Dow had doubled in two years. Besides losing a strong account, because a new Dow sales office in Padua would take over this territory, Aldo was going to miss seeing his friends in this rural part of Italy.

Earlier, telling me how he picked chemistry for a career, Aldo had explained that his career goals combined "earning money, as much as possible," and also "to have fun, because that is much more important." It was the people Aldo enjoyed, not the 100-mile drive to Correggio. He doesn't like the crowded roads or, in Milan, the risk of a 1,500-lira ticket for illegal parking.

To reach his office from home, Aldo rides a bicycle unless he will need his car to call on a customer. By bicycle, it's 15 minutes to the office; by car, it's a 30-minute drive in the morning congestion.

Selling chemicals isn't all fun. Sometimes there are "tremendous troubles," Aldo had learned in his six years with Dow.

"It was roughly when there was the crisis of the TDI shortage that I was put in charge of the VORANOL products, in 1969 and 1970. We don't make TDI, and couldn't supply it to our customers, so the polyol market went down. We went down as well. So as a start it was really tremendous.

"I will let you know the next product that I will be involved with so Dow can plan its strategy for the next crisis. Anytime that I have become involved with a new product, there has been a crisis, really. I get into such tremendous troubles.

"There's the PGI story. [PGI is propylene glycol, industrial grade.] I was put in charge of PGI and there was the crisis in the shortages of all the other products involved with PGI, like maleic and phthalic anhydrides—because PGI goes mainly to the polyester market, and these other products are needed to make fiberglass-reinforced polyesters. So we had the crisis of maleic and phthalic anhydrides, and the market went down.

"Then I started with the VORANOL products, and there was the crisis of TDI. Now, just this year, I have started with styrene—and the shortage of this product is probably worse than all the others."

Aldo was born in Milan and received a technical diploma in chemistry from the Ettore Molinari technical school in Milan.

"After grammar school you have to choose your line to follow for a career. My parents asked for a school that can give this in as short a time as possible, because they were not able to support me for the university, which takes another five years.

"So I chose this five years of chemistry

school, only chemistry, and in fact at 20 years of age I was ready for any kind of job involving chemistry. If I went to the university I wouldn't be wasting my time, but I would have much more time to wait to achieve a certain level of life."

Meanwhile his wife of two years, Annalisa, is completing her university studies for a degree in literature.

Aldo is a dark, slender, 5 feet 11, a full six inches taller than his petite wife, and he looks as though he enjoys sports—which he does, tennis and boating. It also was obvious Aldo enjoys the atmosphere at Corradini, where he can shed jacket and tie and open the top two or three buttons of this shirt in true Italian style.

Before joining Dow he worked in a laboratory doing analyses of pharmaceutical products, then in a plant producing vegetable oil, then in the manufacture of bathroom fixtures. Next came a job with a Dow distributor in Italy, Unione Chimica Europea, which he said does "a tremendous job and is still our biggest customer, handling orders not big enough for Dow to sell directly."

Aldo Polacchini

After two months working in England, going there because of his interest in doing something different, Aldo returned to Italy to join Dow. Now he was trying to interest his old employer, U.C.E., in adding polyols to the products it sells, because that company would be in a better position to provide service for the smaller customers.

"I am quite disappointed in losing Corradini as an account. This is a customer that I have a good relationship with and which will only increase in dollar volume for Dow. We now have 90 per cent of Corradini's total requirements for polyols.

"We do not compete with Corradini in the sale of urethane systems. Sometimes we hear that we have been followed to a foam producer by Corradini, and we say, 'OK, carry on.' If the other company says, 'No, I don't want to buy any more systems, I want to make them myself,' we let Corradini know that is the situation. And if the other company has the technical capability to use the polyols, we supply them.

"So there is a really free interchange of communication with Corradini. They have a really good laboratory for research. And we have increased our share of the business at Corradini at the same time their own business has been growing."

At lunch in Campagnola, the 36-year-old Franco Pecorari, husband of Gustav Corradini's daughter Nelly, related how his father-in-law got into the urethane business. A successful cheese maker, Mr. Corradini, now 66, "had money to invest and heard the possibility of this exciting new material." He no longer sells cheese. But Corradini urethane formulations are sold in Italy and several other countries.

The biggest part of Corradini's business is in formulations for flexible foam, and in foam itself. But the product I was following, RS-350, is used to produce rigid materials, so I asked Franco for examples of applications. These include shoe soles manufactured in Yugoslavia, insulation panels in Greece, pipeline insulation in Egypt, synthetic wood beams in France, pre-polymers for elastomers in South Africa.

Specifically for formulations that include RS-350, Franco named three customer companies that manufacture frames for pictures and mirrors. It was this information that shortly thereafter led me to Cremona, Italy, the hometown of Antonio Stradivari, the violin maker of 250 years ago.

We talked with Franco in new office quarters just being completed at the Corradini plant. The activity suggested he must be enjoying good business, and he said that yes, business was good. We toured the plant, then set out in Franco's new Alfa Romeo to zip off into the countryside.

From my conversion of kilometers into miles, I doubt we were doing more than 60 miles an hour. But on the curvy, narrow roads through the lusciously green farm country it seemed almost as though we were on a race track—first to Franco's spacious new home and then to Campagnola.

At lunch I asked Franco if the bank he had worked in before joining Corradini was part of a multi-city banking chain, or a local bank. That's when I learned this was a communist region. Because of this, apparently, it's axiomatic that banks and most other enterprises be locally-owned. The region's not quite so communist as the "red district" of Bologna, but it's 50 per cent. And I was told that elections here usually go 65 per cent for a communist-socialist coalition.

"These are Italian communists," Franco said. "Many families are communist with two cars and two TV sets, more communist in ideology than in economics," he added after I indicated surprise to find this political orientation in such a prosperous area. It's the south of Italy, south of Rome, where there's high unemployment and more economic problems. In the north, my strong impression was one of prosperity, both industrially and agriculturally.

The Angela Davis controversy in the United States received considerable attention in the lunchtime talk but I admitted to

Franco I had not followed the case very closely. Vietnam and racial conflict in the United States also came up for questions—as they also had among the Dutch on the *Bilderdyk*. And, of course, Watergate—but in a bit different sense. In addition to wondering how it would end, and whether President Richard M. Nixon would stay in office, the Europeans expressed both amazement and admiration for a system that allowed the exposure that was occurring.

It was this conversation that heightened

Nelly and Franco Pecorari
Gustav Corradini

Silla Corradini and Mirio Brozzi

my interest in the visit to the farm, but among the people there was no hint of ill will toward an American. Just the opposite—and probably because these people are by nature friendly and outgoing. Three women, four men, and a boy were tending to various chores; and as I left the farmhouse an 80-year-old woman we had been talking with a few minutes earlier went riding away on a bicycle. She pedaled briskly.

The same friendliness was at the winery, where the large vats are insulated with urethane foam. The three Lini brothers, owners of the winery, annually throw a big springtime party with free wine, food, and music. Aldo and Franco had attended the event the previous month. These two are not only good friends, but had been doubles partners in local tennis tournaments.

Later, when we stopped to buy cheese, the proprietor was not only friendly, but he also spoke English. He'd learned it during World War II—in an American prisoner-of-war camp.

Back at the Corradini plant, and strictly by coincidence, a tank truck driven by Jack and Irma Kayser, of Hulst, near Terneuzen in Holland, was ready to depart for home after unloading a shipment of Dow polyol. Also on hand were Mr. Corradini; his son Silla, 30, who works in sales and technical service for the company; Mirio Brozzi, 32, the company's European sales manager; and Franco's wife, Nelly. I couldn't help noticing beside one building, a stack of drums with the name Dow Corning. The drums contained a silicon-glycol copolymer used in urethane foams to stabilize the size of the foam cells. Because this product had been manufactured, drummed and shipped from my hometown in Michigan, home suddenly seemed not so far away on this Fourth of July—in the pinkish-red region of Italy.

36 | The City of Violins

"A frame is a lot like a suit of clothes. There can be a beautiful girl with a wrong suit. It doesn't polarize the real aspects of the person... The right frame with the right painting doubles the value."

Cremona, Italy, was founded as a Roman colony on the Po River in 218 B.C. Plundered and burned in 69 A.D., it was later rebuilt and, starting in the 13th century, became a city of great architecture. In the 16th century, even before Antonio Stradivari was born, Cremona began a rise to world preeminence in the manufacture of violins.

The art of violin-making still is taught at the Scuola Internationale di Liuteria in Cremona. It was at this school, as a pupil of Nicolo Amati, that Stradivari learned to make violins. Stradivari died in 1737, but the violins made more than 200 years ago by the Amati, Stradivari, and Guarneri families of Cremona are still the most highly-valued in the world.

Violins were the first products of a company started by Francesco Poli in 1899, a company succeeded by the present Cavalli and Poli company in 1907. Cavalli and Poli no longer makes violins, but has long been among the world's leading manufacturers of frames for mirrors and pictures. There have been other products. During World War II the company made wooden toys and, as Nadir Belo well remembers, coffins.

Mr. Belo, 69, also remembers the day in January, 1945, when Allied bombers, aiming at the nearby rail yards, missed their target and hit Cavalli and Poli. Mr. Belo gave the order for dismantling the machinery, and helped carry out the dead and wounded. Several years were required to rebuild the factory.

Giulio Giatti was born in Italy during the war. At 13 he went to Fribourg, Switzerland, to study. He went on to one of Switzerland's best commercial colleges, Maria Hilf, and then to England to the West London College of Commerce, returned to Italy to enroll at the university in Florence, and then traveled to study in Barcelona, Spain. He also served two years in the Italian Army.

At 25, Giulio spoke French, German, English, Italian, and a bit of Spanish. With his university background in the commercial field, he started work for one of the largest textile exporters in Milan. Then a friend suggested he go to Cremona where Cavalli and Poli was looking for "a guy who knows some languages for the export department." Today Giulio, 29 years old, modestly identifies himself as manager of export sales, but actually he manages all the company's sales.

"When I first came here and saw no great offices, and that everything is quite old, near an old rail station, I really didn't know that this was a factory producing picture frames and moldings. I was really astonished by the company because it is very big and is considered to be one of the biggest in the world."

Now Giulio travels the world to sell the products of Cavalli and Poli. And the company's largest customers visit the Cremona factory once or twice a year, "combining it with vacation or holidays and to see new samples or new products.

"Myself, I travel quite a bit, probably too much. We are looking for a salesman because we have the home market, too. The idea would be to let him travel, and I would concentrate my efforts here at the company.

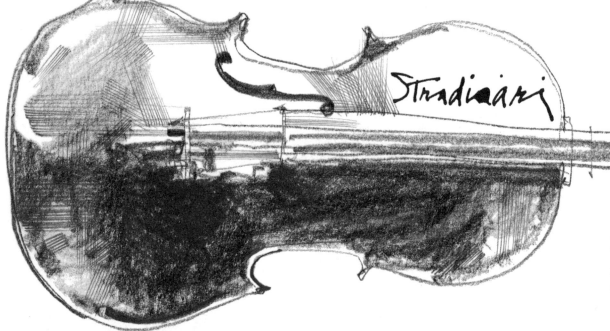

Because now we are studying a new plan of development, trying to go into other fields. This of course takes time. When I'm traveling, I am not concentrating on development of this kind."

In a way, though, it seems traveling is in

Giulio Giatti

Giulio's blood. He attended colleges in four different countries, and earlier in the year, though his bride, Maria, also is an Italian, they decided to go to London for their wedding.

The decision by Cavalli and Poli to start manufacturing frames and frame stock in urethane was made in 1971, following a development project in marketing this type of frame in Germany. Giulio had joined the company only a few months earlier.

"We had quite a big success. First of all, our cost for producing a shaped article is lower with the polyurethane. You only need a mold. It takes much less time to make a frame, only five or ten minutes. The only thing we have changed is the raw material.

"Germany, our best market, is where we first introduced the articles made of synthetic wood. At first they didn't want the article in plastic because they didn't know it. It was the first time they had an article similar to wood—sometimes better than wood, because it doesn't crack. The synthetic material is more stable. Wood is always alive, always changing with temperature, so it cracks.

"We also sell the polyurethane frames in Holland. In England we are just starting with this product. Of course, our articles shouldn't even be considered like some plastic articles that are really junk.

"One of the main strengths of our firm is the finishing department. In a frame like this, 75 per cent is hand labor; the only thing we do by machine is profiling. For the gold leaf and silvering, everything is by hand, leaf after leaf. We do not spray because gold spray is not too shiny, not of the quality done with metal leaf."

Giulio said the company was preparing a new type of catalog, one starting with a history of frame design, and telling which type of

177

molding should be used with which style of painting—for instance, with a Rembrandt. "We want to teach people how to frame. Most of the time, even in well-known galleries with beautiful paintings, there are wrong and awful types of frames.

"A frame is a lot like a suit of clothes. There can be a beautiful girl with a wrong suit. It doesn't polarize the real aspects of the person—or, in this case, the painting. The right frame with the right painting doubles the value."

Because Corradini also supplies urethane systems to two other companies that make picture frames, I asked Giulio how much competition existed in this field.

"We have about four Italian companies selling abroad. Other companies are in Sweden, quite a lot in Belgium, and some in France. We also now have competition from Taiwan, which is starting to do hand-carved picture frames. I've been told the workers in Taiwan are paid $1 a day.

"But our company doesn't have competition in the real sense because we do a high standard of quality. The quality is always accepted in the market. Like, let's say if a Swedish company sells one million feet and we sell 300,000 feet, the volume in dollars is always the same.

"We now have approximately 12,000 to 15,000 items. Too much, too many. If you consider all the kinds of finishing for one article, it goes up three or four times. Now we really want to concentrate on certain articles. We are now market-oriented, and we want our company to be one of the most modern in the world."

When Cavalli and Poli started making frames about 40 years ago, the company recognized that a high quality of wood is required. Today most of this wood comes from Africa and Malaysia, and is becoming

scarce and more costly. The company's normal inventory is a three-year supply.

All of the wood is treated with anti-parasitic agents and fungicides, so Cavalli and Poli's familiarity with chemical products preceded the introduction of urethanes for synthetic wood. Before the wood is worked, it goes through drying cells where the natural process of two years, or eight seasons, is achieved in a few days.

There is an inherent concern for quality among not only the management, but also the workers, Giulio said.

Nadir Belo

"This is a tradition that runs deep," he said. "In Cremona a worker who makes $200 a month will pay $75 for a suit of clothes. He may not buy many, but the Italian wants this quality."

The company's know-how for achieving quality is secret to the extent that a visitor touring the plant is not shown the actual production processing of frames. And there are indications that the company's statement about quality are not just self-serving comments. In 1971, Cavalli and Poli was selected from among all Italian manufacturers for a quality award presented annually.

In adopting urethanes as a basic raw material, the company must develop new technical capabilities. Giulio believes this is being done on a sound basis, expanding use of the material gradually and first introducing this type of frame in Germany and Holland, then England.

"For the natural wood frames, all the material underneath is wood, cut by a machine. All on the surface is a composition, a special material that includes glue and looks like a *pasta*, formed in a mold. It is very hard. Even if you cut it with a saw, it doesn't split. This is part of the know-how in this business."

Thus, whether in wood or urethane, only the prototype frames used in making the molds are hand-carved.

The Cavalli and Poli company is owned by stockholders. Employment at Cavalli and Poli is a tradition running in many Cremona families. Nadir Belo is one of the old-timers. He came to Cremona about 60 years ago, and it was he who wrote the history of painting for the company's new catalog. He started working for Cavalli and Poli in 1922, at 18, and retired as a full-time employee in 1968.

Aside from living most of his life in this city where art has a history of centuries, Belo

has pursued technical study on the subject. At one time, chauffeuring his daughter Flavia to art classes in Milan, he found the instruction so interesting that he sat in on the classes himself. Flavia, married and with two children, is now a teacher of painting and art history in the city of Lodi.

The Cavalli and Poli factory in Cremona was only one of the places in Italy where I saw urethane formulations being used as a substitute for wood. At the F.I.T. company

(Fabbrica Imbottiture & Tappezzati) in Muggia, Leo Gallino, the plant manager, described an upcoming expansion for the molding of various pieces of furniture. F.I.T. also uses RS-350 in formulating its own systems, and at the Coferlegno company in Bagnolo Mella, and the Ellise company in Castenedolo, I saw the complete furniture, including new products just going on the market.

Later, at the Il Bagno Ideale (Ideal Bathroom) store in Milan and the Pietro Passarelli store in Rome, I saw the Coferlegno bathroom furniture on display for sale. A complete set of this furniture costs in the range of $1,000, not items that are sold everyday. And I wanted to find an end-use

buyer-consumer.

So it was that next I turned to the Pieterman company of Schiedam, Holland, a major distributor for the Cavalli and Poli products, to ask where I might find a retailer of picture frames or mirrors. "Pick any city in Germany, and I'll tell you where they are sold," said Joost Pieterman, the company's managing director.

"Berlin," I said, because it was the first German city to come to mind, and also because I was sure Berlin would be one of Europe's most interesting cities. With fond memories of Italy, including weekends in Venice and Como, I was ready to follow the multinational trail of the VORANOL products to yet another country.

37 | "I Am a Berliner"

"The old-time business of poking a knife into the seat of a car to see whether a refugee was hiding...that's pretty much gone...At Checkpoint Charlie now, the formalities take minutes."

Berlin's largest department store is within a mile of the Berlin Wall. A seven-floor building occupying a city block, its merchandise includes everything from lawn mowers to sexy evening gowns—quite an eyeful for visitors from East Germany or other countries in the communist bloc.

The store's full name is Kaufhaus des Westerns, but it is commonly known as the KaDeWe, and it is owned by the Hertie company, headquartered in Frankfurt. Following a late-morning arrival at Tempelhof Airport, I had just a few minutes to spend in the KaDeWe store before its Saturday closing at 2 p.m. There, on the fourth floor, I spotted large mirrors with the Pieterman label. By peeking at the back side, I could tell the frames had been produced in urethane.

On Monday I would be at the KaDeWe store, hoping to find a customer making a purchase of this product that included RS-350 polyol produced in Texas. But before then I would have an opportunity to look around the city. And one of the most interesting visits was with Bob Lochner, the Berlin representative of the American Chamber of Commerce in Germany.

One reason it was interesting is that Bob is well versed on at least one aspect of trade with communist countries, a facet of multinational business that may become increasingly significant in the future.

Bob, besides representing the Chamber in Berlin, is director of the International Institute for Journalists, a German-financed organization for the training of Asian and African journalists. He also is a working journalist, accredited for the American Broadcasting Company and the Swiss news agency, writing occasional reports for the San Francisco *Chronicle*, doing radio commentaries for Radio Frankfurt and the Berlin radio station. I had little doubt I had come across an authoritative source for discussing multinational business at the edge of the Iron Curtain.

During World War II, Bob did European broadcasts in German for the National Broadcasting Company. He joined the United States Foreign Service after the war, working for the United States Information Agency for 26 years until 1971. He had been in Washington as director of Voice of America broadcasts to Europe, and he had headed the American radio station in Berlin for seven years. And he also served two years with the Foreign Service in Vietnam before many Americans had even heard of that country.

Bob has known Germany from his boyhood, living there when his father, Louis Lochner, represented The Associated Press in Berlin from 1921 until 1941.

"The Chamber has a long-range plan to try and push Berlin as a contact point for East-West trade, particularly trade between the United States and the G.D.R. [German Democratic Republic, the official name for East Germany]. Present trade between East Germans and the United States is practically negligible. And everybody expects that as part of the overall East-West trade the United States-East German trade will increase, too, even if modestly.

"The problem for them, obviously, is what can the G.D.R. sell to the United States? What they want from the United States would make up a tremendous shopping list— but they can't afford to pay for it, so the problem is what can they sell in the United States? Many of the products of East Germany are simply not up to world standards and can't be sold in Western countries.

"Their other major problem is that the Soviets take from them what they produce that is of world standard. Of their overall foreign trade, 75 per cent is with the Soviet Union and other communist countries, and ten per cent is with West Germany—which is East Germany's obvious partner, and with whom they have an inter-zonal trade agreement. And then they have another five per cent with the 'third world.' So that leaves ten per cent for all other Western countries.

"But even so, Berlin has some unique advantages to offer in the field of East-West trade. For instance, it's not generally known that the only place in the world where a Western businessman, and his Eastern state counterpart—after all, there are no genuine businessmen there—can agree today on the phone to meet tomorrow is Berlin. West Berlin or East Berlin, let's just say Berlin.

"If the Soviet state functionary wants to visit his Western partner in the Western country, it takes him weeks to obtain a visa, and vice versa. But because of the peculiar status of Berlin, the four-power status, any East European can come to West Berlin for 31 days each year without a visa, without a residence permit. This is absolutely unique.

"Obviously, the Westerner can come to West Berlin without any preparation. The big point is that the East Europeans can come here. Anybody can come here. West Berlin is open to the whole world.

"A second advantage to the Eastern state businessman is that he can save precious foreign exchange. The big state business functionaries, of course, get foreign exchange to go to Washington, London, wherever. But we have heard of cases where a guy in Budapest, Warsaw, or Moscow may say, 'I really have to meet so-and-so from West Germany or the United States,' and his higher-ups say, 'Well, we're short of foreign exchange.'

"If he says, 'I'm going to meet him in

Ka
De
We

Berlin,' then he needs practically no foreign exchange. He can live in East Berlin and pay in Eastern currency, and either meet his Western partner in East Berlin or be invited to West Berlin. This is a very distinct advantage. With increased trade, the need for sudden conferences will increase, and Berlin offers this unique advantage.

"People don't realize that the Wall has become somewhat penetrable. Westerners can, with increasing facility, get into East Berlin. And the West Berliners are now entitled to visit 31 days a year, not just East Berlin, but the rest of East Germany also. So West Berliners are swarming all over East Germany.

"And the G.D.R. has made it a little less onerous to go into East Berlin. The old-time business of poking a knife into the seat of a car to see whether a refugee was hiding, or tearing everything up—that's pretty much gone. If you cross over at Checkpoint Charlie now, the formalities take minutes. Any delay is primarily due to the increasing number of foreigners, since only foreigners can cross at Checkpoint Charlie.

"I go over periodically on Chamber business, and in the course of the Chamber's role to build up East-West trade I have established a rather good personal contact with a section head in the East German Chamber of Foreign Trade. When State Secretary Bail, the first high G.D.R. functionary to visit the United States, went there last November—an informal visit because there are no diplomatic relations yet—my contact in the East German Chamber asked me, on a crash basis, to get him information on four or five big American companies Bail was going to see. And it was as basic as who runs them, the address, the phone number, the Telex number, what they produce, what offices they have in Eastern Europe. So this showed they have practically no information about the United States.

"In several cases I have been able to set up appointments for West German representatives of American companies interested in selling their products to East Germany.

These were specific appointments in East Berlin with the relevant foreign trade organization. As you know, they have individual foreign trade companies in various fields with all sorts of exotic names. And you can't, even by looking at their list, tell for sure which company your product comes under.

"We find ourselves in the most harmonious agreement with the German city officials because anything that helps West Berlin acquire new functions is very much in their interest. We enjoy the support of the West Berlin Chamber of Industry and Commerce, a large organization with a number of experts on trade with East Germany and other East European countries. As you may know, German chambers of commerce are semi-official, financed with public funds, though not part of the bureaucracy."

So much for industrial and wholesale commerce. I asked Bob about a Westerner making purchases in East Berlin, or an Easterner buying in West Berlin.

"The East Germans are delighted to receive Western currency, but there isn't terribly much worth buying in East Berlin. They have the famous Meissen porcelain, and they do produce excellent art books, for instance, much cheaper than the West. As an individual, you face no restrictions. I suppose if you bought a carload, somebody might raise an eyebrow or so, but I don't know of any case.

"East Berliners are not supposed to have any foreign currency. Now there are some shops called intershops where you can get luxury goods—alcohol, cigarettes, cameras, that kind of thing—for Western currency. Inside East Berlin, mind you. These were set up primarily for West Berliners and West Germans who visit their relatives. Rather than have them bring the stuff in from West Berlin, East Germany is trying to latch on to some foreign exchange by having them buy

it on the spot. If you bring similar things from West Berlin, you are subject to certain regulations. You can only bring in 100 grams of coffee, one bottle of liquor on each visit, that kind of thing.

"These luxury goods are sold only against Western currency. As you come into one of these stores, you have to show that you have a Western passport, which in a sense is fantastic. Inside the communist 'paradise,' here is an oasis where the East Germans are not even allowed to enter, where their own currency is not attractive.

"For basic necessities—rent, potatoes, bread—prices are much lower in East Berlin. But for anything in the way of luxury— decent clothing, TV sets, autos, radios—the price jumps up to say ten times what it costs in West Berlin. Gasoline is much more expensive and of inferior quality. The smell of the inferior gasoline is, to me, typical of all communist countries. It pervades the streets.

"In the area around Friedrichstrasse and Checkpoint Charlie, where foreigners and West Berliners cross, some stores show high-quality Western goods in the windows. And the casual visitor says, 'Gee, I always thought they had such poor-quality things, but look— ladies' dresses from Paris.' What they don't show are the prices, and they have just a handful of stores located there precisely to impress the foreign visitor. In reality the really high-quality goods are beyond the reach of all but the elite.

"The shortages are chronic in just about every field. At best, nobody goes hungry and nobody goes unclothed; but as for quality and for choice, it's pitiful. It is an economy that is focused on the absolutely essential. Anything that comes under the general heading of frills, you can't get."

As for the future of the Berlin Wall, Bob

Bob Lochner

sees no hope for it coming down in the foreseeable future.

"One might be optimistic and hope for further liberalization—such as permission for more East Germans to leave the country for visits, which is possible so long as they continue to come back from the visits. And maybe a lowering by five years of the age at which East Germans can leave permanently. Not many choose to do so, because they would lose their East German pensions. But men over 65 and women over 60 can leave now—the reason, of course, being that they are no longer of economic importance. In fact, their pensions represent a cost to the G.D.R.

"Until the G.D.R. can compete economically with the West, the Berlin Wall is a necessity for East Germany because of the big migration that would occur."

Bob Lochner is an American who has lived in Berlin more than he has in the United States, though he attended the University of Chicago and worked in Washington, D.C. So it's no wonder that, of all his varied experiences in working with high officials, he cherishes the memory of translating in Berlin for four men who served the United States as President.

First there was Herbert C. Hoover, who in 1946 undertook for President Harry S Truman to visit various parts of the world to study food supplies and make recommendations for averting a post-war famine. Then there were Dwight D. Eisenhower and Lyndon B. Johnson, before they were elected to the Presidency, and John F. Kennedy, as President in 1963.

Bob recalls that with Kennedy he was walking up the steps of a building near the close of the President's visit. Kennedy wrote out a phrase that he asked Bob to translate into German, and then he practiced it several times. A few minutes later, to the cheers of hundreds of thousands in front of Schoneberg Town Hall, Kennedy called out in German his famous quotation, "I am a Berliner."

John F. Kennedy: *"I am a Berliner."*

38 | Journey's End

"We want the four nations—France, England, Russia, and America—to come to an understanding so people can live a normal life."

The man who sells the Pieterman mirrors to the KaDeWe department store in Berlin is 76 years old. He travels an average of 1,500 miles a week by train, 50 miles a week on foot. He is always carrying a heavy sample case. But he says he doesn't need a car.

I never caught up with George Hendricus Greijer, but I was told about him by Joost Pieterman, managing director of the Pieterman company. Mr. Greijer was born in Amsterdam, and he has been selling the Pieterman mirrors for 25 years, calling on 170 customers in 80 cities.

"Mr. Greijer sells only mirrors with classic frames, most of them manufactured by Cavalli and Poli," Mr. Pieterman said. "Mr. Greijer likes beautiful things, therefore he likes to sell beautiful mirrors. When he applied with us for the position of mirror seller, he was only interested in working with a well-established firm that sells only articles of high quality.

"When there was the change from wooden frames to frames of synthetic material, Mr. Greijer expected objections from customers. But, beyond his expectations, this proceeded without any difficulty. Only one or two per cent of the customers initially had any objections—but these customers bought them, too, and were satisfied.

"The reasons are that the finish of the synthetic frames is the same as the wooden ones, which was our demand; that a layman cannot see a difference between the wooden and synthetic frames; that Mr. Greijer has good relationship with the clients; and the good name of our company. Mr. Greijer is very proud that he, in cooperation with other associates of our export department, has helped to build a good name for our company as a quality supplier.

"In the 25 years that he has been selling our mirrors, Mr. Greijer has traveled about two million miles. He is still active every day in selling."

From the Dow production complex in Texas to Dow's Botlek terminal in Rotterdam; to Corradini in Correggio, Italy; to Cavalli and Poli in Cremona, Italy; back to Holland to the Pieterman company in Schiedam, a Rotterdam suburb; and now to the KaDeWe department store in Berlin. That was the route of the VORANOL RS-350 polyol I followed to and across Europe.

But no longer was there the slightest tinge of Dow identity in the mirrors hanging on the fourth floor of the KaDeWe store. The product forevermore, and rightfully so, would be known as a Pieterman mirror.

"We have built a business in mirrors with classic frames in Holland, Germany, and in the rest of Europe, thanks to the fact that we were sure of a continuing and growing market for this article. The romanticism never gets lost in a person in spite of all indifference and all corruption.

"We are a glass-processing industry, and our mirrors are part of that. Our turnover in mirrors is not more than 15 per cent of our total sales of 20 million Dutch florins [\$7.5 million] in 1972. We produce gauge glasses for domestic and industrial apparatus and safety glass for all purposes. We also produce many glasses for ships and for the furniture industry.

"I am 57 years old and have spent more than 40 years working in our company, which was founded by my father in 1921, when I was five. I also have a dear wife, seven children, and eight grandchildren."

Interesting indeed were all the people I'd talked with so far in the course of this trip. And I still had a great deal of curiosity about the end-use buyer of a mirror, the person I hoped to meet making a purchase at the

KaDeWe store.

This had been truly a multinational journey, even the Lufthansa flight from Rome to Frankfurt. The plane's flight had started in Japan, with stops in Hong Kong, Thailand, India, and Kuwait before reaching the Leonardo da Vinci Airport. It was the first time I'd been on a Boeing 747. If you don't think a 747 is big, ask the woman who a few minutes before takeoff was anxiously searching up and down the aisles looking for a child. I had never known anyone to be lost inside an airplane. After her husband, their other children, and the plane's steward joined the search, the child was finally

found—in one of the plane's 12 washrooms.

The mix of nationalities on board was evident in the passengers' attire, including the turbans from the Middle East. After takeoff, the captain made his announcements in a sequence of German, English, and Italian. And an Oriental stewardess followed with Japanese.

In Berlin there was yet another person whom I did not meet, never talked with, never saw, but will long remember. My experience with this person started after my quick Saturday visit to the KaDeWe store and a double-deck bus tour of East Berlin. Visits to East Berlin are easy, one reason

being that East Germany badly needs Western money. At Checkpoint Charlie, there's a bit of waiting in line and a passport check to accompany the visa payment of a few marks, a small sum for a tourist but substantial for any Berliner who makes the trip frequently.

The sight attracting the most attention at Checkpoint Charlie is the East German border guards' inspection of passenger cars going to West Berlin. They look under the hood and inside the trunk, then go around the vehicle with a long-handled mirror on wheels to make sure no one is hiding on the underside of the car. East German tour guides get on the bus at Checkpoint Charlie, and here you also see people—in some cases families divided by the Wall—in long good-byes as some proceed to West Berlin and others turn back in East Berlin.

Our guide, a teacher and part-time drama teacher, couldn't have been more helpful or more friendly. She settled on English and French as the languages best understood by our group. The visitors to East Berlin this sunny summer day were not just from the West—the United States, Brazil, England, and elsewhere—for at a war memorial park on the outskirts of the city there were uniformed school children on an excursion from Poland.

When I returned to the hotel, I was ready for a nap. After hiding my camera equipment under a jacket in the closet, as had become my habit, I quickly fell asleep. When I awakened, ready for dinner, I dressed and immediately noticed that the wallet in which I carried credit cards and driver's license was missing. After a few minutes of thought, I was sure it must have fallen from my hip pocket while I maneuvered to take pictures from the upper deck of the bus.

Late that night, and early Sunday morning, I checked out quite a few tour buses—but no wallet. Maybe my pocket had been picked, but at least I hadn't lost my money, or my passport, or my air ticket back to the United States. Sunday afternoon, taking pictures along the Berlin Wall, I felt almost nude whenever my hand brushed across my right-rear trousers pocket and felt nothing. Suddenly realizing how strong a habit this had become, I wondered how I could have left the bus and returned to the hotel without noticing the wallet was gone.

At 9 p.m. I had a call from the Hilton's assistant manager, Fernando Gruenberg Stern: "Something terrible has happened.

Elfriede and Ernst Mehlberg

189

The police arrested a man at the hotel this afternoon, and at the police station they found he had two of your credit cards. He stole them from your room."

Inspectors Rudiger Bechtner and Peter Roeper came from the Tiergarten police station to return the two cards and obtain my statement on the incident. I also made a date to take their picture the next day, knowing it would be useful in explaining the incident to anyone suspicious that my loss had occurred under less innocent circumstances.

My amazement was not only in learning the wallet had been stolen, but in realizing that I was asleep in the room when it happened. The door had been locked, but not bolted from the inside. Because the bed was between the door and the chair where I'd draped my trousers, I still wonder what I'd have done had I awakened while the thief was in the room.

Three months later a Dow travel newsletter advised: "Hotel burglaries are not exactly new to Dow travelers. However, the incidents are becoming more frequent. If you awaken when a stranger is in your room you are better off not to attempt heroics." But, considering the throng of people that the European hotels have walking in and out of rooms to deliver breakfast, pick up a tray, return laundry, repair the plumbing—I probably wouldn't recognize a burglar as a burglar if I woke up and saw one.

So the thief is the character in this tale that I never saw, before or after his arrest. And when the weekend ended, I was more anxious than ever to meet the buyer of a Pieterman mirror. But I soon learned this might not be easy.

The administrative people at the KaDeWe store never had heard of The Dow Chemical Company. They thought I should first obtain approval for this project at the company's headquarters in Frankfurt. And the saleslady in the mirror department didn't want me to take any pictures—because she thought I probably was gathering trade information for an American store.

My savior was Ingeborg Neubauer, a Chilean, who with her two teenage children hadn't wanted to stay in a country "where they had no future," although her husband still was in Chile because "he didn't want to start all over again." Mrs. Neubauer knew of Dow Chemical because she had seen the plants Dow had built in Chile.

Mrs. Neubauer, whose languages include English, works in customer service for the KaDeWe store. She suggested that we return to the mirror department so I could show her the type of mirror I was talking about. As we walked toward the display of mirrors, Mrs. Neubauer noticed a couple looking at a large mirror, and yes, I told her, that was a Pieterman mirror. Its frame was oval, gold-leafed and ornate. But no, it then seemed the couple was just inquiring about the price, not buying.

That was disappointing, especially since the department manager said it is usually a few days between sales of this product. I began to wonder how long I might have to wait for a sale. But then yes, the couple was going to buy the mirror after all, and Mrs. Neubauer said she'd be happy to ask them if they would mind a few questions. And the buyers, Ernst and Elfriede Mehlberg, were most gracious. From the store we went to the Hilton, where the assistant manager joined us to translate.

Mr. Mehlberg, 51, a Berlin native, is a plant mechanic for the Fritz Werner Works, which produces industrial machinery. This was the last day of his three-week vacation, most of which the Mehlbergs had spent in Austria. He and his wife had bought new furniture for the bedroom of their apartment, and an interior decorator had suggested this type of mirror to go with the new furniture. It was a gold-leafed mirror priced at 125 marks, or about $52 at the exchange rate then prevailing.

They had been shopping for both carpet and a mirror. And they had with them a drawing of the way the interior decorator had designed their bedroom, and a carpet sample. The drawing had been prepared a year earlier, and Mrs. Mehlberg explained, "It has been so long because it takes quite long in Germany to obtain furniture."

Because I knew that buying all sorts of products, even food, had been more difficult during the Berlin Blockade of 1948-49, I asked if Mr. and Mrs. Mehlberg had experienced many problems at that time. But neither had been in Berlin then. Mr. Mehlberg was a prisoner of the Russians, and Mrs. Mehlberg then lived in East Germany, in the small town of Haselberg.

Mr. Mehlberg had fought on the Eastern Front, in southern Russia, from 1942 until his capture in 1944. He was imprisoned at Zaporozje and released in 1950. Also in 1950, Mrs. Mehlberg left East Germany, before it became difficult to leave. They met in Berlin and were married in 1952. They have lived in their present apartment, on Mehringdamm Avenue south toward Tempelhof Airport, for the past 11 years, and before that they lived just three blocks away.

I asked what, as two individuals in a city that today appears bright and prosperous but which still has several bombed-out buildings as memoirs of the war, and a Wall and armed sentries, and an occasional shooting at the Wall, they would like to say to the world if they had the opportunity.

"For people who live in Berlin, it is very small," said Mr. Mehlberg. "Berlin is an island. If you go out of Berlin it takes too long—all the things you have to do to go through in East Germany. It's easy to cross, but they have special laws."

"Do you know all the problems of Berlin?" Mrs. Mehlberg asked. "Do you know what the people have to accept? People here can't vote for who's going to Parliament. Both Germanys, West and East, were accepted in the United Nations, but now it is a question if Berlin is accepted in the United Nations. Berlin always is special for everything.

"When I want to visit relatives where I was born, I must pay an enormous sum. You must pay ten marks per day per person, plus ten marks for the road. Where in the world do you have to pay money to visit your relatives? Does that make any sense? It's like going in customs because they have to search the car, the luggage, look under the car with a mirror. You can't even take a newspaper to the East.

"We want the four nations—France, England, Russia, and America—to come to an understanding so people can live a normal life."

Somehow it seems fitting that this is where the story of the Dow product ends—at the edge of the free world. The freedom to trade and travel still has various limits. Even in the United States, there are those who would raise new barriers.

While technology is not an unflawed answer to all problems, the world benefits most when the development of technology is unfettered by conflict among nations. And so do the people who are working in multinational business today—even in such ordinary matters as a mattress made in Recife, Brazil, and a mirror frame designed and manufactured in Cremona, Italy. I met a few of those people on this journey east from Brazosport.

ALLIED CHECKPOINT

191